To the Instructor

Thank you for your interest in the Townsend Press vocabulary series—so successful that it now appears in a Fourth Edition. Our goal in this series has been to produce nothing less than excellent books at nothing more than reasonable prices.

About the Book

Notice that the introduction to students (page 1) immediately makes clear to them just why vocabulary study is important. Students are motivated to learn by the four compelling kinds of evidence for word study. The back cover as well convinces students that "a solid vocabulary is a source of power."

You may want to look then at the preface, starting on page vii, which describes in detail the nine distinctive features of the book.

There are thirty chapters in the book, divided into five units. You'll note that while each chapter takes up only four pages, those pages contain a great deal of hands-on practice to help ensure that students master each word. And you'll find that the practice materials themselves are far more carefully done, and more appealing, than the run-of-the-mill items you typically find in a skills text. The quality and interest level of the content will help students truly learn the words, without either boring them or insulting their intelligence.

Supplements to the Book

Adding to the value of *Improving Vocabulary Skills* is the quality of the supplements:

- An **Instructor's Edition**, which you hold in your hand. The *Instructor's Edition* is identical to the student text except that it includes the answers to all of the practices and tests.

- A combined **Instructor's Manual and Test Bank**, free with adoptions of 20 or more copies. This supplement contains a general vocabulary placement test as well as a pretest and a posttest for the book and for each of the five units in the text. It also includes teaching guidelines, suggested syllabi, an answer key, and an additional mastery test for each chapter as well as an additional mastery test for each unit.

- **PowerPoint presentations and Blackboard cartridges** are available for the book and may be downloaded from the "Supplements" area for instructors at **www.townsendpress.com**.

- **Online exercises**, available at **www.townsendpress.com**, which provide a general placement test and two additional tests for each vocabulary chapter in the book. These exercises contain a number of user- and instructor-friendly features, including actual, audible pronunciations of the words; brief explanations of answers; a sound option; frequent mention of the user's first name; a running score at the bottom of the screen; and a record-keeping file.

Adopters of *Improving Vocabulary Skills* can obtain the print supplements by calling our toll-free number, 1-800-772-6410, or by e-mailing Customer Service at **cs@townsendpress.com**.

(Continues on next page)

New Features of the Book

Among the changes in this Fourth Edition of *Improving Vocabulary Skills* are the following:

- **A full-color design.** Color has been carefully used throughout, not as window dressing but to add clarity and readability to the different parts of each chapter and the different sections of the book.

- **Thirty new graphics.** To engage today's visual learners, a full-color illustration has been added to the Final Check story in each chapter.

- **Additional multicultural names and repeated words.** To broaden both the appeal and the effectiveness of the practice materials, ethnic names have been used more frequently, and even more vocabulary words have been repeated in the Final Checks.

- **Revised and updated practice items.** As always, a number of practice items throughout the book have been revised or updated to ensure that each item works as clearly and effectively with students as possible.

A Comprehensive Vocabulary Program

There are nine books in the Townsend Press vocabulary series:

- *Vocabulary Basics* (reading level 4–6)
- *Groundwork for a Better Vocabulary* (reading level 5–8)
- *Building Vocabulary Skills* (reading level 7–9)
- *Building Vocabulary Skills, Short Version* (reading level 7–9)
- *Improving Vocabulary Skills* (reading level 9–11)
- *Improving Vocabulary Skills, Short Version* (reading level 9–11)
- *Advancing Vocabulary Skills* (reading level 11–13)
- *Advancing Vocabulary Skills, Short Version* (reading level 11–13)
- *Advanced Word Power* (reading level 12–14)

Note that the short versions of the three books are limited to 200 words, as opposed to the 260 words and 40 word parts in each of the long versions. For some students and classes, the short versions of the book will provide an easier, more manageable approach to vocabulary development.

Improving Vocabulary Skills

Fourth Edition

Sherrie L. Nist
Professor Emerita, University of Georgia

Townsend Press Reading Series
Groundwork for College Reading with Phonics
Groundwork for College Reading
Ten Steps to Building College Reading Skills
Ten Steps to Improving College Reading Skills
Ten Steps to Advancing College Reading Skills
Ten Steps to Advanced Reading

Townsend Press Vocabulary Series
Vocabulary Basics
Groundwork for a Better Vocabulary
Building Vocabulary Skills
Building Vocabulary Skills, Short Version
Improving Vocabulary Skills
Improving Vocabulary Skills, Short Version
Advancing Vocabulary Skills
Advancing Vocabulary Skills, Short Version
Advanced Word Power

Supplements Available for Most Books
Instructor's Edition
Instructor's Manual and Test Bank
Online Exercises
PowerPoint Presentations
Blackboard Cartridges

Copyright © 2010 by Townsend Press, Inc.
Printed in the United States of America
9 8 7 6 5 4 3 2 1

ISBN-13 (Student Edition): 978-1-59194-190-3
ISBN-10 (Student Edition): 1-59194-190-3
ISBN-13 (Instructor's Edition): 978-1-59194-195-8
ISBN-10 (Instructor's Edition): 1-59194-195-4

Send book orders and requests for desk copies or supplements to:
Townsend Press Book Center
439 Kelley Drive
West Berlin, New Jersey 08091

For even faster service, contact us in any of the following ways:
By telephone: 1-800-772-6410
By fax: 1-800-225-8894
By e-mail: cs@townsendpress.com
Through our website: www.townsendpress.com

Contents

NOTE: Twenty-six of the chapters present ten words apiece. The other four chapters each cover ten word parts and are so marked. For ease of reference, the title of the selection that closes each chapter is included.

Unit Four

Unit Five

Appendixes

Preface: To the Instructor

The problem is all too familiar: *students just don't know enough words.* Reading, writing, and content teachers agree that many students' vocabularies are inadequate for course demands. Weak vocabularies limit students' understanding of what they read and the clarity and depth of what they write.

The purpose of *Improving Vocabulary Skills* and the other books in the Townsend Press vocabulary series is to provide a solid, workable answer to the vocabulary problem. In the course of 30 chapters, *Improving Vocabulary Skills* teaches 260 important words and 40 common word parts. Here are the book's distinctive features:

1 **An intensive words-in-context approach.** Studies show that students learn words best by reading them repeatedly in different contexts, not through rote memorization. The book gives students an intensive in-context experience by presenting each word in **six** different contexts. Each chapter takes students through a productive sequence of steps:

- Students infer the meaning of each word by considering two sentences in which it appears and then choosing from multiple-choice options.
- On the basis of their inferences, students identify each word's meaning in a matching test. They are then in a solid position to deepen their knowledge of a word.
- Finally, they strengthen their understanding of a word by using it three times: in two sentence-length practices and in a passage practice.

Each encounter with a word brings it closer to becoming part of the student's permanent word bank.

2 **Abundant practice.** Along with extensive practice in each chapter, there are a crossword puzzle and a set of unit tests at the end of every six-chapter unit. The puzzle and tests reinforce students' knowledge of the words in each chapter. In addition, most chapters reuse several words from earlier chapters (such repeated words are marked with small circles), allowing for more reinforcement. Last, there are supplementary tests in the *Instructor's Manual and Test Bank* and the online exercises that accompany the book. All this practice means that students learn in the surest possible way: by working closely and repeatedly with each word.

3 **Controlled feedback.** The opening activity in each chapter gives students three multiple-choice options to help them decide on the meaning of a given word. The multiple-choice options also help students complete the matching test that is the second activity of each chapter. A limited answer key at the back of the book then provides answers for the third activity in the chapter. All these features enable students to take an active role in their own learning.

4 **Focus on essential words.** A good deal of time and research went into selecting the words and word parts in each book in the TP vocabulary series. Word frequency lists were consulted, along with lists in a wide range of vocabulary books. In addition, the authors and editors each prepared their own lists. A computer was used to help in the consolidation of the many word lists. A long process of group discussion then led to final decisions about the words and word parts that would be most helpful for students on each reading level.

5 **Appealing content.** Dull practice materials work against learning. On the other hand, meaningful, lively, and at times even funny sentences and passages can spark students' attention and thus enhance their grasp of the material. For this reason, a great deal of effort was put into creating sentences and passages with both widespread appeal and solid context support. We have tried throughout to make the practice materials truly enjoyable for teachers and students alike. Look, for example, at the selection on page 27 that closes the fifth chapter of this book.

6 **Clear format.** The book has been designed so that its very format contributes to the learning process. Each chapter consists of two two-page spreads. In the first two-page spread (the first such spread is on pages 8–9), students can easily refer to all ten words in context while working on the matching test, which provides a clear meaning for each word. In the second two-page spread, students can refer to a box that shows all ten words while they work through the fill-in activities on these pages.

7 **Supplementary materials.**

   a A convenient *Instructor's Edition* is available at no charge to instructors using the book. It is identical to the student book except that it contains answers to all of the activities and tests.

   b A combined *Instructor's Manual and Test Bank* is also offered at no charge to instructors who have adopted the book. This supplement contains a general vocabulary placement test as well as a pretest and a posttest for the book and for each of the five units in the text. It also includes teaching guidelines, suggested syllabi, an answer key, and an additional mastery test for each chapter as well as an additional mastery test for each unit.

   c *PowerPoint presentations and Blackboard cartridges* are available for the book and may be downloaded from the "Supplements" area for instructors at www.townsendpress.com.

   d *Online exercises,* available at the Online Learning Center area of www.townsendpress.com, also accompany the book. These exercises consist of two additional tests for each vocabulary chapter in the book. In addition, they include—at the instructor's option—some of the practice material in the book itself. The program includes a number of user- and instructor-friendly features: brief explanations of answers, a sound option, frequent mention of the user's first name, a running score at the bottom of the screen, a record-keeping file, and actual pronunciation of each word.

   Probably in no other area of reading instruction is the computer more useful than in reinforcing vocabulary. These online exercises take full advantage of the computer's unique capabilities and motivational appeal. Here's how the program works:

   ● Students are tested on the ten words in a chapter, with each word in a sentence context different from any in the book itself.

   ● After students answer each question, they receive immediate feedback: The program states that the answer is right or wrong and why, frequently using the student's first name and providing a running score.

   ● When they complete each test, students receive their scores. If they repeat the test, they then receive a new score, labeled "R" on the scores report, with a number following the "R" indicating how many times they have taken the same test. What is so valuable about this, of course, is that the program gives students immediate additional practice with the words they need to review.

   ● In addition, the online exercise program offers a second, more challenging "Word Definitions" test in which students must identify the meanings of the chapter words without the benefit of context. This test is a final check that students have really learned the words. And, again, there is the option of a retest, with its own score.

   ● Finally, if the instructor so chooses, the online program will provide the student with two of the exercises in the book—Sentence Check 2 and the Final Check. Students can take these exercises online and receive immediate feedback and the option of a retest.

   Once students complete these exercises, their knowledge of each word in the chapter will have been carefully reinforced. And this reinforcement will be the more effective for having occurred in an electronic medium that especially engages today's students.

To obtain a copy of either the *Instructor's Edition* or the *Instructor's Manual and Test Bank*, instructors may contact Customer Service at 1-800-772-6420 or at cs@townsendpress.com.

8 **Realistic pricing.** As with the previous editions, the goal has been to offer the highest possible quality at the lowest possible price. While *Improving Vocabulary Skills* is comprehensive enough to serve as a primary text, its modest price also makes it an inexpensive supplement.

9 **One in a sequence of books.** The most fundamental book in the Townsend Press vocabulary series is *Vocabulary Basics*. It is followed by *Groundwork for a Better Vocabulary* (a slightly more advanced basic text) and then by the three main books in the series: *Building Vocabulary Skills* (also a basic text), *Improving Vocabulary Skills* (an intermediate text), and *Advancing Vocabulary Skills* (a more advanced text). The most advanced book in the Townsend Press vocabulary series is *Advanced Word Power*. There are also short versions of the *Building, Improving*, and *Advancing* books. Suggested grade levels for the books are included in the *Instructor's Manual.* Together, the books can help create a vocabulary foundation that will make any student a better reader, writer, and thinker.

Notes on the Fourth Edition

A number of changes have been made in the fourth edition of *Improving Vocabulary Skills:*

- **A full-color design.** Color has been carefully used throughout, not as window dressing but to add clarity and readability to the different parts of each chapter and the different sections of the book.

- **Thirty new graphics.** To engage today's visual learners, a full-color illustration has been added to the Final Check passage in each chapter.

- **Additional multicultural names and repeated words.** To broaden both the appeal and the effectiveness of the practice materials, ethnic names have been used more frequently, and even more vocabulary words have been repeated in the Final Checks.

- **Revised and updated practice items.** As always, a number of practice items throughout the book have been revised or updated to ensure that each item works as clearly and effectively with students as possible.

Acknowledgments

I am grateful for the enthusiastic comments provided by users of the Townsend Press vocabulary books over the life of the first three editions. I appreciate as well the work done on earlier editions by Eliza Comodromos, Beth Johnson, John Langan, and, in particular, Carole Mohr. I would also like to thank Kathryn Bernstein, Denton Cairnes, and Rick Moore for design, editing, and proofreading assistance with the fourth edition. And I owe special thanks to two TP editors who brought their exceptional talents to this revision. Barbara Solot is responsible for a four-color text design that is as clear as it is inviting. The result of her artistry is a strikingly attractive book that both students and teachers will enjoy. Janet Goldstein, in addition to providing significant design and content input, has lent her extraordinary editing and proofreading skills to this project. Under her guidance, the vocabulary series has been in the best possible hands.

Sherrie L. Nist

Introduction

Why Vocabulary Development Counts

You have probably often heard it said, "Building vocabulary is important." Maybe you've politely nodded in agreement and then forgotten the matter. But it would be fair for you to ask, "*Why* is vocabulary development important? Provide some evidence." Here are four compelling kinds of evidence.

1 Common sense tells you what many research studies have shown as well: vocabulary is a basic part of reading comprehension. Simply put, if you don't know enough words, you are going to have trouble understanding what you read. An occasional word may not stop you, but if there are too many words you don't know, comprehension will suffer. The content of textbooks is often challenge enough; you don't want to work as well on understanding the words that express that content.

2 Vocabulary is a major part of almost every standardized test, including reading achievement tests, college entrance exams, and armed forces and vocational placement tests. Test developers know that vocabulary is a key measure of both one's learning and one's ability to learn. It is for this reason that they include a separate vocabulary section as well as a reading comprehension section. The more words you know, then, the better you are likely to do on such important tests.

3 Studies have indicated that students with strong vocabularies are more successful in school. And one widely known study found that a good vocabulary, more than any other factor, was common to people enjoying successful careers in life. Words are in fact the tools not just of better reading, but of better writing, speaking, listening, and thinking as well. The more words you have at your command, the more effective your communication can be, and the more influence you can have on the people around you.

4 In today's world, a good vocabulary counts more than ever. Far fewer people work on farms or in factories. Far more are in jobs that provide services or process information. More than ever, words are the tools of our trade: words we use in reading, writing, listening, and speaking. Furthermore, experts say that workers of tomorrow will be called on to change jobs and learn new skills at an ever-increasing pace. The keys to survival and success will be the abilities to communicate skillfully and learn quickly. A solid vocabulary is essential for both of these skills.

Clearly, the evidence is overwhelming that building vocabulary is crucial. The question then becomes, "What is the best way of going about it?"

Words in Context: The Key to Vocabulary Development

Memorizing lists of words is a traditional method of vocabulary development. However, you are likely to forget such memorized lists quickly. Studies show that to master a word (or a word part), you must see and use it in various contexts. By working actively and repeatedly with a word, you greatly increase the chance of really learning it.

The following activity will make clear how this book is organized and how it uses a words-in-context approach. Answer the questions or fill in the missing words in the spaces provided.

Inside Front Cover and Contents

Turn to the inside front cover.

● The inside front cover provides a ___pronunciation guide___ that will help you pronounce all the vocabulary words in the book.

Now turn to the table of contents on pages v–vi.

● How many chapters are in the book? ___30___

● Most chapters present vocabulary words. How many chapters present word parts? ___4___

● Four sections follow the last chapter. The first of these sections provides a limited answer key, the second gives helpful information on using ___the dictionary___, the third contains ___topics for discussion and writing___, and the fourth is an index of the 260 words and 40 word parts in the book.

Vocabulary Chapters

Turn to Chapter 1 on pages 8–11. This chapter, like all the others, consists of five parts:

● The *first part* of the chapter, on pages 8–9, is titled ___Ten Words in Context___.

The left-hand column lists the ten words. Under each **boldfaced** word is its ___pronunciation___ (in parentheses). For example, the pronunciation of *absolve* is ___ăb-zŏlv′___. For a guide to pronunciation, see the inside front cover as well as "Dictionary Use" on page 181.

Below the pronunciation guide for each word is its part of speech. The part of speech shown for *absolve* is ___verb___. The vocabulary words in this book are mostly nouns, adjectives, and verbs. **Nouns** are words used to name something—a person, place, thing, or idea. Familiar nouns include *boyfriend, city, hat,* and *truth.* **Adjectives** are words that describe nouns, as in the following word pairs: *former* boyfriend, *large* city, *red* hat, *whole* truth. All of the **verbs** in this book express an action of some sort. They tell what someone or something is doing. Common verbs include *sing, separate, support,* and *imagine.*

To the right of each word are two sentences that will help you understand its meaning. In each sentence, the **context**—the words surrounding the boldfaced word—provides clues you can use to figure out the definition. There are four common types of context clues: examples, synonyms, antonyms, and the general sense of the sentence. Each is briefly described below.

1 Examples

A sentence may include examples that reveal what an unfamiliar word means. For instance, take a look at the following sentence from Chapter 1 for the word *eccentric*:

Bruce is quite **eccentric.** For example, he lives in a circular house and rides to work on a motorcycle, in a three-piece suit.

The sentences provide two examples of what makes Bruce eccentric. The first is that he lives in a circular house. The second is that he rides to work on a motorcycle while wearing a three-piece suit. What do these two examples have in common? The answer to that question will tell you what *eccentric* means. Look at the answer choices below, and in the answer space provided, write the letter of the one you think is correct.

    <u>B</u> *Eccentric* means   A. ordinary.   B. odd.   C. careful.

Both of the examples given in the sentences about Bruce tell us that he is unusual, or odd. So if you wrote *B*, you chose the correct answer.

2 Synonyms

Synonyms are words that mean the same or almost the same as another word. For example, the words *joyful, happy*, and *delighted* are synonyms—they all mean about the same thing. Synonyms serve as context clues by providing the meaning of an unknown word that is nearby. The sentence below from Chapter 2 provides a synonym clue for *irate*.

> If Kate got angry only occasionally, I could take her more seriously, but she's always **irate** about something or other.

Instead of using *irate* twice, the author used a synonym in the first part of the sentence. Find that synonym, and then choose the letter of the correct answer from the choices below.

    <u>C</u> *Irate* means   A. thrilled.   B. selfish.   C. furious.

The author uses two words to discuss one of Kate's qualities: *angry* and *irate*. This tells us that *irate* must be another way of saying "angry." (The author could have written, "but she's always angry about something or other.") Since *angry* can also mean *furious*, the correct answer is *C*.

3 Antonyms

Antonyms are words with opposite meanings. For example, *help* and *harm* are antonyms, as are *work* and *rest*. Antonyms serve as context clues by providing the opposite meaning of an unknown word. For instance, the sentence below from Chapter 1 provides an antonym clue for the word *antagonist*.

> In the ring, the two boxers were **antagonists**, but in their private lives, they were good friends.

The author is contrasting the boxers' two different relationships, so we can assume that *antagonists* and *good friends* have opposite, or contrasting, meanings. Using that contrast as a clue, write the letter of the answer that you think best defines *antagonist*.

    <u>B</u> *Antagonist* means   A. a supporter.   B. an enemy.   C. an example.

The correct answer is *B*. Because *antagonist* is the opposite of *friend*, it must mean "enemy."

4 General Sense of the Sentence

Even when there is no example, synonym, or antonym clue in a sentence, most of the time you can still figure out the meaning of an unfamiliar word. For example, look at the sentence from Chapter 1 for the word *malign*.

> That vicious Hollywood reporter often **maligns** movie stars, forever damaging their public images.

After studying the context carefully, you should be able to figure out what the reporter does to movie stars. That will be the meaning of *malign*. Write the letter of your choice.

    <u>C</u> *Malign* means   A. to praise.   B. to recognize.   C. to speak ill of.

Since the sentence calls the reporter "vicious" and says she damages public images, it is logical to conclude that she says negative things about movie stars. Thus answer *C* is correct.

By looking closely at the pair of sentences provided for each word, as well as the answer choices, you should be able to decide on the meaning of a word. As you figure out each meaning, you are working actively with the word. You are creating the groundwork you need to understand and to remember the word. *Getting involved with the word and developing a feel for it, based upon its use in context, is the key to word mastery.*

It is with good reason, then, that the directions at the top of page 8 tell you to use the context to figure out each word's _____ meaning _____. Doing so deepens your sense of the word and prepares you for the next activity.

● The *second part* of the chapter, on page 9, is titled _____ Matching Words with Definitions _____.

According to research, it is not enough to see a word in context. At a certain point, it is helpful as well to see the meaning of a word. The matching test provides that meaning, but it also makes you look for and think about that meaning. In other words, it continues the active learning that is your surest route to learning and remembering a word.

Note the caution that follows the test. Do not proceed any further until you are sure that you know the correct meaning of each word as used in context.

Keep in mind that a word may have more than one meaning. In fact, some words have quite a few meanings. (If you doubt it, try looking up in a dictionary, for example, the word *make* or *draw*.) In this book, you will focus on one common meaning for each vocabulary word. However, many of the words have additional meanings. For example, in Chapter 13, you will learn that *devastate* means "to upset deeply," as in the sentence "The parents were devastated when they learned that their son had been arrested." If you then look up *devastate* in the dictionary, you will discover that it has another meaning—"to destroy," as in "The hurricane devastated much of Florida." After you learn one common meaning of a word, you will find yourself gradually learning its other meanings in the course of your school and personal reading.

● The *third part* of the chapter, on page 10, is titled _____ Sentence Check 1 _____.

Here are ten sentences that give you an opportunity to apply your understanding of the ten words. After inserting the words, check your answers in the limited answer key at the back of the book. Be sure to use the answer key as a learning tool only. Doing so will help you to master the words and to prepare for the last two activities and the unit tests, for which answers are not provided.

● The *fourth and fifth parts* of the chapter, on pages 10–11, are titled _____ Sentence Check 2 _____ and _____ Final Check _____.

Each practice tests you on all ten words, giving you two more chances to deepen your mastery. In the fifth part, you have the context of an entire passage in which you can practice applying the words.

At the bottom of the last page of this chapter is a box where you can enter your score for the final two checks. These scores should also be entered into the vocabulary performance chart located on the inside back cover of the book. To get your score, count the number of items that you answered correctly in each section. Then add a zero. For example, if you got seven answers right in Sentence Check 2, you would write "70" on the first line in the score box.

Word Parts Chapters

Word parts are the building blocks of many English words. Learning word parts can help you spell and pronounce words, unlock the meanings of unfamiliar words, and remember new words.

This book covers forty word parts—prefixes, suffixes, and roots. **Prefixes** are word parts that are put at the beginning of words. When written separately, a prefix is followed by a hyphen to show that something follows it. For example, the prefix *non* is written like this: *non-*. One common meaning of *non-* is "not," as in the words *nontoxic* and *nonfiction*.

Suffixes are word parts that are added to the end of words. To show that something always comes before a suffix, a hyphen is placed at the beginning. For instance, the suffix *ly* is written like this: *-ly*. A common meaning of *-ly* is "in a certain manner," as in the words *easily* and *proudly*.

Finally, **roots** are word parts that carry the basic meaning of a word. Roots cannot be used alone. To make a complete word, a root must be combined with at least one other word part. Roots are written without hyphens. One common root is *cycl*, which means "circle," as in the words *motorcycle* and *cyclone*.

Each of the four chapters on word parts follows the same sequence as the chapters on vocabulary. Keep the following guidelines in mind as well. To find the meaning of a word part, you should do two things.

1 First decide on the meaning of each **boldfaced** word in "Ten Word Parts in Context." If you don't know a meaning, use context clues to find it. For example, consider the two sentences and the answer options for the word part *quart* or *quadr-* in Chapter 6. Write the letter of your choice.

> Let's cut the apple into **quarters** so all four of us can share it.
>
> The ad said I would **quadruple** my money in two months. But instead of making four times as much money, I lost what I had invested.

   _C_ The word part *quart* or *quadr-* means   A. overly.   B. two.   C. four.

You can conclude that if four people will be sharing one apple, *quarters* means "four parts." You can also determine that *quadruple* means "to multiply by four."

2 Then decide on the meaning each pair of boldfaced words has in common. This will also be the meaning of the word part they share. In the case of the two sentences above, both words include the idea of something multiplied or divided by four. Thus *quart* or *quadr-* must mean _____four_____.

You now know, in a nutshell, how to proceed with the words in each chapter. Make sure that you do each page very carefully. *Remember that as you work through the activities, you are learning the words.*

How many times in all will you use each word? If you look, you'll see that each chapter gives you the opportunity to work with each word six times. Each "impression" adds to the likelihood that the word will become part of your active vocabulary. You will have further opportunities to use the word in the crossword puzzle and tests that end each unit and in the online exercises available at **www.townsendpress.com**.

In addition, many of the words are repeated in context in later chapters of the book. Such repeated words are marked with a small circle (°). For example, which words from Chapter 1 are repeated in the Final Check on page 15 of Chapter 2?

        amiable   _adamant_

Analogies

This book also offers practice in word analogies, yet another way to deepen your understanding of words. An **analogy** is a similarity between two things that are otherwise different. Doing an analogy question is a two-step process. First you have to figure out the relationship in a pair of words. Those words are written like this:

LEAF : TREE

What is the relationship between the two words above? The answer can be stated like this: A leaf is a part of a tree.

Next, you must look for a similar relationship in a second pair of words. Here is how a complete analogy question looks:

LEAF : TREE ::

A. pond : river   C. page : book

B. foot : shoe   D. beach : sky

And here is how the question can be read:

_C_ LEAF is to TREE as

    A. *pond* is to *river.*   C. *page* is to *book.*

    B. *foot* is to *shoe.*   D. *beach* is to *sky.*

To answer the question, you have to decide which of the four choices has a relationship similar to the first one. Check your answer by seeing if it fits in the same wording as you used to show the relationship between *leaf* and *tree:* A ___ is part of a ___. Which answer do you choose?

The correct answer is *C.* Just as a leaf is part of a tree, a page is part of a book. On the other hand, a pond is not part of a river, nor is a foot part of a shoe, nor is a beach part of the sky.

We can state the complete analogy this way: *Leaf* is to *tree* as *page* is to *book.*

Here's another analogy question to try. Begin by figuring out the relationship between the first two words.

_D_ COWARD : HERO ::

    A. soldier : military   C. actor : famous

    B. infant : baby   D. boss : worker

Coward and *hero* are opposite types of people. So you need to look at the other four pairs to see which has a similar relationship. When you think you have found the answer, check to see that the two words you chose can be compared in the same way as *coward* and *hero:* ___ and ___ are opposite types of people.

In this case, the correct answer is *D; boss* and *worker* are opposite kinds of people. (In other words, *coward* is to *hero* as *boss* is to *worker.*)

By now you can see that there are basically two steps to doing analogy items:

1 Find out the relationship of the first two words.

2 Find the answer that expresses the same type of relationship as the first two words have.

Now try one more analogy question on your own. Write the letter of the answer you choose in the space provided.

_A_ SWING : BAT ::

    A. drive : car   C. catch : bat

    B. run : broom   D. fly : butterfly

If you chose answer *A,* you were right. *Swing* is what we do with a *bat,* and *drive* is what we do with a *car.*

Here are some other relationships often found in analogies:

- **Synonyms:** freedom : liberty (*freedom* and *liberty* mean the same thing)

- **Item to category:** baseball : sport (baseball is one kind of sport)

- **Item to description:** school bus : yellow (*yellow* is a word that describes a school bus)

- **Producer to product:** singer: song (a singer is the person who produces a song)

- **Time sequence:** January : March (January occurs two months before March)

A Final Thought

The facts are in. A strong vocabulary is a source of power. Words can make you a better reader, writer, speaker, thinker, and learner. They can dramatically increase your chances of success in school and in your job.

But words will not come automatically. They must be learned in a program of regular study. If you commit yourself to learning words, and you work actively and honestly with the chapters in this book, you will not only enrich your vocabulary—you will enrich your life as well.

Unit One

Chapter 1

absolve	antagonist
adamant	eccentric
amiable	encounter
amoral	epitome
animosity	malign

Chapter 2

curt	retort
demoralize	sabotage
dilemma	subsequent
inclination	wary
irate	zeal

Chapter 3

acclaim	exploit
adjacent	methodical
elicit	obsolete
engross	tangible
escalate	terminate

Chapter 4

deterrent	innovation
implication	revitalize
inequity	sparse
infirmity	subjective
infringe	succinct

Chapter 5

allusion	banal
altruistic	euphemism
appease	mercenary
arbitrary	syndrome
assail	taint

Chapter 6

ann, enn	-ly
audi, audio-	non-
cycl, cyclo-	path, -pathy
-hood	pend
hyper-	quart, quadr-

absolve	antagonist
adamant	eccentric
amiable	encounter
amoral	epitome
animosity	malign

Ten Words in Context

In the space provided, write the letter of the meaning closest to that of each **boldfaced** word. Use the context of the sentences to help you figure out each word's meaning.

1 absolve
(ăb-zŏlv′)
-verb

- Since there was not enough evidence of his guilt, the jury had to **absolve** Mr. Melman of the murder.
- Accused of taking bribes, the mayor said, "In the end, I'll clear my name and be **absolved** of any wrongdoing."

B *Absolve* means
    A. to accuse.   B. to clear of guilt.   C. to inform.

2 adamant
(ăd′ə-mənt)
-adjective

- Ron is **adamant** about not changing plans. He insists we should still camp out even though the weather report now says it will be cold and rainy.
- **Adamant** in his support of gun control, Senator Keen won't give in to pressure from powerful opponents.

A *Adamant* means
    A. firm.   B. uncertain.   C. flexible.

3 amiable
(ā′mē-ə-bəl)
-adjective

- My **amiable** dog greets both strangers and old friends with a happy yip and energetic tail-wagging.
- At first, our history teacher doesn't seem very friendly, but once you get to know her, she shows her **amiable** side.

C *Amiable* means
    A. intelligent.   B. uncaring.   C. good-natured.

4 amoral
(ā-môr′əl)
-adjective

- Jerry is almost totally **amoral**. He cares only about making money and having fun and couldn't care less about right or wrong.
- A former president of Uganda, Idi Amin, was truly **amoral**. He jailed, tortured, and killed innocent opponents without the slightest feeling of guilt.

C *Amoral* means
    A. cowardly.   B. lazy.   C. lacking ethical principles.

5 animosity
(ăn′ə-mŏs′ə-tē)
-noun

- I was shocked when Sandy said she hated Lionel. I'd never realized she felt such **animosity** toward him.
- The bad feelings between the two families go back so many generations that nobody remembers what originally caused the **animosity**.

A *Animosity* means
    A. strong dislike.   B. admiration.   C. great fear.

6 antagonist
(ăn-tăg′ə-nĭst)
-noun

- At the divorce hearing, the husband and wife were such bitter **antagonists** that it was hard to believe they had once loved each other.
- In the ring, the two boxers were **antagonists**, but in their private lives, they were good friends.

B *Antagonist* means
    A. a supporter.   B. an enemy.   C. an example.

7 eccentric
(ĭk-sĕn′trĭk)
-*adjective*

- Bruce is quite **eccentric**. For example, he lives in a circular house and rides to work on a motorcycle, in a three-piece suit.
- Florence Nightingale, the famous nursing reformer, had the **eccentric** habit of carrying a pet owl around in one of her pockets.

_B_ *Eccentric means*   A. ordinary.   B. odd.   C. careful.

8 encounter
(ĕn-koun′tər)
-*noun*

- My **encounter** with Malik in a Los Angeles supermarket surprised me, since I thought he still lived in Chicago.
- I dislike returning to my small hometown, where I am likely to have **encounters** with people who knew me as a troubled kid.

_C_ *Encounter means*   A. a thought.   B. a dinner.   C. a meeting.

9 epitome
(ĭ-pĭt′ə-mē)
-*noun*

- To many, the **epitome** of cuteness is a furry, round-eyed puppy.
- The great ballplayer and civil rights leader Jackie Robinson was the **epitome** of both physical and moral strength.

_A_ *Epitome means*   A. a perfect model.   B. an opposite.   C. a main cause.

10 malign
(mə-līn′)
-*verb*

- That vicious Hollywood reporter often **maligns** movie stars, forever damaging their public images.
- Stacy refuses to **malign** her ex-husband, even though he was the one who insisted on the divorce.

_C_ *Malign means*   A. to praise.   B. to recognize.   C. to speak ill of.

Matching Words with Definitions

Following are definitions of the ten words. Clearly write or print each word next to its definition. The sentences above and on the previous page will help you decide on the meaning of each word.

1. _adamant_   Not giving in; stubborn

2. _amoral_   Lacking a moral sense; without principles

3. _eccentric_   Differing from what is customary; odd

4. _absolve_   To find innocent or blameless

5. _encounter_   A brief or an unexpected meeting

6. _epitome_   A perfect or typical example

7. _antagonist_   An opponent; one who opposes or competes

8. _animosity_   Bitter hostility

9. _malign_   To make evil and often untrue statements about; speak evil of

10. _amiable_   Good-natured; friendly and pleasant

CAUTION: Do not go any further until you are sure the above answers are correct. Then you can use the definitions to help you in the following practices. Your goal is eventually to know the words well enough so that you don't need to check the definitions at all.

Sentence Check 1

Using the answer line provided, complete each item below with the correct word from the box. Use each word once.

| A. absolve | B. adamant | C. amiable | D. amoral | E. animosity |
| F. antagonist | G. eccentric | H. encounter | I. epitome | J. malign |

_____adamant_____ 1. Lilly was ___ in her belief that Sam was a genius at business. Even after his first two companies failed, she still had faith in him.

_____encounter_____ 2. My brothers had planned to meet in the restaurant, but their ___ took place in the parking lot.

_____malign_____ 3. I'm tired of hearing the two candidates for governor ___ each other with stupid insults.

_____amiable_____ 4. Because he doesn't want to lose a sale, Mac remains polite and ___ even when he's annoyed with a customer.

_____amoral_____ 5. Some criminals are truly ___—they don't see that some actions are right and that others are wrong.

_____epitome_____ 6. The ___ of refreshment is drinking an ice-cold lemonade on a sizzling hot day.

_____absolve_____ 7. Jed was ___(e)d of stealing money from the company, but the damage the accusation did to his reputation remained.

_____antagonist_____ 8. The owners of the department store were always competing with each other. They acted more like ____s than partners.

_____animosity_____ 9. I avoid serious discussions with my sister because she shows great ___ toward me if I don't share her opinion.

_____eccentric_____ 10. Today it's not odd for females to learn carpentry, but when my mother went to high school, girls who took wood shop were considered ___.

NOTE: Now check your answers to these items by turning to page 177. Going over the answers carefully will help you prepare for the next two practices, for which answers are not given.

Sentence Check 2

Using the answer lines provided, complete each item below with **two** words from the box. Use each word once.

_____eccentric_____
_____encounter_____ 1–2. The ___ millionaire dressed so shabbily that every ___ with him convinced us that he was poor.

_____animosity_____
_____malign_____ 3–4. Hiroshi feels such ___ toward his sister that he never says a single kind thing about her; he only ___s her.

_____adamant_____
_____antagonist_____ 5–6. Since the congresswoman was ___ in opposing the nuclear power plant, the plant's owners regarded her as their toughest ___.

_____amoral_____ 7–8. Wayne is so ___ that he doesn't even want to be ___(e)d of guilt for all the
_____absolve_____ times he has lied, cheated, and stolen.

_____epitome_____ 9–10. With his friendly air, good-natured laugh and generosity, Santa Claus is the
_____amiable_____ ___ of the ___ grandfather.

Final Check: *Joseph Palmer*

Here is a final opportunity for you to strengthen your knowledge of the ten words. First read the following selection carefully. Then fill in each blank with a word from the box at the top of the previous page. (Context clues will help you figure out which word goes in which blank.) Use each word once.

In 1830, a Massachusetts farmer named Joseph Palmer moved to the city, only to find that people continually reacted to him with anger and hatred. Why? Palmer certainly wasn't a(n) (1)_____amoral_____ man—no, he had a strong sense of right and wrong. He was a friendly and (2)_____amiable_____ person as well. And on the whole, Palmer was the (3)_____epitome_____ of a normal citizen, living a typical life with his family. Yet his neighbors crossed to the other side of the street to avoid an (4)_____encounter_____ with him. Children insulted Palmer and sometimes threw stones at him. Grown men hurled rocks through the windows of his house. Even the local minister (5)_____malign_____(e)d Palmer, telling the congregation that Palmer admired only himself.

One day, four men carrying scissors and a razor attacked Palmer and threw him to the ground. Pulling out a pocketknife, Palmer fought back, slashing at their legs. His (6)_____antagonist_____s fled. Afterward, Palmer was the one arrested and jailed. While in jail, he was attacked two more times. Both times, he fought his way free. After a year—although his accusers still wouldn't (7)_____absolve_____ him of guilt—he was released.

Palmer had won. The cause of all the (8)_____animosity_____ and abuse had been his long, flowing beard. Palmer, (9)_____adamant_____ to the end, had refused to shave.

Thirty years after Palmer's difficulties, it was no longer considered (10)_____eccentric_____ to wear whiskers. Among the many who wore beards then was the President of the United States, Abraham Lincoln.

Scores   Sentence Check 2 _____%   Final Check _____%

Enter your scores above and in the **Vocabulary Performance Chart** on the inside back cover of the book.

curt	retort
demoralize	sabotage
dilemma	subsequent
inclination	wary
irate	zeal

Ten Words in Context

In the space provided, write the letter of the meaning closest to that of each **boldfaced** word. Use the context of the sentences to help you figure out each word's meaning.

1 curt
(kûrt)
-adjective

● The fast-food manager trained workers to give polite, full answers to customers, not **curt** responses.

● Betsy doesn't mean to be **curt**. When she's with other people, she often says just a few quick words to them because she's so shy.

C *Curt* means   A. cautious.   B. courteous.   C. rudely brief.

2 demoralize
(dĭ-môr′ə-līz′)
-verb

● Cara's refusal to date my brother **demoralized** him so completely that for months, he lacked the confidence to ask another woman out.

● When Bonita gained a pound during her diet, it so **demoralized** her that she ate a banana split.

B *Demoralize* means   A. to cheat.   B. to discourage.   C. to excite.

3 dilemma
(dĭ-lĕm′ə)
-noun

● The store manager faced a **dilemma**: either having an elderly, needy man arrested or ignoring store rules about shoplifters.

● In old romantic movies, the heroine's **dilemma** often involves choosing between a rich boyfriend and the poor man she really loves.

A *Dilemma* means   A. a hard choice.   B. a great danger.   C. a benefit.

4 inclination
(ĭn-klə-nā′shən)
-noun

● My **inclination** is to major in nursing, but I'm going to speak to a few nurses before I make my final decision.

● That two-year-old has some irritating habits, such as her **inclination** to say "no" to everything.

A *Inclination* means   A. a preference.   B. a reason.   C. a fate.

5 irate
(ī-rāt′)
-adjective

● If Kate got angry only occasionally, I could take her more seriously, but she's always **irate** about something or other.

● Ray gets mad when his wife misplaces the TV's remote control, and she becomes equally **irate** when he writes a check and forgets to record it in the checkbook.

C *Irate* means   A. thrilled.   B. selfish.   C. furious.

6 retort
(rĭ-tôrt′)
-verb

● When I told my parents I'd put the dishes in the dishwasher the next morning, my father **retorted**, "Maybe we should serve you dinner in the mornings, too."

● "What do you want?" the young woman asked Dracula. "Only to drink in your charms," he **retorted**.

B *Retort* means   A. to approve.   B. to reply.   C. to ask.

7 sabotage
(săb′ə-tŏzh′)
-verb

- Terrorist groups train their members to **sabotage** airports and other public places.
- A fired programmer **sabotaged** the company's network by infecting it with a computer virus.

C *Sabotage* means
  A. to develop. B. to invest in. C. to do harm to.

8 subsequent
(sŭb′sĭ-kwənt′)
-adjective

- "I was hired as a stock boy," said the company president. "My **subsequent** jobs took me steadily up the company ladder."
- The first few times Janet drove on a highway, she was terrified, but on **subsequent** trips, she felt more relaxed.

B *Subsequent* means
  A. first. B. following. C. previous.

9 wary
(wâr′ē)
-adjective

- "There's no such thing as a free lunch" means that we should be **wary** about promises of getting something for nothing.
- I'm a little **wary** of people who, when they first meet me, treat me as if I'm their best friend.

A *Wary* means
  A. careful. B. tired. C. welcoming.

10 zeal
(zēl)
-noun

- Velma attacked her food with such **zeal** that I thought she hadn't eaten for a week!
- My neighbor has so much **zeal** about keeping our neighborhood clean that he sweeps our sidewalk if we don't do it ourselves.

B *Zeal* means
  A. resistance. B. passion. C. skill.

Matching Words with Definitions

Following are definitions of the ten words. Clearly write or print each word next to its definition. The sentences above and on the previous page will help you decide on the meaning of each word.

1. _____inclination_____   A tendency, or preference, to think, act, or behave in a certain way; a leaning

2. _____curt_____   Rudely brief when speaking to someone; abrupt

3. _____wary_____   Cautious; on guard

4. _____retort_____   To reply, especially in a quick, sharp, or witty way

5. _____demoralize_____   To lower the spirits of; weaken the confidence or cheerfulness of

6. _____dilemma_____   A situation requiring a difficult choice

7. _____subsequent_____   Following, in time or order; next; later

8. _____zeal_____   Enthusiastic devotion; intense enthusiasm

9. _____sabotage_____   To deliberately destroy or damage

10. _____irate_____   Very angry

CAUTION: Do not go any further until you are sure the above answers are correct. Then you can use the definitions to help you in the following practices. Your goal is eventually to know the words well enough so that you don't need to check the definitions at all.

Sentence Check 1

Using the answer line provided, complete each item below with the correct word from the box. Use each word once.

A. **curt**	B. **demoralize**	C. **dilemma**	D. **inclination**	E. **irate**
F. **retort**	G. **sabotage**	H. **subsequent**	I. **wary**	J. **zeal**

_____dilemma_____ 1. Rob's ___ was whether to go to work feeling sick or to stay home and lose a day's pay.

_____wary_____ 2. Be ___ when something sounds too good to be true—it probably is.

_____inclination_____ 3. I have to watch my budget because I have a(n) ___ to overspend.

_____curt_____ 4. The director cut off most of the auditioning singers with a(n) ___ response: "Thank you. That will be all."

_____sabotage_____ 5. The striking miners planned to ___ one of the mines by blowing up the main entrance.

_____demoralize_____ 6. Because Devan expected to get an A on his research paper, receiving a grade of C truly ___(e)d him.

_____subsequent_____ 7. The team played miserably in the first game of the season, but they managed to win all ___ games.

_____irate_____ 8. My father always became ___ when any of his children came home after curfew. One time he began yelling at me even before my date had left.

_____zeal_____ 9. If adolescents could apply to their studies just a bit of the ___ they feel for music and video games, their grades would improve dramatically.

_____retort_____ 10. When the wisecracking waiter said, "That hat looks ridiculous, lady," the woman stated, "I didn't come here to be insulted." "That's what you think!" ___(e)d the waiter.

NOTE: Now check your answers to these items by turning to page 177. Going over the answers carefully will help you prepare for the next two practices, for which answers are not given.

Sentence Check 2

Using the answer lines provided, complete each item below with **two** words from the box. Use each word once.

_____irate_____
_____curt_____

1–2. Already angry, the customer became even more ___ when he received only this ___ response: "No returns."

_____inclination_____
_____retort_____

3–4. When I answer my phone and hear someone demand, "Who is this?" my ___ is to ___, "I'm the person whose phone was ringing. Who is *this*?"

_____sabotage_____
_____wary_____

5–6. Because of terrorist attempts to ___ flights, airline security workers are ___ of even innocent-looking passengers.

_____ zeal _____

_____ demoralize _____

_____ subsequent _____

_____ dilemma _____

7–8. I began the semester with great ___ for my chemistry class, but the realization that I didn't have the necessary background quickly ___(e)d me.

9–10. Margo intended to accept the job offer to be a salad chef, but a(n) ___ offer for an office position has presented her with a(n) ___: Should she take the interesting restaurant job, which pays poorly, or the higher-paying job that may not interest her much?

Final Check: *Telephone Salespeople*

Here is a final opportunity for you to strengthen your knowledge of the ten words. First read the following selection carefully. Then fill in each blank with a word from the box at the top of the previous page. (Context clues will help you figure out which word goes in which blank.) Use each word once.

If my carpets need cleaning or I want a new cellphone plan, I will do some comparison shopping first. I am not likely to buy anything suddenly just because a complete stranger has phoned—usually during the dinner hour—to sell it. For this and other reasons, I have always been (1)_____ wary _____ of telephone salespeople. I don't like their cheerful, overly amiable° voices and their nervy suggestions as to how I might easily pay for whatever it is they are selling. My (2)_____ inclination _____ is to get off the phone as soon as possible.

My husband, however, creates a(n) (3)_____ dilemma _____ for me when he takes these calls. He doesn't want what is being sold either, but he feels sorry for the telemarketers. He doesn't want to (4)_____ demoralize _____ them with such a(n) (5)_____ curt _____ reply as "No." When they begin their sales pitches, he is overcome by their (6)_____ zeal _____ for their products and therefore listens politely. Then he (7)_____ sabotage _____s my efforts to discourage (8)_____ subsequent _____ calls by suggesting that the salespeople call back later to talk to his wife! I don't know who gets more (9)_____ irate _____ when that happens—I or the salespeople, disappointed when they realize we never intended to buy a thing. More than once, when I've finally said "No sale" for the last time to an adamant° telemarketer who had been refusing to take "no" for an answer, he or she has (10)_____ retort _____(e)d, "Well, thanks for wasting my time."

| Scores | Sentence Check 2 _____% | Final Check _____% |

acclaim	exploit
adjacent	methodical
elicit	obsolete
engross	tangible
escalate	terminate

Ten Words in Context

In the space provided, write the letter of the meaning closest to that of each **boldfaced** word. Use the context of the sentences to help you figure out each word's meaning.

1 acclaim
(ə-klām′)
-noun

- Any subway system that is clean, quiet, and safe deserves **acclaim**.
- Although Vincent Van Gogh's paintings are now worth millions of dollars, the artist received little **acclaim** in his lifetime and died in poverty.

B *Acclaim* means   A. criticism.   B. praise.   C. change.

2 adjacent
(ə-jā′sənt)
-adjective

- Because their desks are **adjacent**, Jeff and Kellie often exchange looks and comments.
- If you keep your dishes in a cupboard that's **adjacent** to the dishwasher, you won't have to walk too far when putting away the clean dishes.

A *Adjacent* means   A. close.   B. similar.   C. separated.

3 elicit
(ĭ-lĭs′ĭt)
-verb

- The movie star's violet eyes always **elicit** admiration and wonder.
- The basketball player's three-point shot to win the game in its final seconds **elicited** a roar of delight from the excited fans.

C *Elicit* means   A. to stop.   B. to follow.   C. to bring out.

4 engross
(ĕn′grōs′)
-verb

- The suspenseful TV movie so **engrossed** Bryan that he didn't even budge when he was called to dinner.
- The fascinating single-file march of black ants along the sidewalk **engrossed** me for several minutes.

A *Engross* means   A. to hold the interest of.   B. to disgust.   C. to bore.

5 escalate
(ĕs′kə-lāt′)
-verb

- The fight between the two hockey players **escalated** into an all-out battle among members of both teams.
- "We need to **escalate** our fund-raising efforts," the theater manager said. "Otherwise, the company won't survive."

A *Escalate* means   A. to expand.   B. to delay.   C. to weaken.

6 exploit
(ĕks-ploit′)
-verb

- At the turn of the century, factory owners **exploited** children by making them work in terrible conditions for as many as eighteen hours a day.
- Although Ricky is the English teacher's son, he refuses to **exploit** his status. He works as hard as anyone else in the class.

B *Exploit* means   A. to forget.   B. to take advantage of.   C. to be sad about.

7 methodical
(mə-thŏd′ĭ-kəl)
-adjective

- A **methodical** way to store spices is to shelve them in alphabetical order.
- Juanita is so **methodical** about her diet that she classifies the foods in each meal into different nutritional categories.

_C_ _Methodical_ means   A. accidental.   B. out-of-date.   c. orderly.

8 obsolete
(ŏb′sə-lēt′)
-adjective

- Cellphones are so common now that they have made pagers almost **obsolete**.
- In the United States, the automobile quickly made travel by horse and carriage **obsolete**.

_C_ _Obsolete_ means   A. popular.   B. useful.   c. extinct.

9 tangible
(tăn′jə-bəl)
-adjective

- The sculptor loved making her ideas **tangible** by giving them form in metal and stone.
- Corn-chip crumbs, empty soda bottles, and dirty napkins were **tangible** evidence that a party had taken place the night before.

_B_ _Tangible_ means   A. clever.   B. solid.   c. hidden.

10 terminate
(tûr′mə-nāt′)
-verb

- As the clock's hands inched toward 3:00, the students waited impatiently for the bell to **terminate** the last class before spring vacation.
- The referee should have **terminated** the boxing match when he first saw the weaker fighter losing the ability to defend himself.

_A_ _Terminate_ means   A. to end.   B. to revive.   c. to begin.

Matching Words with Definitions

Following are definitions of the ten words. Clearly write or print each word next to its definition. The sentences above and on the previous page will help you decide on the meaning of each word.

1. _____elicit_____ To draw forth

2. _____terminate_____ To stop; bring to an end

3. _____methodical_____ Orderly; systematic

4. _____adjacent_____ Close; near (to something)

5. _____tangible_____ Able to be touched; having form and matter

6. _____obsolete_____ No longer active or in use; out of date

7. _____escalate_____ To increase or intensify

8. _____acclaim_____ Great praise or applause; enthusiastic approval

9. _____engross_____ To hold the full attention of; absorb

10. _____exploit_____ To use selfishly or unethically; take unfair advantage of

CAUTION: Do not go any further until you are sure the above answers are correct. Then you can use the definitions to help you in the following practices. Your goal is eventually to know the words well enough so that you don't need to check the definitions at all.

Sentence Check 1

Using the answer line provided, complete each item below with the correct word from the box. Use each word once.

| A. acclaim | B. adjacent | C. elicit | D. engross | E. escalate |
| F. exploit | G. methodical | H. obsolete | I. tangible | J. terminate |

tangible   1. A wedding ring is a(n) ___ expression of a couple's commitment to each other.

obsolete   2. If solar energy becomes as cheap and plentiful as sunshine, nuclear energy, which is expensive, may become ___.

acclaim   3. With movies like *Saving Private Ryan, Forrest Gump, Cast Away,* and *Charlie Wilson's War* to his credit, actor Tom Hanks has won Oscars and the ___ of admiring critics.

adjacent   4. Our house is ___ to one with a high wooden fence, so our view on that side is completely blocked.

escalate   5. The shouting match between Rose and her brother ___(e)d until it was so loud that the neighbors complained.

engross   6. Sometimes an article I'm reading on the bus will ___ me so much that I'll pass my stop.

exploit   7. When workers feel ___(e)d by their employers, they often go on strike for larger salaries and better working conditions.

methodical   8. Diana is very ___ when it comes to cooking. She reads the recipe carefully, gathers all the ingredients, and gets out the utensils before beginning.

terminate   9. When Luke was caught stealing money on the job, the company ___(e)d his employment and brought him up on criminal charges.

elicit   10. In one disturbing survey, the question "Which do you like better, TV or Daddy?" ___(e)d this response from a number of children: "TV."

NOTE: Now check your answers to these items by turning to page 177. Going over the answers carefully will help you prepare for the next two practices, for which answers are not given.

Sentence Check 2

Using the answer lines provided, complete each item below with **two** words from the box. Use each word once.

engross
elicit   1–2. The gifted ice skater's routine ___(e)d the audience. It was the epitome° of grace and power combined. At the end, a long, rapid spin ___(e)d a burst of applause.

obsolete
terminate   3–4. Although hand-crafted furniture is almost ___, mass production hasn't yet ___(e)d all demand for it.

tangible
acclaim   5–6. Workers want ___ rewards such as a good salary and a health-care program, but they also welcome less concrete benefits, such as ___ for a job well done.

exploit

escalate

methodical

adjacent

7–8.   The more the British ___(e)d the American colonies by taxing them unfairly, the more the colonists' animosity° toward the British ___(e)d.

9–10. Patty's ___ approach to gardening is to arrange all the plants in a row, with each one ___ to the one that will be planted after it.

Final Check: _A Cruel Sport_

Here is a final opportunity for you to strengthen your knowledge of the ten words. First read the following selection carefully. Then fill in each blank with a word from the box at the top of the previous page. (Context clues will help you figure out which word goes in which blank.) Use each word once.

As Alex sat down in the carnival tent, the lights dimmed. A spotlight revealed a short, heavy man holding a thick chain. He tugged the chain, and an old, muzzled bear appeared. The man, the animal's owner, announced that the bear's name was Sally. He said he would give a hundred dollars to anyone who wrestled Sally to the floor.

"That's disgusting! You have no right to (1)___exploit___ an animal that way!" a woman called out. Several voices joined her in protest. A number of people walked out of the tent. Alex wanted to leave, too, but he was too shocked to move. He had thought bear wrestling was (2)___obsolete___, given up long ago as a cruel sport.

But the man's offer (3)___elicit___(e)d one drunken response. "I'll do it!" a big man yelled, winning the (4)___acclaim___ of Sally's owner, who congratulated him warmly. The drunk began swinging at Sally. She backed away. "Knock her on her rear!" the owner shouted with zeal°. When Sally finally raised a paw to defend herself, her antagonist° could see that she had no claws. Feeling very brave now, he (5)___escalate___(e)d his attack.

The horrible scene (6)___engross___(e)d Alex, who could barely believe his eyes. The man sitting (7)___adjacent___ to Alex rose to his feet and left, muttering "This shouldn't be allowed. I'm calling the police."

Meanwhile, the drunken man knocked Sally over. Her owner then (8)___terminate___(e)d the match and handed Sally a bucket of food. The (9)___methodical___ way in which he conducted his act showed Alex he had done it many, many times before.

Finally, the owner led Sally away. The animal's drooping head and her labored walk were (10)___tangible___ expressions of her misery. As Sally passed him, Alex saw two police officers enter the tent. He hoped with all his heart that the law could prevent another such amoral° display of cruelty to this living creature.

Scores   Sentence Check 2 _____%   Final Check _____%

Enter your scores above and in the **Vocabulary Performance Chart** _on the inside back cover of the book._

CHAPTER 4

deterrent	innovation
implication	revitalize
inequity	sparse
infirmity	subjective
infringe	succinct

Ten Words in Context

In the space provided, write the letter of the meaning closest to that of each **boldfaced** word. Use the context of the sentences to help you figure out each word's meaning.

1 deterrent
(dĭ-tûr′ənt)
-*noun*

- As a **deterrent** to burglars, my father put a sign on our lawn that says, "Beware of pit bull."
- If the dangers of skydiving aren't a big enough **deterrent** for Ben, maybe the high cost will be.

_B_ *Deterrent* means   A. a reward.   B. a prevention.   C. a reason.

2 implication
(ĭm-plĭ-kā′shən)
-*noun*

- When the boss said that company profits were down, the **implication** was that nobody would be getting a raise.
- When the salesman winked, the **implication** was that he would give Joaquin a special deal on a car.

_C_ *Implication* means   A. a minor fault.   B. a demand.   C. something suggested.

3 inequity
(ĭn-ĕk′wĭt-ē)
-*noun*

- In South Africa, Mahatma Gandhi experienced an **inequity** that was all too common at the time—he was thrown off a "whites only" train.
- Most Americans consider it an **inequity** that some millionaires pay less in taxes than ordinary citizens do.

_A_ *Inequity* means   A. an injustice.   B. a physical weakness.   C. a question.

4 infirmity
(ĭn-fûr′mə-tē)
-*noun*

- Rick uses a wheelchair, but he doesn't let his **infirmity** keep him from traveling.
- Certain **infirmities**, such as arthritis and diabetes, are more likely to affect the elderly.

_B_ *Infirmity* means   A. a relationship.   B. a disability.   C. a secret.

5 infringe
(ĭn-frĭnj′)
-*verb*

- The protesters may picket the nuclear power plant as long as they don't **infringe** on other people's right to enter and exit freely.
- When my mother is doing her homework, no one is allowed to **infringe** on her quiet time.

_A_ *Infringe on* means   A. to interfere with.   B. to protect.   C. to recognize.

6 innovation
(ĭn′ə-vā′shən)
-*noun*

- When commercial bakers first offered sliced bread, it was considered an exciting **innovation**.
- The high cost of college has led to such financial **innovations** as savings accounts for children's education begun while the children are still infants.

_A_ *Innovation* means   A. something new.   B. a weakness.   C. an imitation.

20

7 revitalize
(rē-vĭt′əl-īz′)
-verb

- When DeShawn is tired after work, he finds a brief nap **revitalizes** him for an evening out with friends.
- The City Council hopes to **revitalize** the currently lifeless shopping district by offering tax breaks for new businesses.

A *Revitalize* means   A. to refresh.   B. to amuse.   C. to tire out.

8 sparse
(spărs)
-adjective

- There are thick pine forests at the foot of the mountain, but higher up, the trees become **sparse**.
- Unfortunately, the turnout for the team's first pep rally was **sparse**. Organizers hope to have better attendance at the next one.

B *Sparse* means   A. long.   B. thin.   C. crowded.

9 subjective
(səb-jĕk′tĭv)
-adjective

- Martina, a highly **subjective** judge of her son's abilities, feels he's brilliant in every respect. The boy's father, however, has a less emotional view of him.
- The reporter refused to write about his friend's trial. He knew any story he wrote would be too **subjective** to be published as an unbiased article.

A *Subjective* means   A. one-sided.   B. boring.   C. impersonal.

10 succinct
(sək-sĭngkt′)
-adjective

- Text messages are usually **succinct**. People don't want to type any more words than necessary to get their messages across.
- "What's new?" is a **succinct** way of asking, "Has anything of interest happened to you lately, my friend?"

C *Succinct* means   A. wordy.   B. prejudiced.   C. brief and clear.

Matching Words with Definitions

Following are definitions of the ten words. Clearly write or print each word next to its definition. The sentences above and on the previous page will help you decide on the meaning of each word.

1. _____inequity_____   Injustice; unfairness; an instance of injustice

2. _____innovation_____   A new custom, method, or invention; something newly introduced

3. _____subjective_____   Based on personal opinions, feelings, and attitudes; not objective

4. _____deterrent_____   Something that discourages or prevents a certain action

5. _____succinct_____   Expressed clearly in a few words; to the point; concise

6. _____revitalize_____   To renew the strength and energy of; restore to a vigorous, active condition

7. _____infirmity_____   A physical weakness or defect; ailment

8. _____sparse_____   Distributed thinly; not thick or crowded

9. _____infringe_____   To intrude or trespass on; to go beyond the limits considered proper

10. _____implication_____   An idea that is communicated indirectly, through a suggestion or hint

CAUTION: Do not go any further until you are sure the above answers are correct. Then you can use the definitions to help you in the following practices. Your goal is eventually to know the words well enough so that you don't need to check the definitions at all.

Sentence Check 1

Using the answer line provided, complete each item below with the correct word from the box. Use each word once.

A. deterrent	B. implication	C. inequity	D. infirmity	E. infringe
F. innovation	G. revitalize	H. sparse	I. subjective	J. succinct

infirmity 1. Although Marie joked about her broken leg, it was an ___ that kept her from work for a month.

implication 2. When a restaurant's tables have ashtrays, the ___ is that smoking is permitted.

infringe 3. Our democratic rights do not include the freedom to ___ on other people's rights.

succinct 4. "Now" is a ___ way of saying, "At this particular point in time."

sparse 5. Our grass is ___ along a path at the corner of the lot, where kids take a shortcut through our yard.

innovation 6. An interesting ___ in food packaging is a bottle from which salad dressing is sprayed, rather than poured.

revitalize 7. The seminar for company employees ___(e)d my aunt's interest in her job by giving her new skills and suggesting new goals.

subjective 8. *The Diary of Anne Frank* is a ___ view of events during World War II, from the point of view of a young Jewish girl in hiding.

inequity 9. The company was accused of creating a(n) ___ by paying women less than men for doing the same work.

deterrent 10. The fact that Beethoven was totally deaf by age 50 was not a(n) ___ to his composing, at the age of 53, one of his most ambitious and beloved works, the *Ninth Symphony*.

NOTE: Now check your answers to these items by turning to page 177. Going over the answers carefully will help you prepare for the next two practices, for which answers are not given.

Sentence Check 2

Using the answer lines provided, complete each item below with **two** words from the box. Use each word once.

sparse
revitalize 1–2. When the candidate for mayor saw the ___ turnout for his speech, he knew he had to do something to ___ his campaign.

innovation
infringe 3–4. Future ___s in technology, particularly on the Internet, may make it easier for a government to ___ on the privacy of citizens' computer records.

infirmity
deterrent 5–6. Although arthritis can be a painful ___, Aunt Fern refuses to let it be a(n) ___ to her active lifestyle. For example, she continues to go square-dancing every week.

_____subjective_____   7–8. All editorials are ___—they represent someone's opinions. In an editorial, for
_____inequity_____   example, writers are free to argue against the ___ of police brutality, instead
                            of just reporting on it.

_____implication_____   9–10. A sign may be brief and still have several ___s. For example, the ___ sign
_____succinct_____   "Dangerous Curve" suggests that drivers should be wary° and slow down,
                            that the curve ahead is sharp, and that bad accidents have happened there
                            before.

Final Check: *Bald Is Beautiful*

Here is a final opportunity for you to strengthen your knowledge of the ten words. First read the following
selection carefully. Then fill in each blank with a word from the box at the top of the previous page.
(Context clues will help you figure out which word goes in which blank.) Use each word once.

While I was looking through a men's hair-care magazine,
I noticed many ads for toupees and hair thickeners. The
(1)_____implication_____ seemed to be that a man's baldness
is a major (2)_____infirmity_____. Well, I'm not going to
let anyone (3)_____infringe_____ on a man's right
to be bald, or to demoralize° those who have already lost
their hair. Listen, all you baldies. You may feel it's a serious
(4)_____inequity_____ that some heads have only
(5)_____sparse_____ hair while others are thickly covered,
but I think bald men—including my father—are terrifically
attractive. Sure, that's just my (6)_____subjective_____
opinion, but I'm not alone. I know another woman whose
boyfriend went so far as to shave his head in order to
(7)_____revitalize_____ their tired romance. My thick-haired boyfriend hasn't offered to go quite
that far, but I wouldn't offer any (8)_____deterrent_____ to him if he had an inclination° to do the
same thing. I know drug companies manufacture medications to produce hair on bald heads, but that's
one (9)_____innovation_____ I would discourage any man from using. I'd even like to see the day
when toupees are as obsolete° as hoop skirts. I hate to see all those beautiful, shiny bald heads covered up.
Or, to be more (10)_____succinct_____: bald is beautiful.

| Scores | Sentence Check 2 _____% | Final Check _____% |

allusion	banal
altruistic	euphemism
appease	mercenary
arbitrary	syndrome
assail	taint

Ten Words in Context

In the space provided, write the letter of the meaning closest to that of each **boldfaced** word. Use the context of the sentences to help you figure out each word's meaning.

1 allusion
(ə-lo͞o′zhən)
-noun

- After I suggested that Monty have fruit for dessert instead of chocolate cake, he responded, "Is that an **allusion** to my weight?"
- Ramon didn't have the courage to come right out and ask Lia to marry him. Instead, he made only an **allusion** to marriage by asking, "Wouldn't it be easier if we had to fill out just one tax return?"

_B_ *Allusion to* means   A. a contrast to.   B. a hint about.   C. an answer for.

2 altruistic
(ăl′tro͞o-ĭs′tĭk)
-adjective

- When an enemy approaches, ground squirrels show **altruistic** behavior. They risk their own lives to give alarm calls to nearby relatives.
- "I'm not often **altruistic**," Brett admitted. "I usually put my own welfare first."

_A_ *Altruistic* means   A. unselfish.   B. cheerful.   C. greedy.

3 appease
(ə-pēz′)
-verb

- My sister was so outraged when I accidentally dropped and broke her cell phone that nothing I could say or do would **appease** her.
- Roger was furious when he saw me out with another guy, but I quickly **appeased** him by explaining that the "date" was my cousin.

_C_ *Appease* means   A. to annoy.   B. to heal.   C. to calm.

4 arbitrary
(är′bĭ-trĕr′ē)
-adjective

- Professor Miller's students were angry that he graded essays in an **arbitrary** way, rather than using clear-cut standards.
- Parents should not enforce rules according to their moods. Such **arbitrary** discipline only confuses children.

_C_ *Arbitrary* means   A. steady.   B. slow.   C. impulsive.

5 assail
(ə-sāl′)
-verb

- The storm **assailed** us with hail and heavy rain.
- The two candidates continuously **assailed** each other with accusations of dishonesty.

_A_ *Assail* means   A. to attack.   B. to confuse.   C. to support.

6 banal
(bə-năl′)
-adjective

- The film, with its overused expressions and unimaginative plot, was the most **banal** I had ever seen.
- "Nice to see you" may be a **banal** comment, but what it lacks in originality it makes up for in friendliness.

_B_ *Banal* means   A. greedy.   B. unoriginal.   C. clever.

7 euphemism
(yōō'fə-mĭz'əm)
-noun

● Common **euphemisms** include "final resting place" (for *grave*), "intoxicated" (for *drunk*), and "powder room" (for *toilet*).

● The Central Intelligence Agency is on record as having referred to assassination with the **euphemism** "change of health."

B *Euphemism* means   A. a harsh term.   B. a term that doesn't offend.   C. a foreign term.

8 mercenary
(mûr'sə-něr'ē)
-adjective

● Ed is totally **mercenary**. His philosophy is, "Pay me enough, and I'll do anything."

● The con man pretended to love the wealthy widow, but he actually married her for **mercenary** reasons.

C *Mercenary* means   A. jealous.   B. angry.   C. greedy.

9 syndrome
(sĭn'drōm)
-noun

● Headaches are usually harmless, but as part of a **syndrome** including fever and a stiff neck, they may be a sign of a serious illness.

● Jet lag is a **syndrome** resulting from flying long distances; it often includes exhaustion, headache, and loss of appetite.

A *Syndrome* means   A. a group of symptoms.   B. a cause.   C. something required.

10 taint
(tānt)
-verb

● The involvement of organized crime has **tainted** many sports, including boxing and horse racing.

● The government scandal **tainted** the reputations of everyone involved.

B *Taint* means   A. to benefit.   B. to damage.   C. to start.

Matching Words with Definitions

Following are definitions of the ten words. Clearly write or print each word next to its definition. The sentences above and on the previous page will help you decide on the meaning of each word.

1. _____arbitrary_____   Determined by personal judgment, not rule or reason; based on impulse
2. _____mercenary_____   Motivated only by financial gain; greedy
3. _____allusion_____   An indirect reference
4. _____syndrome_____   A group of symptoms typical of a particular disease or condition
5. _____euphemism_____   A mild or vague term used as a substitute for one considered offensive or unpleasant
6. _____appease_____   To calm, especially by giving in to the demands of
7. _____banal_____   Lacking originality; overused; commonplace
8. _____taint_____   To stain the honor of someone or something
9. _____assail_____   To attack physically or verbally
10. _____altruistic_____   Unselfishly concerned for the welfare of others; unselfish

CAUTION: Do not go any further until you are sure the above answers are correct. Then you can use the definitions to help you in the following practices. Your goal is eventually to know the words well enough so that you don't need to check the definitions at all.

Sentence Check 1

Using the answer line provided, complete each item below with the correct word from the box. Use each word once.

A. **allusion**	B. **altruistic**	C. **appease**	D. **arbitrary**	E. **assail**
F. **banal**	G. **euphemism**	H. **mercenary**	I. **syndrome**	J. **taint**

_____mercenary_____ 1. There have been people ___ enough to sell their own children for the right price.

_____allusion_____ 2. "Someone hasn't shown me his report card," my mother said, making a(n) ___ to my brother.

_____altruistic_____ 3. It takes a(n) ___ person to adopt a disabled child.

_____assail_____ 4. The mugger ___ed his victims with a baseball bat.

_____euphemism_____ 5. The local undertaker insists on using a(n) ___ for the chapel of his funeral parlor. He calls it the "slumber room."

_____taint_____ 6. The report that the halfback was addicted to drugs ___(e)d the team's image.

_____appease_____ 7. The only thing that would ___ the dead boy's parents was imprisonment of the drunk driver who had killed him.

_____syndrome_____ 8. Abraham Lincoln is thought to have had Marfan's ___, a group of symptoms which includes unusually long bones and abnormal blood circulation.

_____arbitrary_____ 9. The judge's harsh sentence was ___. Rather than being based on past similar cases or on the seriousness of the crime, it was based on the judge's opinion of the defendant.

_____banal_____ 10. "You're special" probably appears on thousands of greeting cards, but when someone says it to you and means it, it never seems ___.

NOTE: Now check your answers to these items by turning to page 177. Going over the answers carefully will help you prepare for the next two practices, for which answers are not given.

Sentence Check 2

Using the answer lines provided, complete each item below with **two** words from the box. Use each word once.

_____Altruistic_____
_____mercenary_____
1–2. ___ people tend to place the public welfare above their own self-interest. In contrast, ___ people will exploit° anyone for a profit—they will even sell harmful products.

_____assail_____
_____appease_____
3–4. The angry customer loudly ___(e)d the salesman for having sold her a broken clock. The salesman quickly ___(e)d her by giving her a full refund.

_____syndrome_____
_____taint_____
5–6. A certain rare ___ includes a very odd symptom—an uncontrollable urge to use obscene language. This disease can ___ a victim's reputation, because some people who hear the foul language won't understand the reason for it.

_____arbitrary_____
_____euphemism_____
7–8. My boss judges performance in a(n) ___ manner, praising and scolding according to his moods. And when he says, "Please stay a few minutes longer today," "a few minutes" is a(n) ___ for "an hour."

_____banal_____   9–10. The critic hated stale language. Instead of writing a(n) ___ comment such
_____allusion_____   as "That ballerina is light on her feet," he made an interesting ___ to the
                                   dancer's movements: "She was never heavier than moonlight."

Final Check: *No Luck with Women*

Here is a final opportunity for you to strengthen your knowledge of the ten words. First read the following selection carefully. Then fill in each blank with a word from the box at the top of the previous page. (Context clues will help you figure out which word goes in which blank.) Use each word once.

My older brother, Mark, has no luck with women. He doesn't understand why. I do.

To begin with, when he first meets a woman, he goes into one of two styles of conversation. The first is to (1)_____assail_____ her with a stream of personal questions: "What's your name? Where do you live? Is that your real hair color? What kind of work do you do? Do you want to have kids someday? Are you seeing anyone? Would you like to have dinner with me?" Naturally, most women find this surprising and annoying. His other approach is to say the most (2)_____banal_____ things imaginable:

"Nice day, isn't it? I thought it might rain this morning, but it didn't. It might rain tomorrow, but who knows. Last week was nice weather, too." By this time the poor girl has either walked away or passed out from boredom.

Another thing Mark often does in his encounters° with women is to say things that make him sound totally (3)_____mercenary_____, as if money were the most important thing in the world to him. He makes frequent (4)_____allusion_____s to his own salary, asks the woman how much she makes, and complains about the prices of everything on a menu. When he takes a date to a movie, he sometimes embarrasses her by trying to get his money back from the theater manager afterward, claiming he hadn't liked the movie. Naturally, this sort of behavior somewhat (5)_____taint_____s him in the woman's eyes, and he rarely gets a second date. When one of his former girlfriends complained to me about Mark's behavior, I tried to (6)_____appease_____ her by telling her that underneath it all, Mark is really a nice guy. She replied by saying that she didn't have the inclination° to dig that far down.

Mark, of course, finds women's reactions to him completely (7)_____arbitrary_____. He shakes his head and says, "Women are just not reasonable. Here I am, as nice as can be, and they act as if I have some horrible, contagious (8)_____syndrome_____." I try to be a(n) (9)_____altruistic_____ sister and help the guy out. I point out how his behaviors turn women off, using gentle (10)_____euphemism_____s such as "You're a special, unusual person, Mark. You're just a little eccentric°." Maybe I need to come right out and let him hear the truth, even if it makes him mad: "You're *weird*, Mark."

Scores	Sentence Check 2 _____%	Final Check _____%

Enter your scores above and in the **Vocabulary Performance Chart** on the inside back cover of the book.

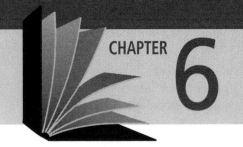

ann, enn	-ly
audi, audio-	non-
cycl, cyclo-	path, -pathy
-hood	pend
hyper-	quart, quadr-

Ten Word Parts in Context

Common word parts—also known as *prefixes, suffixes*, and *roots*—are used in forming many words in English. Figure out the meanings of the following ten word parts by looking *closely* and *carefully* at the context in which they appear. Then, in the space provided, write the letter of the meaning closest to that of each word part.

1 ann, enn

● This year's **annual** family reunion will be held at a campground.

● Our town is having a big **bicentennial** parade exactly two hundred years after the day the town was founded.

B The word part *ann* or *enn* means   A. four.   B. year.   C. hang.

2 audi, audio-

● The bride's softly spoken wedding vows were not **audible** to those at the back of the church.

● The sound system in the new **auditorium** is so good that music can be heard clearly even in the upper balconies.

C The word part *audi* or *audio-* means   A. condition.   B. feeling.   C. hearing.

3 cycl, cyclo-

● When Bob asked his parents if he could buy a new "two-wheeler," they didn't realize he meant a **motorcycle**.

● A **cyclone** travels in a circular motion.

A The word part *cycl* or *cyclo-* means   A. circle.   B. four.   C. condition.

4 -hood

● When children reach **adulthood**, how much help should their parents give them?

● For my great-grandmother, **womanhood** began early—she was married at 15.

A The word part *-hood* means   A. state of.   B. sound.   C. not.

5 hyper-

● Trina is **hypersensitive** to conflict. When people disagree with her, she thinks they are rejecting her personally.

● On the Internet, pages are written in **hypertext**—a special language that includes links to related text, images, and sound.

B The word part *hyper-* means   A. opposite of.   B. more than normal.   C. fourth.

6 -ly

● One cannot **easily** drown in Utah's Great Salt Lake because the lake's high percentage of salt helps people float.

● During the American Revolution, many brides **proudly** wore red, instead of white, as a symbol of rebellion.

B The word part *-ly* means   A. fourth.   B. in a certain way.   C. opposite of.

7 non-

- The paints used in elementary schools are **nontoxic** so that a child who might swallow some won't be poisoned.
- The story about the aliens was supposed to be **nonfiction**, but it sounded made-up to me.

B The word part *non-* means

    A. condition.   B. not.   C. overly.

8 path, -pathy

- When Ricardo's marriage fell apart, Ben's reaction was very **empathic** because he had also been rejected by a loved one.
- Felicia and her mother claim to have powers of **telepathy**. They say that they know each other's feelings and thoughts without being told.

A The word part *path* or *-pathy* means

    A. feeling.   B. hearing.   C. the opposite.

9 pend

- The children's swing is an old tire that's **suspended** from a strong oak branch.
- I can't sit and watch the swinging **pendulum** of a grandfather clock without starting to feel sleepy.

C The word part *pend* means

    A. suffering.   B. to listen.   C. to hang.

10 quart, quadr-

- Let's cut the apple into **quarters** so all four of us can share it.
- The ad said I would **quadruple** my money in two months. But instead of making four times as much money, I lost what I had invested.

C The word part *quart* or *quadr-* means

    A. overly.   B. two.   C. four.

Matching Word Parts with Definitions

Following are definitions of the ten word parts. Clearly write or print each word part next to its definition. The sentences above and on the previous page will help you decide on the meaning of each word part.

1. _____quart, quadr-_____ Four, fourth

2. _____path, -pathy_____ Feeling, suffering

3. _____-ly_____ In a certain manner

4. _____audi, audio-_____ Hearing, sound

5. _____pend_____ To hang

6. _____-hood_____ State, condition

7. _____ann, enn_____ Year

8. _____hyper-_____ More than normal; overly; excessively

9. _____cycl, cyclo-_____ Circle

10. _____non-_____ Not; the opposite of

CAUTION: Do not go any further until you are sure the above answers are correct. Then you can use the definitions to help you in the following practices. Your goal is eventually to know the word parts well enough so that you don't need to check the definitions at all.

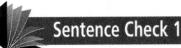

Sentence Check 1

Using the answer line provided, complete each *italicized* word below with the correct word part from the box. Use each word part once.

A. ann	B. audi, audio-	C. cycl, cyclo-	D. -hood	E. hyper-
F. -ly	G. non-	H. path, -pathy	I. pend	J. quart, quadr-

___audience___ 1. Chen loves playing the piano, especially when he has a(n) (. . . *ence*) ___ listening to him.

___sympathetic___ 2. It's hard for me to be (*sym . . . etic*) ___ when my sister complains, because she causes so many of her problems herself.

___childhood___ 3. Because of therapy, Grace is a well-adjusted adult, but her (*child . . .*) ___ years were troubled and unhappy.

___pendant___ 4. When I lost one of my diamond earrings, I had the other one made into a(n) (. . . *ant*) ___ to hang around my neck.

___quartet___ 5. The children's odd (. . . *et*) ___ consisted of a toy-drum player, a building-block clapper, a piano player, and a bell ringer.

___nonessential___ 6. We were told to bring only necessary equipment on our camping trip, so I was surprised to see how much (. . . *essential*) ___ gear others brought.

___happily___ 7. Mrs. Baker said she and her husband had been (*happi . . .*) ___ married for forty-seven years. But Mr. Baker, correcting her, said 1977 wasn't so great.

___unicycle___ 8. One of the most difficult vehicles to ride is also one of the simplest: a (*uni . . . e*) ___, a vehicle with only one wheel.

___annually___ 9. The supervisor said that workers would be evaluated (. . . *ually*) ___ for possible promotions. So if they don't get a promotion one year, they might get one the next.

___hypertension___ 10. My grandmother has (. . . *tension*) ___, which is abnormally high blood pressure.

NOTE: Now check your answers to these items by turning to page 177. Going over the answers carefully will help you prepare for the next two practices, for which answers are not given.

Sentence Check 2

Using the answer line provided, complete each *italicized* word in the sentences below with the correct word part from the box. Use each word part once.

___manhood___
___depends___
1–2. Some males act as if their (*man . . .*) ___ really (*de . . . s*) ___ on how many touchdowns they score or home runs they hit, rather than on maturity and strength of character.

___cyclist___
___helplessly___
3–4. The (. . . *ist*) ___ stood (*helpless . . .*) ___ staring at the tire he had chained to the tree. The rest of the bike had been stolen.

___nondrinker___
___hypercritical___
5–6. Stan, a (. . . *drinker*) ___, is (. . . *critical*) ___ of anyone who touches alcohol. He is adamant° in his belief that taking even a single drink is the sign of a self-destructive personality.

_____audiovisual_____   7–8. The nursing class watched an (. . . *visual*) ___ show about the horrible
_____pathetic_____   conditions in a mental institution of the 1950s. The patients looked (. . . *etic*)
                               ___; clearly, they were suffering.

_____quarterly_____   9–10. For my research report, I used two online articles—one from a (. . . *erly*)
_____annual_____   ___, posted four times a year; and the other from an (. . . *ual*) ___ that
                               appears only every January.

Final Check: *A Taste of Parenthood*

Here is a final opportunity for you to strengthen your knowledge of the ten word parts. First read the
following selection carefully. Then complete each *italicized* word in the parentheses below with a word
part from the box at the top of the previous page. (Context clues will help you figure out which word part
goes in which blank.) Use each word part once.

I have a lot of (*sym* . . .) (1)_____sympathy_____ for
parents of twins, triplets, and (. . . *uplets*) (2)_____quadruplets_____.
I just spent the weekend baby-sitting for my four nieces and
nephews.

First, I altruistically° offered to watch my brother's two
children so that he and his wife could go away for the weekend for
their sixth wedding (. . . *iversary*) (3)_____anniversary_____.
Then my sister called and said that her husband, an actor, had a
chance to (. . . *tion*) (4)_____audition_____ for a big part
in a TV drama. He had to fly to California for the weekend. She said
she'd love to go along if I could watch their children, aged two
and three. I (*willing* . . .) (5)_____willingly_____ agreed.

What a time I had! I soon learned that the word *baby-sitting*
has a false implication°—I did very little sitting that weekend.
The children's activity was (. . . *stop*) (6)_____nonstop_____. It seemed as if they never sat down,
and nothing engrossed° them for more than a few minutes. They went from pedaling their tiny (*tri* . . . *es*)
(7)_____tricycles_____ to building with their blocks to banging their toy drums. They "washed" the
dishes, let the dog loose, and made mud pies in the tomato garden. By Sunday, I was convinced they
were all (. . . *active*) (8)_____hyperactive_____. In addition, all weekend I was assailed° with endless
questions: "Why can't I stay up late?" "Do I have to brush my teeth?" "What do ants eat?"

Besides all the activity and questions, I had to cope with the knowledge that four little ones were
entirely (*de* . . . *ent*) (9)_____dependent_____ on me for their needs. What if one got hurt? What if they got
sick? Fortunately, we survived without a disaster.

I can't imagine what it must be like for parents with two or more children. I guess I'm not ready to have
kids yet—not even one. At least my responsibilities were terminated° on Sunday night. But (*parent* . . .)
(10)_____parenthood_____ is for keeps. I think I'll wait.

| Scores | Sentence Check 2 _____ % | Final Check _____ % |

The box at the right lists twenty-five words from Unit One. Using the clues at the bottom of the page, fill in these words to complete the puzzle that follows.

Word list:
absolve
acclaim
adjacent
altruistic
amiable
animosity
arbitrary
banal
demoralize
deterrent
eccentric
epitome
escalate
inclination
infringe
innovation
mercenary
obsolete
retort
sparse
subsequent
succinct
taint
terminate
zeal

ACROSS

1. To stain the honor of someone or something
4. To stop; bring to an end
5. To lower the spirits of
6. To reply, especially in a quick, sharp, or witty way
7. Friendly and pleasant
9. Motivated only by financial gain; greedy
11. Distributed thinly
13. Close; near (to something)
15. A tendency to think, act, or behave in a certain way
18. Lacking originality; overused
20. Enthusiastic devotion; intense enthusiasm
21. A perfect or typical example
22. To intrude or trespass on; to go beyond proper limits
23. Determined by personal judgment; based on impulse

DOWN

2. Great praise or applause; enthusiastic approval
3. Something that prevents or discourages a certain action
8. To find innocent or blameless
10. Differing from what is customary; odd
12. Expressed clearly in a few words
13. Unselfishly concerned for the welfare of others; unselfish
14. To increase or intensify
15. A new custom, method, or invention; something newly introduced
16. No longer active or in use; out-of-date
17. Following in time or order; next; later; succeeding
19. Bitter hostility

PART A

Choose the word that best completes each item and write it in the space provided.

__*escalates*__ 1. In the winter, the price of tomatoes ___ while their quality goes down.

    A. elicits   B. appeases   C. escalates   D. absolves

__*euphemism*__ 2. A common ___ for *corpse* is "remains."

    A. syndrome   B. dilemma   C. euphemism   D. zeal

__*mercenary*__ 3. The taxi driver was so ___ that he charged his own mother for a ride.

    A. mercenary   B. amiable   C. curt   D. wary

__*inequity*__ 4. Do you consider it an ___ that only one percent of Americans own 40 percent of the nation's wealth?

    A. allusion   B. inclination   C. inequity   D. acclaim

__*obsolete*__ 5. You probably thought that mail delivery by mule was ___, but it still exists in the Grand Canyon.

    A. adamant   B. curt   C. tangible   D. obsolete

__*succinct*__ 6. You can make your essays ___ by going through them carefully to remove all unnecessary words.

    A. succinct   B. adamant   C. tangible   D. eccentric

__*epitome*__ 7. New York's firefighters and police were the ___ of courage during the attack on the World Trade Center on September 11, 2001. Many of them lost their lives while attempting to save others.

    A. encounter   B. epitome   C. animosity   D. innovation

__*deterrent*__ 8. As a(n) ___ to stealing, a chain of restaurants requires its employees to wear uniforms without pockets.

    A. deterrent   B. acclaim   C. innovation   D. inference

__*absolved*__ 9. The suspect realized that if she wanted to be ___ of the charges, she'd better hire a detective to find the real murderer.

    A. assailed   B. demoralized   C. tainted   D. absolved

__*inclination*__ 10. You might have a stronger ___ to work for high grades if you were a student in a special program in the Cleveland public high schools, where each A earns forty dollars toward college tuition.

    A. animosity   B. infirmity   C. inclination   D. syndrome

(Continues on next page)

PART B

On the answer line, write the letter of the choice that best completes each item.

___D___ 11. You would have an **encounter** with an old friend from grade school if you
     A. contacted him by e-mail.   C. forgot about him.
     B. missed him.   D. ran into him at the mall.

___A___ 12. The office manager **maligned** her boss by saying,
     A. "He's not only stupid but also dishonest."   C. "He's the nicest boss I've ever had."
     B. "I wish I had a sports car like his."   D. "I think he could be a little more efficient."

___C___ 13. Which of the following would be considered an **innovation** if it were put on the market today?
     A. An electric blanket   C. An automobile that drives itself
     B. A fax machine   D. A hand plow

___C___ 14. Our English teacher says spring fever is a **syndrome** that includes
     A. March through June.   C. an urge to stare sleepily out the window.
     B. beautiful daffodils.   D. allergy pills.

___B___ 15. "You have **tainted** the name of our family forever," Ellen's father told her, "and you should be
     A. proud."   C. amused."
     B. ashamed."   D. thanked."

___D___ 16. The nurse **exploited** her elderly patient by
     A. giving him a bath and changing his sheets.   C. complaining to her husband about him.
     B. reading aloud to him every day.   D. tricking him into giving his fortune to her.

___A___ 17. A **curt** response when someone asked you to dance would be
     A. "No way."
     B. "That'd be great. Thanks."
     C. "I'd really like to, but I've already been asked by someone else."
     D. "I wouldn't dance with you if we were the last two human beings left alive on Earth."

___B___ 18. When the Lees moved to a new neighborhood, they were faced with an unfortunate **dilemma**:
     A. They discovered that a large family of squirrels was living in the attic of their new home.
     B. They had to choose between a terrible public school or a private one that was very expensive.
     C. They had friendly neighbors on one side and rude ones on the other.
     D. There was enough sun in their back yard for good-sized vegetable and flower gardens.

___B___ 19. When we put out a can of tuna for the stray cat in our yard, the **wary** animal
     A. gobbled it down as though it were starving.
     B. sniffed it suspiciously and took a long time before deciding to eat it.
     C. didn't seem hungry.
     D. ate it and promptly fell asleep.

___C___ 20. When the teacher smiled at the class and said, "If I were you, I'd study Chapter 2 tonight," the **implication** was that
     A. most of the students had already studied that chapter.
     B. most of the class members were poor students.
     C. the teacher would test the class on that chapter the next day.
     D. the chapter was not very interesting.

Score   (Number correct) _____ x 5 = _____%

PART A

Complete each item with a word from the box. Use each word once.

A. **acclaim**	B. **adamant**	C. **allusion**	D. **antagonist**	E. **appease**
F. **demoralize**	G. **elicit**	H. **infringe**	I. **retort**	J. **revitalize**
K. **sabotage**	L. **sparse**	M. **zeal**		

___sabotage___   1. An unhappy employee ___(e)d the company's assembly line by spilling coffee on a gear box.

___infringe___   2. Do you think that supermarket tabloids ___ on celebrities' privacy?

___antagonist___   3. The ___s in the debate took opposing sides on the question of outlawing cigarettes.

___zeal___   4. Today's children develop a ___ for electronic devices early. Even two-year-olds spend several hours a day in front of a TV or computer screen.

___elicit___   5. Apparently, the chance to be President of the United States doesn't ___ much enthusiasm from most Americans—89 percent say they wouldn't want the job.

___revitalize___   6. A "perm" involves the contradictory steps of burning hair to a lifeless state and then smearing on conditioners to ___ it.

___acclaim___   7. Although Marilyn Monroe received great ___ from adoring fans and critics, she never received an Academy Award.

___adamant___   8. Our congressional representative, ___ in her opposition to pesticides, often reminds voters that pesticides kill about fourteen thousand people each year.

___retort___   9. When a woman told Winston Churchill, "If you were my husband, I'd put poison in your tea," he ___(e)d, "If I were your husband, I'd drink it."

___demoralize___   10. Although failure ___s some people, it encourages others to try harder.

___sparse___   11. The plants look ___ now, but within a year or two they'll multiply and fill in the empty spaces.

___allusion___   12. "Gina isn't the only athlete in the family," Clarence said, making a(n) ___ to Gina's father, a bowling champion.

___appease___   13. When Kathleen stood Evan up for the prom, an apology did not ___ him. He's suing her for the cost of his rented tux and the prom tickets.

(Continues on next page)

PART B

Write **C** if the italicized word is used **correctly**. Write **I** if the word is used **incorrectly**.

___I___ 14. Ants have the *infirmity* of being able to survive under water for up to two weeks.

___C___ 15. When the evidence in a case is unclear, a jury's decision may be *arbitrary*, based on only the jurors' "gut feeling."

___I___ 16. Movie reviews are never *subjective*—they represent the personal opinions of critics.

___I___ 17. If you worry about the environment, you're *eccentric*. According to a recent poll, over three-fourths of Americans are concerned about the environment.

___C___ 18. Phyllis is very *methodical* in her efforts to be the life of any party. She keeps a file box of jokes, indexed by occasion.

___C___ 19. A wedding ring is a *tangible* expression of a couple's commitment to each other.

PART C

On the answer line, write the letter of the word that is the **synonym** of the boldfaced word.

Example: __A__ irate   A. angry   B. calm   C. well-informed

__B__ 20. **terminate**   A. begin   B. end   C. grow

__C__ 21. **amoral**   A. ethical   B. costly   C. unprincipled

__A__ 22. **amiable**   A. friendly   B. natural   C. unfriendly

PART D

On the answer line, write the letter of the word that is the **antonym** of the boldfaced word.

Example: __B__ irate   A. angry   B. calm   C. well-informed

__C__ 23. **assail**   A. flow   B. attack   C. defend

__A__ 24. **subsequent**   A. previous   B. hidden   C. following

__C__ 25. **animosity**   A. liveliness   B. hatred   C. sympathy

Score   (Number correct) _____   x 4 = _____%

Enter your score above and in the **Vocabulary Performance Chart** on the inside back cover of the book.

Each item below starts with a pair of words in CAPITAL LETTERS. For each item, figure out the relationship between these two words. Then decide which of the choices (A, B, C, or D) expresses a similar relationship. Write the letter of your choice on the answer line.

_A_ 1. ABSOLVE : BLAME ::
    A. reduce : enlarge   C. trial : verdict
    B. blame : punish   D. wish : desire

_D_ 2. AMORAL : CRIMINAL ::
    A. pastor : church   C. uneducated : professor
    B. murderer : victim   D. brave : explorer

_B_ 3. ANTAGONIST : TEAMMATE ::
    A. coworker : relative   C. scholar : athlete
    B. opponent : supporter   D. teammate : coach

_C_ 4. DILEMMA : SOLUTION ::
    A. puzzle : piece   C. breakdown : repair
    B. confusion : bewilderment   D. size : color

_A_ 5. SABOTAGE : TERRORIST ::
    A. entertain : magician   C. terrorize : frighten
    B. destroy : carpenter   D. magic : illusion

_A_ 6. WARY : CAUTIOUS ::
    A. jealous : envious   C. jealous : rival
    B. excessive : minimal   D. minimize : exaggerate

_C_ 7. IRATE : FRIENDLY ::
    A. peaceful : calming   C. sweet : sour
    B. plentiful : abundant   D. warrior : weapon

_C_ 8. ACCLAIM : CRITIC ::
    A. test : question   C. loyalty : dog
    B. statement : silence   D. symptom : disease

_C_ 9. ADJACENT : NEARBY ::
    A. neighboring : distant   C. optimistic : cheerful
    B. familiar : strange   D. optimist : whiner

_D_ 10. ENGROSS : FASCINATING ::
    A. popular : well-known   C. boring : thrilling
    B. common : rare   D. bore : monotonous

(Continues on next page)

_A_ 11. INFIRMITY : STRENGTH ::
    A. joy : unhappiness   C. sadness : depression
    B. disappointment : emotion   D. depression : suicide

_B_ 12. METHODICAL : ORGANIZED ::
    A. careful : sloppy   C. simple : elaborate
    B. careful : orderly   D. insult : anger

_A_ 13. OBSOLETE : MODEL T ::
    A. well-known : Disney World   C. spotlight : flashlight
    B. old-fashioned : modern   D. nutritious : chewing gum

_D_ 14. TANGIBLE : DREAMS ::
    A. weather : snowy   C. frequent : often
    B. probable : likely   D. intentional : accident

_D_ 15. TERMINATE : EMPLOYMENT ::
    A. chimney : house   C. remember : forget
    B. begin : commence   D. quit : school

_A_ 16. ESCALATE : INTENSIFY ::
    A. labor : work   C. enlarge : preserve
    B. compliment : insult   D. increase : adjust

_C_ 17. SPARSE : THICK ::
    A. acorn : oak tree   C. confusing : clear
    B. recent : modern   D. amusing : intelligent

_D_ 18. SUCCINCT : WORDY ::
    A. talkative : chatty   C. alarming : frightening
    B. brief : hurried   D. welcome : unwanted

_D_ 19. ALTRUISTIC : UNSELFISH ::
    A. saint : holy   C. generous : stingy
    B. artist : painting   D. wealthy : rich

_A_ 20. BANAL : UNORIGINAL ::
    A. surprising : unexpected   C. copied : original
    B. pleasant : distasteful   D. match : fire

Score   (Number correct) _____ x 5 = _____%

Enter your score above and in the **Vocabulary Performance Chart** on the inside back cover of the book.

PART A

Listed in the left-hand column below are ten common word parts, followed by words in which the parts are used. In each blank, write in the letter of the correct definition on the right.

Word Parts	Examples	Definitions
_E_ 1. **ann, enn**	annual, bicentennial	A. In a certain manner
_I_ 2. **audi, audio-**	audible, auditorium	B. Feeling, suffering
_C_ 3. **cycl, cyclo-**	motorcycle, cyclone	C. Circle
_G_ 4. **-hood**	adulthood, womanhood	D. To hang
_J_ 5. **hyper-**	hypersensitive, hypertext	E. Year
_A_ 6. **-ly**	easily, proudly	F. Four, fourth
_H_ 7. **non-**	nontoxic, nonfiction	G. State, condition
_B_ 8. **path, -pathy**	empathic, telepathy	H. Not; the opposite of
_D_ 9. **pend**	suspend, pendulum	I. Hearing, sound
_F_ 10. **quart, quadr-**	quarter, quadruple	J. More than normal; overly

PART B

Using the answer line provided, complete each *italicized* word in the sentences below with the correct word part from the box. Not every word part will be used.

A. **ann**	B. **audi-**	C. **cycl-**	D. **-hood**	E. **hyper-**
F. **-ly**	G. **non-**	H. **-pathy**	I. **pend**	J. **quadr-**

boyhood   11. Mickey Mouse had no (*boy . . .*) ___ —he was "born" as an adult.

cycle   12. I enjoy riding an exercise bike because I don't have to (*. . . e*) ___ uphill.

sympathy   13. My dog didn't know why I was crying, but I could tell that she felt (*sym . . .*) ___ for me—she began to whine softly.

suspended   14. The spider, (*sus . . . ed*) ___ from the ceiling on its own silken thread, dangled above a bowl of popcorn.

nonsense   15. Children's rhymes include such (*. . . sense*) ___ words as "Hickory, dickory, dock."

(Continues on next page)

PART C

Use your knowledge of word parts to determine the meaning of the **boldfaced** words. On the answer line, write the letter of each meaning.

___A___   16. Ned **secretly** slipped a note under Anna's plate.

     A. in a secret manner   B. at a secret time   C. without being secret

___B___   17. Should I buy a **quart** or a gallon of chocolate milk?

     A. a third of a gallon   B. a fourth of a gallon   C. a half gallon

___C___   18. The public library's **biennial** hobby show will take place next month.

     A. happening every two weeks   B. happening every two months   C. happening every two years

___B___   19. My mother was troubled by **hyperthyroidism**.

     A. too little activity   B. too much activity   C. a missing thyroid gland
       of the thyroid gland   of the thyroid gland

___A___   20. There's a problem at the television station. Only the **audio** portion of the show is coming through.

     A. sound   B. picture   C. top

Score   (Number correct) _____ x 5 = _____%

Enter your score above and in the **Vocabulary Performance Chart** on the inside back cover of the book.

Unit Two

Chapter 7

calamity	persevere
comprehensive	ponder
conventional	rehabilitate
flagrant	turmoil
fluctuate	venture

Chapter 8

attest	enigma
attribute	exemplify
discern	mobile
dispatch	nocturnal
enhance	orient

Chapter 9

concurrent	hypothetical
confiscate	nominal
constitute	predominant
decipher	prerequisite
default	recession

Chapter 10

degenerate	sanctuary
implausible	scrutiny
incoherent	sinister
intercede	suffice
intricate	vulnerable

Chapter 11

blatant	gloat
blight	immaculate
contrive	plagiarism
garble	qualm
gaunt	retaliate

Chapter 12

-ate	forc, fort
bio-	hum
claim, clam	pater, patri-
fin	semi-
flex, flect	-ward

CHAPTER 7

calamity	persevere
comprehensive	ponder
conventional	rehabilitate
flagrant	turmoil
fluctuate	venture

Ten Words in Context

In the space provided, write the letter of the meaning closest to that of each **boldfaced** word. Use the context of the sentences to help you figure out each word's meaning.

1 calamity
(kə-lăm′ĭ-tē)
-noun

● The survivors of the earthquake slowly rebuilt their homes and lives after the **calamity**.

● Our neighbor's house burned down one night in May. Ever since that **calamity**, some of the children on our street have been afraid to go to bed at night.

_B_ *Calamity* means   A. an activity.   B. a tragedy.   C. a risk.

2 comprehensive
(kŏm′prē-hĕn′sĭv)
-adjective

● That article on sightseeing in Charleston was not **comprehensive**. It failed to mention many points of interest in that wonderful city.

● The company's **comprehensive** insurance plan covers most health services, including hospitals, doctors, and dentists.

_A_ *Comprehensive* means   A. complete.   B. familiar.   C. continuous.

3 conventional
(kən-vĕn′shə-nəl)
-adjective

● Two **conventional** Valentine's Day gifts are roses and chocolates.

● Jorge wanted to propose to Ramona in the **conventional** manner, so in the middle of a restaurant, he got down on one knee and asked, "Will you marry me?"

_C_ *Conventional* means   A. out-of-the-way.   B. useful.   C. usual.

4 flagrant
(flā′grənt)
-adjective

● The use of campaign funds for the congressman's private business was a **flagrant** violation of the law.

● In **flagrant** disregard of his parents' stated wishes, Art wore a T-shirt and jeans to their dinner party.

_A_ *Flagrant* means   A. obvious.   B. acceptable.   C. minor.

5 fluctuate
(flŭk′chōō-āt′)
-verb

● My weight used to **fluctuate** between 150 and 190 pounds. Now it's steady, at 170 pounds.

● Desert temperatures can **fluctuate** by as much as fifty degrees between daytime and nighttime.

_B_ *Fluctuate* means   A. to continue.   B. to vary.   C. to follow.

6 persevere
(pûr′sə-vîr′)
-verb

● "I know you're tired," Jack said, "but we've got to **persevere** and get to the camp before the storm hits."

● It was not easy to attend English classes while working at two jobs, but Nina **persevered** until she could speak English well.

_C_ *Persevere* means   A. to surrender.   B. to hold back.   C. to keep going.

7 ponder
(pŏn′dər)
-*verb*

● Too often we don't take time to **ponder** the possible consequences of our actions.

● Over the years, Mr. Madigan rarely took time to **ponder** the meaning of life. Since his heart attack, however, he's thought a lot about what is important to him.

<u>C</u> *Ponder* means   A. to wait for.   B. to ignore.   C. to think about.

8 rehabilitate
(rē′hə-bĭl′ə-tāt)
-*verb*

● Most prisons make little effort to **rehabilitate** inmates so that they can lead productive, wholesome lives after their release.

● My grandfather learned to walk, write, and speak again in a program that **rehabilitates** stroke victims.

<u>B</u> *Rehabilitate* means   A. to pay back.   B. to return to normal life.   C. to depend upon.

9 turmoil
(tûr′moil)
-*noun*

● Without a teacher, the sixth-grade class was in **turmoil**, until the principal entered the room and the students quickly came to order.

● After the **turmoil** of crying babies, active children, and trying to feed 120 people, I'm glad when our family reunions end.

<u>B</u> *Turmoil* means   A. discussion.   B. disorder.   C. harmony.

10 venture
(vĕn′chər)
-*verb*

● "I'll **venture** going on any ride in this amusement park except the Twister," said Nick. "I'll risk getting sick to my stomach, but I won't risk my life."

● "At tomorrow's staff meeting," my older sister said, "I will **venture** to say what I really think—and cross my fingers that I don't get fired."

<u>A</u> *Venture* means   A. to dare.   B. to remember.   C. to imagine.

Matching Words with Definitions

Following are definitions of the ten words. Clearly write or print each word next to its definition. The sentences above and on the previous page will help you decide on the meaning of each word.

1. _____flagrant_____   Shockingly obvious; outrageous

2. _____venture_____   To take the risk of; dare

3. _____comprehensive_____   Including all or much

4. _____rehabilitate_____   To restore to a normal life through therapy or education

5. _____persevere_____   To continue with an effort or plan despite difficulties

6. _____turmoil_____   Complete confusion; uproar

7. _____calamity_____   An event bringing great loss and misery

8. _____fluctuate_____   To vary irregularly; to go up and down or back and forth

9. _____ponder_____   To consider carefully; think deeply about

10. _____conventional_____   Customary; ordinary

CAUTION: Do not go any further until you are sure the above answers are correct. Then you can use the definitions to help you in the following practices. Your goal is eventually to know the words well enough so that you don't need to check the definitions at all.

Sentence Check 1

Using the answer line provided, complete each item below with the correct word from the box. Use each word once.

A. calamity	B. comprehensive	C. conventional	D. flagrant	E. fluctuate
F. persevere	G. ponder	H. rehabilitate	I. turmoil	J. venture

_____calamity_____ 1. Tracy is so vain that she considers it a ___ if a pimple appears anywhere on her face.

_____ponder_____ 2. Too many people have a child without taking time to ___ parenthood. They give less thought to having a baby than to buying a sofa.

_____flagrant_____ 3. When Charlene lost her job because she spoke up for a fellow employee, it was a ___ violation of her rights.

_____comprehensive_____ 4. Our history exam will be ___; it will cover everything we've studied since September.

_____conventional_____ 5. Nobody in Doug's family has a ___ job. His mother is a drummer, his father is a magician, and his uncle is a wine taster.

_____persevere_____ 6. Learning the new software program was difficult, but when Maria saw how useful it would be in her work, she was glad she had ___(e)d.

_____rehabilitate_____ 7. It took many months of therapy to ___ my aunt after she lost her sight, but now she can get around her home and neighborhood on her own.

_____turmoil_____ 8. The day we moved, the apartment was in ___. Boxes and people were everywhere, and the baby wouldn't stop crying.

_____fluctuate_____ 9. The way my dog's appetite ___(e)d this week worries me. One day she hardly ate anything, and the next day she gulped down everything I gave her.

_____venture_____ 10. Instead of hiring a lawyer, the defendant will ___ to plead her own case in court.

NOTE: Now check your answers to these items by turning to page 177. Going over the answers carefully will help you prepare for the next two practices, for which answers are not given.

Sentence Check 2

Using the answer lines provided, complete each item below with **two** words from the box. Use each word once.

_____venture_____
_____calamity_____
1–2. The one time my cousin ___(e)d skydiving, the result was a ___. Her parachute didn't open, and she was injured so badly in the fall that she almost died.

_____rehabilitate_____
_____persevere_____
3–4. A drug-treatment center can ___ most addicts. Among the failures are addicts who don't ___ with the treatment and leave the center early.

_____conventional_____
_____flagrant_____
5–6. When he drives alone, Marshall's behavior is very ___; he obeys all the traffic rules. But when his friends are with him, he shows off with ___ violations of the speed limit.

_____ponder_____

___comprehensive___   7–8. "We need to ___ all we might do to help families in trouble," said the social worker to her staff. "We must plan a ___ program, not just a narrow plan dealing with only one part of their lives."

_____fluctuate_____   9–10. The boss's moods and orders ___ so wildly at times that they throw the department into ___. As a result, productivity is at an all-time low, and it will take a new boss to revitalize° this office.

_____turmoil_____

Final Check: *Accident and Recovery*

Here is a final opportunity for you to strengthen your knowledge of the ten words. First read the following selection carefully. Then fill in each blank with a word from the box at the top of the previous page. (Context clues will help you figure out which word goes in which blank.) Use each word once.

We tried to stop Anna from jumping, but her (1)___flagrant___ disregard of our warnings led to a (2)___calamity___ that would change her life forever. She dove off a rock into a river none of us was sure was deep enough. When she hit the bottom, she broke her back.

I visited Anna at the hospital every day for the next few weeks. I saw her mood (3)___fluctuate___ between anger and quiet depression. Her whole life seemed in (4)___turmoil___; she was too confused and demoralized° to think reasonably about her future.

Within about a month, however, I began to see a change in Anna. She had moved to Henner House to participate in a very (5)___comprehensive___ program, designed to meet all the needs of patients like Anna. The program (6)___rehabilitate___s accident victims so that they can subsequently° return to fulfilling lives. Anna gained hope once she saw she could learn to do such everyday tasks as cooking, cleaning, and bathing. After learning how to get around indoors, she (7)___venture___(e)d traveling around the city in her wheelchair. The more she did, the better she felt. The staff also helped Anna plan for her future. They urged her to (8)___ponder___ her goals and how she might meet them. At times, it was difficult for her to (9)___persevere___ with the program, but she didn't quit.

Now, ten months later, Anna is able to live a somewhat (10)___conventional___ life. Her infirmity° is not a deterrent°; she is able to do many of the ordinary things she used to do—work, drive, and live in an apartment with a friend. Yes, her life has changed forever. But Anna is once again glad to be alive.

Scores	Sentence Check 2 _____%	Final Check _____%

attest	enigma
attribute	exemplify
discern	mobile
dispatch	nocturnal
enhance	orient

Ten Words in Context

In the space provided, write the letter of the meaning closest to that of each **boldfaced** word. Use the context of the sentences to help you figure out each word's meaning.

1 attest
(ə-tĕst′)
-verb

- Anyone who has seen the Golden Gate Bridge in the rose-gold light of sunset can **attest** to its beauty.
- Witnesses **attest** to the fact that rainfall makes the ground of Death Valley so slippery that boulders slide across it.

A *Attest to* means
A. to declare to be true.
B. to wish for.
C. to forget easily.

2 attribute
(ăt′rə-byōōt′)
-noun

- A three-hundred-page novel written in 1939 has the odd **attribute** of containing no *e*, the most common letter in English.
- Some cars have computerized **attributes** such as windshield wipers that automatically turn on when it rains.

C *Attribute* means
A. a tendency.
B. a defect.
C. a characteristic.

3 discern
(dĭ-sûrn′)
-verb

- An experienced jeweler can easily **discern** whether a diamond is genuine or fake.
- People who are red-green colorblind can **discern** the colors of traffic lights by recognizing shades of gray.

A *Discern* means
A. to see clearly.
B. to disregard.
C. to change.

4 dispatch
(dĭ-spăch′)
-verb

- I wanted to **dispatch** the letter as quickly as possible, so I took it to the post office instead of dropping it into a mailbox.
- At work Harold is treated like an errand boy. His boss often **dispatches** him to the deli for sandwiches or donuts.

B *Dispatch* means
A. to represent.
B. to send.
C. to drive.

5 enhance
(ĕn-hăns′)
-verb

- Our gym teacher **enhanced** her appearance with a more attractive hairstyle.
- The college catalogue stated that the writing course would "**enhance** all students' writing skills" by improving their grammar and style.

A *Enhance* means
A. to make better.
B. to recognize.
C. to reduce.

6 enigma
(ĭ-nĭg′mə)
-noun

- How the thief entered our house was an **enigma** until we remembered that the cellar door had been left unlocked.
- The "singing sands" of Scotland remained an **enigma** until scientists learned that footsteps caused the round grains of sand and the surrounding air pockets to make musical vibrations.

B *Enigma* means
A. a comfort.
B. a puzzle.
C. an error.

7 exemplify
(ĭg-zĕm′plə-fī′)
-verb

- The many IRS employees who give citizens inaccurate information **exemplify** governmental incompetence.
- Mr. Ramirez, who emphasizes original thinking and freedom of expression, **exemplifies** the best in teaching.

A *Exemplify* means   A. to illustrate.   B. to save.   C. to oppose.

8 mobile
(mō′bəl)
-adjective

- My parents own a **mobile** home, which can be moved from place to place.
- Every morning when I was in the hospital, a volunteer wheeled a **mobile** library into my room.

C *Mobile* means   A. active.   B. expensive.   C. movable.

9 nocturnal
(nŏk-tûr′nəl)
-adjective

- I know when my brother has enjoyed one of his **nocturnal** feasts because I find a stack of dishes in the sink in the morning.
- Since owls are **nocturnal**, they are rarely seen during the day.

C *Nocturnal* means   A. noisy.   B. busy.   C. of the night.

10 orient
(ôr′ē-ĕnt)
-verb

- When coming up from the subway, I often need to look at a street sign to **orient** myself.
- Certain cars let drivers **orient** themselves in unfamiliar places with the help of an electronic map that shows the car's location.

A *Orient* means   A. to locate.   B. to welcome.   C. to question.

Matching Words with Definitions

Following are definitions of the ten words. Clearly write or print each word next to its definition. The sentences above and on the previous page will help you decide on the meaning of each word.

1. _____enigma_____ A mystery or puzzle

2. _____dispatch_____ To send to a specific place or on specific business

3. _____nocturnal_____ Of, about, or happening in the night; active at night

4. _____attest_____ To make a statement about something on the basis of personal experience; bear witness; testify

5. _____orient_____ To determine one's location or direction; to locate in relation to a direction (east, west, etc.)

6. _____discern_____ To recognize; detect

7. _____enhance_____ To improve; add to the strength, beauty, or value of something

8. _____mobile_____ Moving or able to move from place to place

9. _____attribute_____ A quality or feature of a person or thing

10. _____exemplify_____ To be an example of; represent; be typical of

CAUTION: Do not go any further until you are sure the above answers are correct. Then you can use the definitions to help you in the following practices. Your goal is eventually to know the words well enough so that you don't need to check the definitions at all.

Sentence Check 1

Using the answer line provided, complete each item below with the correct word from the box. Use each word once.

A. attest	B. attribute	C. discern	D. dispatch	E. enhance
F. enigma	G. exemplify	H. mobile	I. nocturnal	J. orient

_____enhance_____   1. Fresh garlic may not ___ the breath, but it certainly improves spaghetti sauce.

_____attest_____   2. A witness ___(e)d to the truth of the defendant's claim that she had loved the murdered man.

_____dispatch_____   3. When I was younger, my mother used to ___ me to the store for milk or some missing cooking ingredient as often as twice a day.

_____exemplify_____   4. The lives of such reformers as Susan B. Anthony, Mahatma Gandhi, and Martin Luther King ___ greatness.

_____enigma_____   5. Science does not have enough evidence to solve the ___ of whether or not there is other intelligent life in the universe.

_____nocturnal_____   6. The convicts decided on a(n) ___ escape. The darkness would hide them as they fled through the forest.

_____discern_____   7. Sue's hairpiece is so natural-looking that it's impossible to ___ where the hairpiece ends and her own hair begins.

_____orient_____   8. The positions of the stars help sailors ___ themselves on the open seas.

_____mobile_____   9. My mother is unable to walk, but with her wheelchair she is ___ enough to get around her apartment, move along a sidewalk, and even shop at a mall.

_____attribute_____   10. Giant kelp, a form of seaweed, has some amazing ___s. Not only is it the world's fastest-growing vegetable, but the more it is cut, the faster it grows.

NOTE: Now check your answers to these items by turning to page 177. Going over the answers carefully will help you prepare for the next two practices, for which answers are not given.

Sentence Check 2

Using the answer lines provided, complete each item below with **two** words from the box. Use each word once.

_____enhance_____
_____discern_____   1–2. Because Helen Keller could not hear or see, the keenness of her other senses was ___(e)d by use. It is said that she could ___ who was in a room simply by using her sense of smell.

_____mobile_____
_____orient_____   3–4. A ___ robot that collects and delivers mail throughout the office building ___s itself with electric eyes.

_____attribute_____
_____exemplify_____   5–6. In fables, animals often illustrate human ___s. In the story of the race between the tortoise and the hare, the tortoise is meant to ___ the human qualities of being slow but steady. Despite competing against a much speedier antagonist°, he perseveres° and defeats the overly confident hare.

_____dispatch_____   7–8. The reason the boss likes to ___ Oliver on lengthy errands is no ___.
_____enigma_____   Everyone knows that the office functions better with Oliver out of the way.

_____attest_____   9–10. Anyone who has ever gone to college can ___ to the fact that during final
_____nocturnal_____   exams, many students become ___ animals. They study all night before an
                                       exam and then, once the test is over, sleep the rest of the day.

Final Check: *Animal Senses*

Here is a final opportunity for you to strengthen your knowledge of the ten words. First read the following selection carefully. Then fill in each blank with a word from the box at the top of the previous page. (Context clues will help you figure out which word goes in which blank.) Use each word once.

Animals possess sensory powers that humans lack. Homing pigeons fly with great speed and accuracy when (1)_____dispatch_____(e)d with messages to faraway places. How do pigeons (2)_____orient_____ themselves in unfamiliar regions? This remains something of a(n) (3)_____enigma_____. The mystery, however, is partly explained by a pigeon's ability to see ultraviolet light, which reveals the sun's position even through clouds. In addition, pigeons can hear sound waves that have traveled hundreds of miles. These waves (4)_____enhance_____ a pigeon's sense of direction by indicating distant mountains and seas. Pigeons even appear to (5)_____discern_____ changes in the earth's magnetic field.

Bats have impressive (6)_____attribute_____s equally worthy of acclaim°. As (7)_____nocturnal_____ animals, they search for food in complete darkness. They do so by screeching in tones higher than any human can hear and then locating prey by the returning echoes.

Scorpions also (8)_____exemplify_____ the night hunter. Tiny leg hairs enable them to feel vibrations in the sand made by a (9)_____mobile_____ insect as far as two feet away.

People with knowledge of the pigeon, bat, and scorpion can (10)_____attest_____ to the fact that such "innovations"° as the magnetic compass, radar, and the motion detector are nothing new.

| Scores | Sentence Check 2 _____% | Final Check _____% |

concurrent	hypothetical
confiscate	nominal
constitute	predominant
decipher	prerequisite
default	recession

Ten Words in Context

In the space provided, write the letter of the meaning closest to that of each **boldfaced** word. Use the context of the sentences to help you figure out each word's meaning.

1 concurrent
(kən-kûr′ənt)
-adjective

● Having mistakenly registered for two **concurrent** classes, Joe had to drop one of them and choose a course that met at a different time.

● **Concurrent** with the closing of the steel mill was the opening of a new toy factory in town. As a result, most of the workers laid off from the mill found jobs at the new factory.

A *Concurrent* means   A. occurring at the same time.   B. resulting.   C. noticeable.

2 confiscate
(kŏn′fĭs-kāt′)
-verb

● "Hand 'em over," my father said. Just as we were really starting to have fun, he **confiscated** our entire supply of water balloons.

● Chinese drug agents once **confiscated** $2 million worth of heroin that had been wrapped in plastic and inserted into live goldfish. The agents seized the drugs as they were being sent out of the country.

B *Confiscate* means   A. to distribute widely.   B. to take possession of.   C. to overlook.

3 constitute
(kŏn′stĭ-tōot)
-verb

● In my opinion, a good movie, a pizza, and animated conversation **constitute** a perfect night out.

● Twelve business and professional people **constitute** the board of directors of the women's shelter. Among other things, they help raise funds for the shelter.

C *Constitute* means   A. to repeat.   B. to oppose.   C. to form.

4 decipher
(dĭ-sī′fər)
-verb

● Why do contracts have to use language that's so difficult to **decipher**?

● If your teacher can't **decipher** your handwriting, you'll need to write your papers on a computer.

A *Decipher* means   A. to figure out.   B. to find.   C. to improve.

5 default
(dĭ-fôlt′)
-verb

● We won our case against the appliance repairman because he **defaulted** by failing to appear in court.

● Eli's mother said, "I'll co-sign on your car loan, but you have to make every payment. If you **default**, it will hurt my credit rating."

B *Default* means   A. to act as expected.   B. not to do something required.   C. to begin.

6 hypothetical
(hī′pō-thĕt′ĭ-kəl)
-adjective

● Imagine the **hypothetical** situation of going to live alone on an island. Which books and CDs would you take along?

● Law schools hold pretend court sessions with **hypothetical** cases so that students can practice their skills.

C *Hypothetical* means   A. sure to happen.   B. dangerous.   C. imaginary.

7 nominal
(nŏm′ə-nəl)
-*adjective*

- Except for a **nominal** registration fee, the camp for needy children is entirely free.
- Professor Banks gave us only **nominal** extra credit for participating in psychology experiments. She wanted our course grade to be based mainly on our test scores.

B *Nominal* means   A. enormous.   B. very little.   C. helpful.

8 predominant
(prĭ-dŏm′ə-nənt)
-*adjective*

- Rock is the **predominant** music on that radio station, but country music is also played.
- Although the **predominant** type of car in New York City in 1900 used gasoline, a third of the cars ran on electricity.

B *Predominant* means   A. rare.   B. main.   C. temporary.

9 prerequisite
(prē-rĕk′wĭ-zĭt)
-*noun*

- You can't take Spanish Literature I unless you've taken the **prerequisite**, Spanish III.
- Since she was allergic to cigarette smoke, Kaylin told Troy that his quitting smoking was a **prerequisite** for their marrying.

A *Prerequisite* means   A. a requirement.   B. a penalty.   C. a method.

10 recession
(rĭ-sēsh′ən)
-*noun*

- While seashore businesses in the North suffer a **recession** in the winter, they do very well from spring to fall.
- The department store laid off twenty workers during the **recession**, but it rehired them when business improved.

C *Recession* means   A. a rapid growth.   B. a sale.   C. an economic setback.

Matching Words with Definitions

Following are definitions of the ten words. Clearly write or print each word next to its definition. The sentences above and on the previous page will help you decide on the meaning of each word.

1. _____constitute_____   To make up; be the parts of

2. _____default_____   To fail to do something required

3. _____predominant_____   Most common or most noticeable

4. _____prerequisite_____   Something required beforehand

5. _____confiscate_____   To seize with authority; legally take possession of

6. _____decipher_____   To interpret or read (something confusing or hard to make out)

7. _____nominal_____   Slight; very small compared with what might be expected

8. _____concurrent_____   Happening or existing at the same time; simultaneous

9. _____recession_____   A temporary decline in business

10. _____hypothetical_____   Supposed for the sake of argument or examination; imaginary; theoretical

CAUTION: Do not go any further until you are sure the above answers are correct. Then you can use the definitions to help you in the following practices. Your goal is eventually to know the words well enough so that you don't need to check the definitions at all.

Sentence Check 1

Using the answer line provided, complete each item below with the correct word from the box. Use each word once.

| A. concurrent | B. confiscate | C. constitute | D. decipher | E. default |
| F. hypothetical | G. nominal | H. predominant | I. prerequisite | J. recession |

predominant 1. Anger was the ___ emotion among voters when they first heard that their taxes would be raised again.

concurrent 2. Although the two robberies were ___—both occurred at midnight on Friday— one man had planned them both.

constitute 3. One hundred senators and 435 members of the House of Representatives ___ the United States Congress.

prerequisite 4. A ___ for taking the driver's road test is passing a written test on the state's driving laws.

nominal 5. The town library charges only a ___ fine for late books but a higher fine for late DVDs.

decipher 6. Karim has such terrible handwriting that his wife couldn't ___ his message saying she should meet him at the restaurant.

recession 7. When the shoe factory closed, our little town went into a ___ because the laid-off workers had no money to spend at local businesses.

default 8. The phone company refused to install a phone in Glen's new apartment because he had ___(e)d on several of his previous bills.

confiscate 9. After Justine borrowed the family car without permission for the third time, her parents ___(ed) her driver's license.

hypothetical 10. To teach young children safety, many parents explain what to do in ___ situations, such as if a stranger asks them to go for a ride.

NOTE: Now check your answers to these items by turning to page 178. Going over the answers carefully will help you prepare for the next two practices, for which answers are not given.

Sentence Check 2

Using the answer lines provided, complete each item below with **two** words from the box. Use each word once.

nominal
concurrent 1–2. This summer, local children can sign up for art or music lessons for a ___ fee of $3. They can't take both, though, since the classes will be ___.

constitute
predominant 3–4. Although cancer and heart disease ___ the leading threats to life in the United States, car accidents are the ___ cause of death for teenagers.

prerequisite
decipher 5–6. "It seems as if a degree in accounting is a ___ for understanding our tax laws," said Ken. "How else could anyone ___ the tax codes?"

<u>   default   </u>

<u>   confiscate   </u>

<u>   hypothetical   </u>

<u>   recession   </u>

7–8. The small print on the Bryants' mortgage stated that if they should ___ on payments, the bank had the right to ___ their house.

9–10. When Ms. Howe was interviewed for the job of store manager, the regional manager asked her a question about a ___ situation. "Imagine that our business is in a ___," he said. "What would you do to enhance° sales?"

Final Check: *Money Problems*

Here is a final opportunity for you to strengthen your knowledge of the ten words. First read the following selection carefully. Then fill in each blank with a word from the box at the top of the previous page. (Context clues will help you figure out which word goes in which blank.) Use each word once.

My neighbor, Martha, ran into my house crying and angry. "My car has been stolen!" she gasped. "I saw them take it!"

I called the police for her, and she told an officer the license number and car model. "The (1)___predominant___ color of the car is brown," she added, "but it has a black roof. I had it parked in the lot adjacent° to the beauty shop I own. I saw two men tow it away."

"You saw them tow it away?" the officer asked. "Have you (2)___default___(e)d on your car loan?"

"What do you mean?" Martha asked.

"If you haven't been making your payments, the bank or dealer has the right to (3)___confiscate___ the car."

Martha admitted that she hadn't made any payments for three months. Later she told me she'd gotten notices in the mail but threw them away because their language was too complicated to (4)___decipher___. She also said she was having money problems. (5)___Concurrent___ with the car loan was a big home-improvement loan. She also had five credit-card bills and regular living expenses to pay. To top it all off, the city was suffering from a (6)___recession___, so her income was down, something her laid-off employees could certainly attest° to. She was about $12,000 in debt.

At my suggestion, Martha visited a debt counselor, who helped her develop a comprehensive° plan to pay her bills. The only (7)___prerequisite___s for this free service were a regular job and a willingness to pay one's debts in full. The counselor and Martha planned what would (8)___constitute___ a reasonable budget, based on Martha's income and expenses. They then wrote to the companies she owed to arrange to pay a (9)___nominal___ amount each month until the whole debt was paid. They also discussed what she would do in several (10)___hypothetical___ situations, such as if her refrigerator died or her income changed.

Now, Martha is getting back on her feet again—in more ways than one, since she never got the car back.

Scores	Sentence Check 2 _____%	Final Check _____%

degenerate	sanctuary
implausible	scrutiny
incoherent	sinister
intercede	suffice
intricate	vulnerable

Ten Words in Context

In the space provided, write the letter of the meaning closest to that of each **boldfaced** word. Use the context of the sentences to help you figure out each word's meaning.

1 degenerate
(dĭ-jĕn′ər-āt′)
-verb

- Mr. Freedman's family was called to the nursing home when the old man's condition began to **degenerate**. It was feared he didn't have long to live.
- Mel's relationship with his parents **degenerated** when he dropped out of school against their wishes and became a bartender.

_C_ _Degenerate_ means   A. to improve.   B. to remain the same.   C. to get worse.

2 implausible
(ĭm-plô′zə-bəl)
-adjective

- As **implausible** as it may sound, southern Florida sometimes does get snow.
- Insurance companies hear such **implausible** excuses for auto accidents as "I hit the telephone pole when I was blinded by the lights of a flying saucer."

_A_ _Implausible_ means   A. unbelievable.   B. acceptable.   C. valuable.

3 incoherent
(ĭn′kō-hîr′ənt)
-adjective

- If Mitch doesn't get some sleep soon, he'll become completely **incoherent**. He's so tired that he's already having trouble expressing his thoughts clearly.
- My sister talks a lot in her sleep, but she's so **incoherent** then that we can never figure out what she's saying.

_B_ _Incoherent_ means   A. calm.   B. unclear.   C. inconvenient.

4 intercede
(ĭn′tər-sēd′)
-verb

- When the principal said Harry couldn't play in Friday's football game, the coach **interceded**, hoping to change the principal's mind.
- Inez's parents refused to come to her wedding until her brother **interceded** and persuaded them to come after all.

_B_ _Intercede_ means   A. to give in to someone.   B. to plead for someone.   C. to examine closely.

5 intricate
(ĭn′trĭ-kĭt)
-adjective

- _War and Peace_ is a long, **intricate** novel that weaves together the detailed life stories of many individuals.
- It's amazing to see the **intricate** gold and silver jewelry that ancient Indians made with only simple tools. It obviously required great patience and skill to create such complex ornaments.

_C_ _Intricate_ means   A. simple.   B. uninteresting.   C. complicated.

6 sanctuary
(săngk′chōō-ĕr′ē)
-noun

- Old, unused trains in Grand Central Station serve as a nighttime **sanctuary** for some of New York City's homeless.
- When the houseful of children becomes too noisy, Ned finds the laundry room to be a **sanctuary**, a place where he can read in quiet.

_B_ _Sanctuary_ means   A. a reminder.   B. a shelter.   C. a challenge.

7 scrutiny
(skrōōt′ən-ē)
-noun

- Store security guards give careful **scrutiny** to people carrying large bags, since the bags may be used for shoplifting.
- Before being published, a book comes under the **scrutiny** of a proofreader, who examines it for grammar and spelling errors.

A *Scrutiny* means   A. attention.   B. protection.   C. permission.

8 sinister
(sĭn′ĭs-tər)
-adjective

- In the movie, a mad scientist thought up the **sinister** scheme of releasing a deadly virus. His evil plot failed when he died from the virus himself.
- The creepy novel *The Boys from Brazil* tells of a **sinister** plot to clone dozens of copies of Adolf Hitler who would then take over the world.

B *Sinister* means   A. illogical.   B. evil.   C. inconsiderate.

9 suffice
(sə-fīs′)
-verb

- The amount of research you've done may **suffice** for a high-school term paper, but not for a college essay.
- I forgot to buy something for lunch tomorrow, but the leftover meatloaf will **suffice**.

B *Suffice* means   A. to be wasted.   B. to be adequate.   C. to be examined.

10 vulnerable
(vŭl′nər-ə-bəl)
-adjective

- Homes in heavily wooded areas are especially **vulnerable** to termites.
- Because they tend to have brittle bones, the elderly are **vulnerable** to fractures.

A *Vulnerable* means   A. open.   B. safe.   C. attracted.

Matching Words with Definitions

Following are definitions of the ten words. Clearly write or print each word next to its definition. The sentences above and on the previous page will help you decide on the meaning of each word.

1. _____intricate_____ Having many parts arranged in a complicated way; complex

2. _____suffice_____ To be good enough

3. _____degenerate_____ To worsen; deteriorate

4. _____sanctuary_____ A place of safety, protection, or relief

5. _____intercede_____ To make a request or plead on behalf of someone else

6. _____vulnerable_____ Open to damage or attack; susceptible

7. _____implausible_____ Difficult to believe; unlikely

8. _____sinister_____ Evil; wicked

9. _____scrutiny_____ Close inspection; careful examination

10. _____incoherent_____ Unable to speak in an orderly, logical way

CAUTION: Do not go any further until you are sure the above answers are correct. Then you can use the definitions to help you in the following practices. Your goal is eventually to know the words well enough so that you don't need to check the definitions at all.

Sentence Check 1

Using the answer line provided, complete each item below with the correct word from the box. Use each word once.

| A. **degenerate** | B. **implausible** | C. **incoherent** | D. **intercede** | E. **intricate** |
| F. **sanctuary** | G. **scrutiny** | H. **sinister** | I. **suffice** | J. **vulnerable** |

suffice 1. Ken's cartoons ___ for the school newspaper, but they wouldn't be good enough for the city papers.

sinister 2. In the *Batman* movies, the Joker's name is misleading, for he's a(n) ___ man who takes pleasure in doing evil.

vulnerable 3. People who live in big cities are more ___ to muggings than are residents of small towns.

intricate 4. The leaves outside the window created a(n) ___ lacy shadow on my bedroom wall.

implausible 5. Although it seems ___, the seemingly dead desert really does blossom after a rainstorm.

sanctuary 6. People who allow an escaped convict to use their home as a ___ may face criminal charges themselves.

incoherent 7. My brother was so upset that he was ___. It wasn't until he calmed down that I understood what he was saying: that he had been fired.

scrutiny 8. Unclaimed bags at airports receive the ___ of security officers watching for drugs or explosives.

degenerate 9. When I don't have company, my apartment tends to ___ into a jumble of papers, clothes, and school supplies.

intercede 10. When Dad informed my little sister that she had to be home from her date no later than ten o'clock, Mom ___(e)d and gave her a midnight curfew.

NOTE: Now check your answers to these items by turning to page 178. Going over the answers carefully will help you prepare for the next two practices, for which answers are not given.

Sentence Check 2

Using the answer lines provided, complete each item below with **two** words from the box. Use each word once.

vulnerable
sanctuary 1–2. Birds feel ___ to attack when they are out in the open where shrubbery is sparse°. To attract them to your bird feeder, put it near a ___ of thickly growing trees and large bushes.

implausible
suffice 3–4. To get into the party, Malcolm made up a flagrant° lie—a(n) ___ story about having lost our invitations in a fire. However, the unlikely tale did not ___ to get us in.

intricate
degenerate 5–6. When a complicated musical piece is played by a talented orchestra, audiences can appreciate the ___ structure. But when poor musicians try the piece, it usually ___s into noise.

_____ sinister
_____ incoherent

7–8. As he left the bank, the robber shot and wounded an elderly man on mere impulse. Shocked by the ___ act, the bank clerk was at first ___. However, after calming down, she was able to clearly tell the police about the robbery and the totally arbitrary° shooting.

_____ scrutiny
_____ intercede

9–10. The children's eager ___ of the carefully arranged candies and cookies brought a curt° warning from their mother: "Look, but don't touch!" However, their grandmother ___(e)d and convinced her that it would be an inequity° to give all the goodies to company and none to the children.

Final Check: *The New French Employee*

Here is a final opportunity for you to strengthen your knowledge of the ten words. First read the following selection carefully. Then fill in each blank with a word from the box at the top of the previous page. (Context clues will help you figure out which word goes in which blank.) Use each word once.

One summer, Nan worked in a factory with an employee who had recently arrived from France, a soft-spoken young man named Jean-Louis. He spoke little English, but Nan's basic French (1)_____ suffice _____(e)d for simple conversations and helpful translations.

However, one day when she was called to the foreman's office, she wished she knew no French at all. FBI agents were there with Jean-Louis. After explaining that Jean-Louis may have been more (2)_____ sinister _____ than the innocent young man he appeared to be, the foreman left her there to translate for the agents. The agents said Jean-Louis had been on the run after committing several jewel thefts in France. They had already been to Jean-Louis's apartment and confiscated° a diamond necklace and some expensive watches. Nan struggled to translate their questions, which were often too (3)_____ intricate _____ for her limited vocabulary. At times, she became so nervous that she was nearly (4)_____ incoherent _____. When Jean-Louis finally deciphered° what Nan was saying, he said the police were maligning° him. He claimed he was being mistaken for his no-good twin brother, who was responsible for the robberies, and therefore he was innocent—he should be absolved° of all blame. The angry FBI agents found Jean-Louis's story (5)_____ implausible _____. The conversation soon (6)_____ degenerate _____(e)d into a shouting match, with everyone yelling at poor Nan. When her boss heard the racket, he (7)_____ intercede _____(e)d, appeased° the agents, and got them to excuse her.

Nan then went to the ladies' room, a (8)_____ sanctuary _____ from the turmoil° of all the shouting. After the agents left with Jean-Louis, she was calm enough to go back to work. But she felt (9)_____ vulnerable _____ for days as she wondered if she was under the (10)_____ scrutiny _____ of jewel thieves who might blame her for Jean-Louis's arrest.

| Scores | Sentence Check 2 _____% | Final Check _____% |

Enter your scores above and in the **Vocabulary Performance Chart** on the inside back cover of the book.

blatant	gloat
blight	immaculate
contrive	plagiarism
garble	qualm
gaunt	retaliate

Ten Words in Context

In the space provided, write the letter of the meaning closest to that of each **boldfaced** word. Use the context of the sentences to help you figure out each word's meaning.

1 blatant
(blā′tənt)
-adjective

● Eva is a **blatant** bargain-hunter. Not only does she wait for end-of season sales, but she chooses an already-reduced item and then asks if the salesperson will accept a lower price.

● The company's disregard of the environment is **blatant**. It makes no effort to stop polluting coastal waters with garbage.

A *Blatant* means   A. unmistakable.   B. scrambled.   C. not noticeable.

2 blight
(blīt)
-noun

● Nothing has hurt our country more than the **blight** of drugs.

● There are two ways of looking at TV: as a valuable source of information or as a **blight** that dulls the mind.

C *Blight* means   A. something that assists.   B. something that is new.   C. something that harms.

3 contrive
(kən-trīv′)
-verb

● My eight-year-old son could write a book titled *101 Ways I Have **Contrived** to Stay Up Past My Bedtime.*

● Jill has to **contrive** a way to get a day off from work for her friend's wedding. She's already used up her vacation time.

A *Contrive* means   A. to think up.   B. to mix up.   C. to avoid.

4 garble
(găr′bəl)
-verb

● The new reporter **garbled** the newspaper story; the result was an article that made no sense at all.

● The company had **garbled** the bike's assembly instructions so badly that we were constantly confused about which step to do next.

C *Garble* means   A. to read.   B. to lose.   C. to jumble.

5 gaunt
(gônt)
-adjective

● Abraham Lincoln's beard made his **gaunt** face look fuller.

● Sharon's eating disorder, called anorexia nervosa, has made her so **gaunt** that she looks like a walking skeleton.

A *Gaunt* means   A. very thin.   B. wide.   C. confused.

6 gloat
(glōt)
-verb

● The coach told his team, "There's only one thing worse than a sore loser, and that's a mean winner. Don't **gloat**."

● Neil's sister always tattles on him and then **gloats** when he's punished, saying, "I told you so."

B *Gloat* means   A. to apologize fully.   B. to be overly self-satisfied.   C. to pay back.

7 immaculate
(ĭ-măk′yə-lĭt)
-adjective

- It's amazing that while Carolyn's appearance is always **immaculate**, her apartment often seems very dirty.
- Don't expect a child to come home from a birthday party with **immaculate** clothing. Children usually manage to get as much birthday cake on their clothing as in their mouths.

B *Immaculate* means   A. uncomfortable.   B. spotless.   C. soiled.

8 plagiarism
(plā′jĕ-rĭz′əm)
-noun

- When the author saw a movie with the same plot as one of her novels, she sued for **plagiarism**.
- The teacher warned her students that using an author's exact words as one's own is **plagiarism**.

B *Plagiarism* means   A. creativity.   B. the stealing of ideas.   C. planning.

9 qualm
(kwŏm)
-noun

- Lorenzo is so honest that he has **qualms** about telling "little white lies." For instance, it bothers him to say he likes a friend's new haircut when he really doesn't.
- After hiding Kwan's bike as an April Fool's joke, I began to have **qualms**. What if she thought it was stolen and called the police?

A *Qualm* means   A. a guilty feeling.   B. a proud memory.   C. a clever plan.

10 retaliate
(rĭ-tăl′ē-āt′)
-verb

- When I broke my sister's stereo, she **retaliated** by taking my iPod earphones and refusing to give them back.
- When Ron refused to pay his younger brother for washing his car, he **retaliated** by washing it again—with its windows open.

B *Retaliate* means   A. to forgive.   B. to take revenge.   C. to confuse.

Matching Words with Definitions

Following are definitions of the ten words. Clearly write or print each word next to its definition. The sentences above and on the previous page will help you decide on the meaning of each word.

1. _____qualm_____ An uneasy feeling about how right or proper a particular action is

2. _____garble_____ To mix up or confuse (as a story or message); scramble

3. _____gloat_____ To feel or express delight or self-satisfaction, often spitefully

4. _____blight_____ Something that weakens, damages, or destroys

5. _____plagiarism_____ Using someone else's writings or ideas as one's own

6. _____contrive_____ To plan cleverly; think up

7. _____retaliate_____ To return an injury for an injury; pay back

8. _____blatant_____ Very obvious, often offensively so

9. _____immaculate_____ Perfectly clean

10. _____gaunt_____ Thin and bony

CAUTION: Do not go any further until you are sure the above answers are correct. Then you can use the definitions to help you in the following practices. Your goal is eventually to know the words well enough so that you don't need to check the definitions at all.

Sentence Check 1

Using the answer line provided, complete each item below with the correct word from the box. Use each word once.

A. **blatant**	B. **blight**	C. **contrive**	D. **garble**	E. **gaunt**
F. **gloat**	G. **immaculate**	H. **plagiarism**	I. **qualm**	J. **retaliate**

___immaculate___ 1. A(n) ___ house may be a sign that someone has nothing better to do than clean.

___blight___ 2. Child abuse is a ___ on the physical and mental health of our youth.

___gloat___ 3. My aunt refuses to drive Mr. Elson to bingo because he ___s so much when he wins, which is often.

___blatant___ 4. The F's and D's on my brother's report card are ___ evidence of how little he has studied this term.

___contrive___ 5. Emilio still hopes to ___ a way to get Rita to go out with him, even though she's refused him four times.

___garble___ 6. When my friend Jamee left a message with my little brother, inviting me to go to the mall, my brother ___(e)d it so badly that the message I got was "Jamee wants you to go play ball."

___retaliate___ 7. Every time the Hatfields harmed the McCoys, the McCoys would ___, so the feud went on for years.

___gaunt___ 8. Rescued after being lost at sea for nine days, the men were terribly ___, but they put on weight rapidly.

___qualm___ 9. My parents say it is foolish to give spare change to panhandlers, but I always feel a ___ when I walk by them and give nothing.

___plagiarism___ 10. Mark Twain joked that charges of ___ were ridiculous because no one can be completely original. He wrote, "We mortals can't create—we can only copy."

NOTE: Now check your answers to these items by turning to page 178. Going over the answers carefully will help you prepare for the next two practices, for which answers are not given.

Sentence Check 2

Using the answer lines provided, complete each item below with **two** words from the box. Use each word once.

___immaculate___
___blatant___ 1–2. The living room looked ___ except for a lump under the carpet, a(n) ___ sign that my son had taken a shortcut in cleaning up.

___retaliate___
___qualm___ 3–4. After the bully struck him, Jules wanted to ___ by throwing a rock, but he had ___s about doing anything so dangerous.

___gaunt___
___contrive___ 5–6. The little girl was so ___ after her illness that her parents carefully ___(e)d fattening meals that were sure to arouse her appetite.

<u>_plagiarism_</u>   7–8. "At least I know you aren't guilty of ___," said my teacher. "Nobody else
<u>_garble_</u>   would have ___(e)d the report so badly that it's impossible to follow."

<u>_blight_</u>   9–10. Willie is a ___ on our school. Not only does he start fights with opposing
<u>_gloat_</u>   players on the basketball court, but he also ___s after he's benched, as if
              he's proud of causing such turmoil°. In fact, although he's a great player, the
              coach is pondering° kicking him off the team.

Final Check: *A Cruel Teacher*

Here is a final opportunity for you to strengthen your knowledge of the ten words. First read the following selection carefully. Then fill in each blank with a word from the box at the top of the previous page. (Context clues will help you figure out which word goes in which blank.) Use each word once.

It has been twenty years since I was in Mr. Brill's tenth-grade biology class, but I still get nervous thinking about it. Mr. Brill was a tall, (1)_____ _gaunt_ _____ man who resembled the skeleton at the back of the room. His meanness was (2)_____ _blatant_ _____. For his most difficult questions, he would call on the shyest kids, those most vulnerable° to the pain of embarrassment. And when they nervously (3)_____ _garble_ _____(e)d their answers, he would (4)_____ _gloat_ _____, as if their poor performance were a personal victory for him. The discomfort of some of his victims was almost tangible°, nearly as solid as the wooden pointer which he sometimes loudly slammed across his desk just to shock us. He seemed to (5)_____ _contrive_ _____ situations just to make us miserable. For example, if our fingernails were not (6)_____ _immaculate_ _____, we were sent out of class. As if we needed clean hands to dissect a frog! One time I worked extremely hard on a paper for class, but he accused me of (7)_____ _plagiarism_ _____. He said I must have copied it because I was too dumb to write anything that good. Without a (8)_____ _qualm_ _____, he gave me an F, which ruined my average and demoralized° me for the rest of the year. All of us students would imagine ways to get even with him, but we were too afraid to (9)_____ _retaliate_ _____. Why a teacher like that was allowed to continue teaching was an enigma° to us, one I still have not figured out. In all the years since, I've never met a person who was such a (10)_____ _blight_ _____ on the teaching profession.

| Scores | Sentence Check 2 _____% | Final Check _____% |

Enter your scores above and in the **Vocabulary Performance Chart** on the inside back cover of the book.

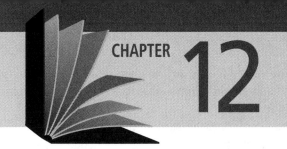

-ate	forc, fort
bio-	hum
claim, clam	pater, patri-
fin	semi-
flex, flect	-ward

Ten Word Parts in Context

Figure out the meanings of the following ten word parts by looking *closely* and *carefully* at the context in which they appear. Then, in the space provided, write the letter of the meaning closest to that of each word part.

1 -ate

- Teachers often find it difficult to **motivate** students to want to learn.
- The TV history series **fascinated** viewers with such details as a seventeenth-century English children's hospital that gave each child two gallons of beer per week.

<u>A</u> The word part *-ate* means   A. cause to become.   B. call.   C. end.

2 bio-

- Helen Keller wrote a touching **autobiography** titled *The Story of My Life*.
- **Biology** is the science of living things, both plant and animal.

<u>B</u> The word part *bio-* means   A. bend.   B. life.   C. partly.

3 claim, clam

- In 2008, American theater critics **acclaimed** *In the Heights*, which won four Tony awards, as the best musical of the year.
- The **exclamation** point emphasizes passionate, sudden, and surprised outcries, such as "Aha!" and "That hurts!"

<u>A</u> The word part *claim* or *clam* means   A. cry out.   B. father.   C. partly.

4 fin

- The **final** word in many prayers is *amen*, which means "May it be so."
- "Ooooooooh! Aaaaaaaah!" the crowd exclaimed, enjoying the spectacular five-minute **finale** that closed the Fourth of July fireworks display.

<u>C</u> The word part *fin* means   A. strong.   B. toward.   C. end.

5 flex, flect

- Gymnasts must be extremely **flexible** so that they can bend their bodies into many positions.
- When they enter church, Catholics **genuflect**—that is, they bend one knee, as a sign of reverence.

<u>A</u> The word part *flex* or *flect* means   A. bend.   B. father.   C. person.

6 forc, fort

- The burglar **forcibly** entered the home by breaking the kitchen window.
- The children made a high wall of pressed snow to **fortify** themselves against a snowball attack by the kids across the street.

<u>C</u> The word part *forc* or *fort* means   A. person.   B. direction of.   C. strong.

7 hum

● "We have done all that is **humanly** possible to save your grandmother's life," said the doctor.

● A resident of the shelter for the homeless complained, "The treatment here is not **humane**. We want to be treated like people, not objects."

B   The word part *hum* means   A. in the direction of.   B. having to do with people.   C. call.

8 pater, patri-

● Mike just became a father, so he is taking six months' **paternity** leave to help care for the baby.

● The soldiers' **patriotism** was so strong that they risked their lives to defend their fatherland.

C   The word part *pater* or *patri-* means   A. partly.   B. toward.   C. father.

9 semi-

● My grandfather is only **semiretired**—he works part-time as a plumber.

● I use **semisweet** chocolate in my frosting to keep it from being too bitter or too sweet.

A   The word part *semi-* means   A. partly.   B. of living things.   C. toward.

10 -ward

● Everyone at the fair looked **skyward** in horror as the colorful hot-air balloon exploded.

● The children tried walking to school **backward** but gave up before even reaching the end of their block.

B   The word part *-ward* means   A. call.   B. in the direction of.   C. of living things.

Matching Word Parts with Definitions

Following are definitions of the ten word parts. Clearly write or print each word part next to its definition. The sentences above and on the previous page will help you decide on the meaning of each word part.

1.   flex, flect   Bend

2.   semi-   Partly; half

3.   bio-   Life; of living things

4.   pater, patri-   Father

5.   -ate   Cause to become

6.   -ward   In the direction of; toward

7.   claim, clam   Call; cry out

8.   forc, fort   Strong

9.   hum   Person; having to do with people

10.   fin   End

CAUTION: Do not go any further until you are sure the above answers are correct. Then you can use the definitions to help you in the following practices. Your goal is eventually to know the word parts well enough so that you don't need to check the definitions at all.

Sentence Check 1

Using the answer line provided, complete each *italicized* word below with the correct word part from the box. Use each word part once.

| A. -ate | B. bio- | C. claim, clam | D. fin | E. flex |
| F. forc, fort | G. hum | H. pater, patri- | I. semi- | J. -ward |

_____exclaimed_____ 1. Little Jesse loudly (*ex . . . ed*) ___ that his father was the smartest man on the block.

_____biorhythm_____ 2. A (*. . . rhythm*) ___ is any cycle of periodic changes in life, such as daily changes in body temperature.

_____patricide_____ 3. The jury found the disturbed young man, who had shot his father, guilty of (*. . . cide*) ___.

_____homeward_____ 4. After a cold, rainy weekend of camping, the Boy Scouts were relieved to head (*home . . .*) ___.

_____inflexible_____ 5. My mother was so (*in . . . ible*) ___ that she never once bent the rule and let me stay out past curfew.

_____forceful_____ 6. The candidate's (*. . . eful*) ___ speech in favor of reduced military spending made a powerful impression on me.

_____semiprivate_____ 7. Uncle Carlos was in a (*. . . private*) ___ room in the hospital. The other man in the room had also suffered a heart attack.

_____finalists_____ 8. There are only two (*. . . alists*) ___ in the last episode of *American Idol*.

_____humanitarian_____ 9. Bishop Desmond Tutu of South Africa received the Nobel Peace Prize for his (*. . . anitarian*) ___ efforts to bring justice to his country's people.

_____humiliated_____ 10. In 1961, administrators of New York's Museum of Modern Art were (*humili . . . d*) ___ to learn that for weeks a painting had been displayed upside down.

NOTE: Now check your answers to these items by turning to page 178. Going over the answers carefully will help you prepare for the next two practices, for which answers are not given.

Sentence Check 2

Using the answer line provided, complete each *italicized* word in the sentences below with the correct word part from the box. Use each word part once.

_____downward_____
_____reflex_____ 1–2. I looked (*down . . .*) ___ and watched the doctor tap my knee to see if its (*re . . .*) ___ was normal.

_____paternal_____
_____enforces_____ 3–4. My supervisor, Mr. Kane, is (*. . . nal*) ___. He (*en . . . es*) ___ the rules in a fatherly way—firmly but kindly. In addition, my coworkers are all very amiable°, making for an extremely friendly atmosphere.

_____semiconscious_____
_____Finally_____ 5–6. After the accident, my brother was (*. . . conscious*) ___ for several hours. (*. . . ally*)___, around midnight, he became fully alert and mobile° enough to walk out of the hospital on his own.

_____ biography _____

_____ human _____

7–8. When the teacher asked students to write a (. . . *graphy*) ___, she meant the life story of a (. . . *an*) ___. But Harry wrote the life story of Tarzan, his pet snake.

_____ proclamation _____

_____ integrate _____

9–10. In 1863, Abraham Lincoln issued a (*pro . . . ation*) ___ freeing the slaves. But it would be almost one hundred years after his announcement before real efforts were made to (*integr . . .*) ___ black people into society's mainstream.

Final Check: *It's Never Too Late*

Here is a final opportunity for you to strengthen your knowledge of the ten word parts. First read the following selection carefully. Then complete each *italicized* word in the parentheses below with a word part from the box at the top of the previous page. (Context clues will help you figure out which word part goes in which blank.) Use each word part once.

I almost fell out of my chair last night when my father (*pro . . . ed*) (1)_____ proclaimed _____, "I quit my job today. I'm going to college." He realizes that people may think him eccentric° to start school at his age, but he's willing to appear odd because he's tired of (. . . *skilled*) (2)_____ semiskilled _____ work in a factory. He wants a job that requires more skill and training. Both of my (. . . *nal*) (3)_____ paternal _____ grandparents died when Dad was a child, so he and his brothers were forced to quit school early to work. Dad finished high school at night. Now he will venture° working only part-time in order to (*educ . . .*) (4)_____ educate _____ himself further. He still isn't sure what his major will be, but he has always liked science. He definitely wants to take a (. . . *logy*) (5)_____ biology _____ course because all living things interest him. He'd like to focus

his (*ef . . . s*) (6)_____ efforts _____ in a field that benefits (. . . *anity*) (7)_____ humanity _____, such as physical therapy, where he could help rehabilitate° people with certain infirmities°. He's also thinking about nursing. Most men of his generation think of nursing as women's work, so Dad's interest in this field shows me he is more (. . . *ible*) (8)_____ flexible _____ in his thinking than I ever realized. Whatever his choice, he is looking (*for . . .*) (9)_____ forward _____ to classes with great zeal°. I know that when he (. . . *ishes*) (10)_____ finishes _____ his schooling, no one will be prouder of him than I already am.

| Scores | Sentence Check 2 _____% | Final Check _____% |

The box at the right lists twenty-five words from Unit Two. Using the clues at the bottom of the page, fill in these words to complete the puzzle that follows.

Word box:
- attribute
- blatant
- calamity
- concurrent
- contrive
- conventional
- decipher
- default
- discern
- dispatch
- enigma
- fluctuate
- gaunt
- immaculate
- implausible
- intercede
- mobile
- nominal
- ponder
- qualm
- recession
- scrutiny
- sinister
- suffice
- turmoil

ACROSS

5. Perfectly clean
6. Thin and bony
7. An event bringing great loss and misery
8. A quality or feature of a person or thing
9. To consider carefully
11. An uneasy feeling about how right or proper a particular action is
18. Customary; ordinary
22. To be good enough
23. A temporary decline in business
24. A mystery or puzzle
25. To send to a specific place or a specific business

DOWN

1. To plan cleverly; think up
2. To vary irregularly; to go up and down or back and forth
3. Difficult to believe; unlikely
4. Very obvious, often offensively so
10. Slight; very small compared to what might be expected
12. Moving or able to move from place to place
13. To make a request or plead on behalf of someone else
14. Close inspection; careful examination
15. To interpret or read (something confusing or hard to make out)
16. Happening or existing at the same time; simultaneous
17. Complete confusion; uproar
19. To recognize; detect
20. To fail to do something required
21. Evil; wicked

66

PART A

Choose the word that best completes each item and write it in the space provided.

_____nocturnal_____ 1. According to legend, vampires are ___ creatures who cannot survive in daylight.

       A. incoherent   B. immaculate   C. nocturnal   D. conventional

_____rehabilitate_____ 2. The counseling program to ___ addicts includes job training.

       A. rehabilitate   B. contrive   C. ponder   D. exemplify

_____degenerate_____ 3. Unless figure skaters practice regularly, their skills will ___.

       A. retaliate   B. degenerate   C. confiscate   D. decipher

_____implausible_____ 4. It may sound ___, but a camel can drink twenty-five gallons of water at a time.

       A. implausible   B. gaunt   C. mobile   D. nominal

_____concurrent_____ 5. Movie subtitles should be ___ with the spoken words they are translating.

       A. flagrant   B. hypothetical   C. incoherent   D. concurrent

_____immaculate_____ 6. Even the most ___ people have microscopic creatures clinging to their hair.

       A. sinister   B. immaculate   C. incoherent   D. intricate

_____blight_____ 7. Measles remains a serious ___ worldwide, killing over a million people each year.

       A. blight   B. plagiarism   C. qualm   D. prerequisite

_____dispatch_____ 8. The Peace Corps continues to ___ American volunteers to live and work in developing nations.

       A. discern   B. garble   C. dispatch   D. default

_____default_____ 9. The government student loan program is in serious trouble because many students ___ on their payments.

       A. suffice   B. attest   C. intercede   D. default

_____flagrant_____ 10. In a race across New Jersey in 1901, drivers traveling up to thirty miles an hour were arrested for their ___ disregard of the speed limit, which was eight miles an hour.

       A. flagrant   B. hypothetical   C. conventional   D. immaculate

(Continues on next page)

PART B

On the answer line, write the letter of the choice that best completes each item.

___C___ 11. **Conventional** business clothing for a man includes
    A. Bermuda shorts and a Hawaiian shirt.   C. a suit and tie.
    B. jeans and a sleeveless tank top.   D. swimming trunks.

___B___ 12. In order to **attest** to what it feels like to walk on the moon's surface, a person must
    A. have read about an astronaut who did it.   C. be a scientist who has studied the moon.
    B. have walked there himself or herself.   D. have a good imagination.

___C___ 13. A person who has lost his or her eyesight can become more **mobile** by
    A. learning to read Braille.   C. learning to get around with a Seeing Eye
    B. becoming depressed and refusing to go out.   dog.
        D. listening to the radio.

___C___ 14. A usual **prerequisite** to getting a driver's license is
    A. purchasing a car.   C. passing a driving test.
    B. committing many traffic offenses.   D. refusing to have one's photograph taken.

___D___ 15. When her brother and sister argue, Rachel often **intercedes** by
    A. leaving the house.   C. ignoring them both.
    B. covering her ears.   D. helping each see the other's point of
        view.

___D___ 16. College students who don't eat properly and don't get much sleep are **vulnerable** to
    A. good health.   C. driving places.
    B. their doctors.   D. illness.

___A___ 17. The parrot **garbled** its words,
    A. making us all laugh at its mixed-up speech.   C. embarrassing us with its dirty words.
    B. amazing us by speaking so clearly.   D. boring us by repeating the same few
        words.

___B___ 18. Which of the following **constitutes** a good breakfast?
    A. A neighborhood diner
    B. Orange juice and bran flakes with milk and bananas
    C. Spaghetti with anchovy sauce
    D. Customers at a pancake house

___A___ 19. The tennis player's performance **fluctuated** during the tournament. It
    A. was magnificent one day, awful the next, and average the following day.
    B. was consistently excellent.
    C. began well but went steadily downhill all week.
    D. started badly but became better every day.

___C___ 20. Since she wanted to **gloat** about her promotion at work, Kris
    A. didn't mention it to anyone.
    B. worked harder than ever to show that she deserved it.
    C. said to a coworker, "Sorry, loser. I got it."
    D. became very nervous about her new responsibilities.

Score   (Number correct) _____ x 5 = _____%

PART A

Complete each item with a word from the box. Use each word once.

A. **attribute**	B. **calamity**	C. **decipher**	D. **enigma**	E. **exemplify**
F. **nominal**	G. **orient**	H. **qualm**	I. **recession**	J. **retaliate**
K. **scrutiny**	L. **sinister**	M. **suffice**		

_____calamity_____ 1. The sinking of the ship *Titanic*, which struck an iceberg, was a(n) ___ in which nearly 1,600 people died.

_____orient_____ 2. People who can't read must ___ themselves in a city by relating to familiar places, not signs.

_____suffice_____ 3. "A hint to my daughter to take out the garbage won't ___," Alonso insisted. "She needs to be told to do it."

_____decipher_____ 4. I don't know who sent me the birthday card because I couldn't ___ the signature.

_____recession_____ 5. A shortage of a single product, such as sugar, could cause a(n) ___ in several industries.

_____scrutiny_____ 6. Don't buy a used car unless you examine it closely and also have a mechanic give it careful ___.

_____nominal_____ 7. Although our library charges only a ___ fee to use a computer, I don't think it should charge students any fee at all.

_____attribute_____ 8. In some religions, gods and goddesses represent various human ___s, such as strength, beauty, and wisdom.

_____qualm_____ 9. Through the years, people with ___s about having cheated on their income taxes have sent gifts of money to the IRS.

_____retaliate_____ 10. The citizens in that small country ___(e)d against their communist dictator, who had ordered mass murders, by executing him.

_____sinister_____ 11. One of the oddest ___ plots of all time was thought up by a wealthy Frenchman. He fed his victims rich foods until they died of overeating.

_____enigma_____ 12. The thousands of oak leaves that covered the ground in a Scottish town in 1889 were a(n) ___. The nearest oak trees were eight miles away.

_____exemplify_____ 13. Lightning bolts, which travel at millions of miles an hour and produce five times the heat of the sun's surface, ___ nature's tremendous energy.

(Continues on next page)

PART B

Write **C** if the italicized word is used **correctly**. Write **I** if the word is used **incorrectly**.

_I_   14. The *turmoil* of a smooth, clear lake always makes me feel at peace.

_I_   15. A wonderfully *incoherent* speaker, Abraham Lincoln was widely admired for his powerful speeches.

_I_   16. James Bond was about to step into his enemy's trap when a beautiful woman, a former enemy who had fallen in love with him, *pondered* him to escape.

_C_   17. The Democratic and Republican parties are *predominant* in the United States, but other parties are also represented on the ballots.

_C_   18. Shortly before his birthday, Hollis *contrived* to get his parents to walk past the toy store so that he could point out the PlayStation 3 games displayed in the window.

_I_   19. Each year, thousands of Americans who think themselves too *gaunt* have some fat surgically removed.

PART C

On the answer line, write the letter of the word that is the **synonym** of the boldfaced word.

Example: _C_ **nominal**   A. personal   B. enormous   C. slight

_B_   20. **confiscate**   A. give back   B. seize   C. combine

_A_   21. **enhance**   A. improve   B. lead   C. weaken

_B_   22. **comprehensive**   A. limited   B. broad   C. irregular

PART D

On the answer line, write the letter of the word that is the **antonym** of the boldfaced word.

Example: _B_ **nominal**   A. personal   B. enormous   C. slight

_C_   23. **intricate**   A. complicated   B. musical   C. simple

_B_   24. **persevere**   A. look   B. give up   C. persist

_C_   25. **blatant**   A. strange   B. obvious   C. hidden

Score   (Number correct) _____ x 4 = _____ %

Enter your score above and in the **Vocabulary Performance Chart** on the inside back cover of the book.

Each item below starts with a pair of words in CAPITAL LETTERS. For each item, figure out the relationship between these two words. Then decide which of the choices (A, B, C, or D) expresses a similar relationship. Write the letter of your choice on the answer line.

_C_ 1. CALAMITY : SUFFERING ::
   A. magnet : repels   C. tragedy : sadness
   B. tragedy : joy   D. table : chair

_A_ 2. PERSEVERE : QUIT ::
   A. open : shut   C. drink : thirsty
   B. perspire : sweat   D. continue : persist

_B_ 3. VENTURE : EXPLORER ::
   A. see : blind person   C. cow : milk
   B. teach : professor   D. ocean : ship

_D_ 4. CONVENTIONAL : UNCOMMON ::
   A. conduct : experiment   C. owner : possesses
   B. thoughtful : considerate D. quiet : noisy

_A_ 5. MOBILE : UNMOVING ::
   A. rapid : slow   C. excited : lively
   B. write : words   D. wet : water

_B_ 6. ENIGMA : MYSTERIOUS ::
   A. baseball : bat   C. funny : serious
   B. joke : funny   D. clue : detective

_B_ 7. OWL : NOCTURNAL ::
   A. tiger : cat   C. day : night
   B. tiger : fierce   D. child : adult

_A_ 8. DISCERN : LOOK ::
   A. hear : listen   C. cold : touch
   B. smell : taste   D. ignore : see

_B_ 9. DECIPHER : CODE ::
   A. surgeon : doctor   C. puzzle : piece
   B. untangle : knot   D. evident : clear

_D_ 10. CONFISCATE : SEIZE ::
   A. confuse : clarify   C. take : give
   B. cry : funeral   D. contribute : give

(Continues on next page)

_A_   11. HYPOTHETICAL : ACTUAL ::
      A. brave : cowardly   C. old : ancient
      B. scary : frightening   D. problem : solve

_C_   12. DEFAULT : LOAN ::
      A. pass : course   C. break : promise
      B. pay : salary   D. tax : income

_C_   13. INTRICATE : COMPLEX ::
      A. difficult : simple   C. circular : round
      B. headlight : car   D. scold : soothe

_D_   14. DEGENERATE : IMPROVE ::
      A. solve : equation   C. ride : train
      B. generous : giving   D. grow : shrink

_B_   15. IMPLAUSIBLE : UNLIKELY ::
      A. straight : crooked   C. furniture : house
      B. unfortunate : unlucky   D. unfortunate : lucky

_A_   16. SANCTUARY : SAFETY ::
      A. hideout : secrecy   C. wheel : steer
      B. enclosed : exposed   D. dinner : breakfast

_A_   17. GAUNT : PLUMP ::
      A. tall : short   C. precious : jewelry
      B. thin : skinny   D. fruit : nutrition

_B_   18. BLIGHT : DESTROYS ::
      A. flood : dries   C. pianist : piano
      B. medicine : heals   D. agreement : disagree

_C_   19. QUALM : CONSCIENCE ::
      A. love : hatred   C. cramp : muscle
      B. room : fireplace   D. pain : health

_D_   20. PLAGIARISM : IDEAS ::
      A. criminal : crime   C. writing : paper
      B. host : party   D. shoplifting : merchandise

Score   (Number correct) _____ x 5 = _____%

Enter your score above and in the **Vocabulary Performance Chart** on the inside back cover of the book.

UNIT TWO: Test 4 (Word Parts)

PART A

Listed in the left-hand column below are ten common word parts, followed by words in which the parts are used. In each blank, write in the letter of the correct definition on the right.

Word Parts	Examples	Definitions
_E_ 1. **-ate**	motivate, fascinate	A. Father
_J_ 2. **bio-**	autobiography, biology	B. Call; cry out
_B_ 3. **claim, clam**	acclaim, exclamation	C. Partly
_D_ 4. **fin**	final, finale	D. End
_I_ 5. **flex, flect**	flexible, genuflect	E. Cause to become
_H_ 6. **forc, fort**	forcibly, fortify	F. In the direction of; toward
_G_ 7. **hum**	humanly, humane	G. Person; having to do with people
_A_ 8. **pater, patri-**	paternity, patriotism	H. Strong
_C_ 9. **semi-**	semiretired, semisweet	I. Bend
_F_ 10. **-ward**	skyward, backward	J. Life; of living things

PART B

Using the answer line provided, complete each *italicized* word in the sentences below with the correct word part from the box. Not every word part will be used.

A. **-ate**	B. **bio-**	C. **clam**	D. **fin**	E. **flex**
F. **fort**	G. **hum**	H. **patri-**	I. **semi-**	J. **-ward**

activate _____ 11. To (*activ . . .*) ___ yeast, put it in a warm liquid.

inwardly _____ 12. When I meditate, I focus (*in . . . ly*) ___ by mentally repeating a nonsense word.

fortified _____ 13. In the seventeenth century, England (*. . . ified*) ___ its weakening wool trade by passing a law that all corpses must be buried in wool.

final _____ 14. The French king Louis XIV's (*. . . al*) ___ words before his death were to his servants: "Why do you weep? Did you think I was immortal?"

humanoid _____ 15. Why are robots often given a (*. . . anoid*) ___ appearance? Are we more comfortable with "smart" machines that resemble us?

(Continues on next page)

PART C

Use your knowledge of word parts to determine the meaning of the **boldfaced** words. On the answer line, write the letter of each meaning.

___B___ 16. The dining club is **semipublic**.

    A. fully public   B. partly public   C. private

___C___ 17. A **patriarchy** is a form of social organization in which families are headed by

    A. the strongest.   B. the oldest.   C. the father.

___A___ 18. My chemistry teacher also teaches **biochemistry**, which is the chemistry of

    A. life processes.   B. lakes.   C. weather.

___B___ 19. Albert Einstein **claimed** that his brain was his laboratory.

    A. realized   B. made known   C. silently wished

___C___ 20. The company I work for has decided to experiment with **flextime** for employees.

    A. longer work hours   B. shorter work hours   C. adjustable work hours

Score   (Number correct) _____ x 5 = _____%

Unit Three

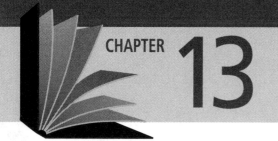

curtail	indispensable
devastate	intermittent
digress	rigor
incentive	squander
incorporate	succumb

Ten Words in Context

In the space provided, write the letter of the meaning closest to that of each **boldfaced** word. Use the context of the sentences to help you figure out each word's meaning.

1 curtail
(kər-tāl′)
-*verb*

- Upon hearing reports of a huge snowstorm, the principal **curtailed** the school day so students could go home early.
- I need to **curtail** my volunteer activities so that I can spend more time earning money to pay back a loan.

_B_ *Curtail* means
    A. to combine.
    B. to shorten.
    C. to extend.

2 devastate
(dĕv′əs-tāt′)
-*verb*

- Learning that their son had been arrested for armed robbery **devastated** the Huttons. They couldn't believe he'd do such a terrible thing.
- Vera is so fond of Andy. She'll be **devastated** to hear he has cancer.

_C_ *Devastate* means
    A. to thrill.
    B. to annoy.
    C. to upset greatly.

3 digress
(dī-grĕs′)
-*verb*

- Professor Rubin never **digresses** during a lecture. Even his jokes relate to the day's topic.
- I tried to teach my three-year-old niece our phone number, but we **digressed** to a discussion of whether Winnie the Pooh has a telephone.

_B_ *Digress* means
    A. to listen carefully.
    B. to go off the subject.
    C. to get up.

4 incentive
(ĭn-sĕn′tĭv)
-*noun*

- The insurance company offers an **incentive**—a free vacation—to encourage its representatives to make more sales.
- The thought of myself in a bathing suit next summer provides me with an adequate **incentive** to exercise.

_A_ *Incentive* means
    A. encouragement.
    B. liberty.
    C. change.

5 incorporate
(ĭn-kôr′pər-āt′)
-*verb*

- Jerry **incorporated** all of his favorite desserts into one: a chocolate-covered banana-cream pecan pie.
- Since the number of young children has gone down in my neighborhood, the two elementary schools have been **incorporated** into one.

_B_ *Incorporate* means
    A. to give up.
    B. to join together.
    C. to raise.

6 indispensable
(ĭn-dĭ-spĕn′sə-bəl)
-*adjective*

- Because there's no bus or train service nearby, a car is **indispensable** in my neighborhood.
- When you're broke, you find that many things you thought were **indispensable** aren't actually necessary after all.

_B_ *Indispensable* means
    A. free.
    B. needed.
    C. expensive.

7 intermittent
(ĭn′tər-mĭt′ənt)
-*adjective*

- You have to work steadily with your dog to train him well. **Intermittent** practice won't work.
- Dora realized that her weight loss on a diet would be **intermittent**, so she didn't give up when the losses stopped. She knew they would start again.

A   *Intermittent* means   A. irregular.   B. too much.   C. steady.

8 rigor
(rĭg′ər)
-*noun*

- New Marines must go through the **rigors** of boot camp, such as completing an obstacle course and running several miles a day.
- The **rigor** of working at two part-time jobs while going to school proved too much for Jamal. Exhausted, he quit both jobs.

C   *Rigor* means   A. a gamble.   B. an expense.   C. a hardship.

9 squander
(skwŏn′dər)
-*verb*

- It's sad to see such a wonderful artist **squander** her talent designing labels for baked-bean cans.
- The company lunchroom now closes promptly at one o'clock so that workers can't **squander** time on long lunch breaks.

B   *Squander* means   A. to share.   B. to misuse.   C. to upset.

10 succumb
(sə-kŭm′)
-*verb*

- Leah **succumbed** to her daughter's begging and bought her a pet lizard for her birthday.
- Once the suspect was arrested, he quickly **succumbed** and confessed to stealing the car stereo.

A   *Succumb* means   A. to yield.   B. to delay.   C. to anger.

Matching Words with Definitions

Following are definitions of the ten words. Clearly write or print each word next to its definition. The sentences above and on the previous page will help you decide on the meaning of each word.

1. _____squander_____   To waste; spend or use foolishly

2. _____curtail_____   To cut short or reduce

3. _____incentive_____   Something that moves one to take action or work harder; a motivation

4. _____digress_____   To turn aside, or stray, especially from the main topic in speaking or writing

5. _____rigor_____   Great hardship or difficulty; harshness; severity

6. _____devastate_____   To upset deeply; overwhelm

7. _____succumb_____   To give in; stop resisting

8. _____indispensable_____   Necessary

9. _____incorporate_____   To unite into a single whole; combine

10. _____intermittent_____   Starting and stopping from time to time; off-and-on

CAUTION: Do not go any further until you are sure the above answers are correct. Then you can use the definitions to help you in the following practices. Your goal is eventually to know the words well enough so that you don't need to check the definitions at all.

Sentence Check 1

Using the answer line provided, complete each item below with the correct word from the box. Use each word once.

A. **curtail**	B. **devastate**	C. **digress**	D. **incentive**	E. **incorporate**
F. **indispensable**	G. **intermittent**	H. **rigor**	I. **squander**	J. **succumb**

Intermittent   1. ___ rain kept interrupting the ballgame.

devastate   2. The sight of her bandaged husband in an oxygen tent ___(e)d Claire.

incorporate   3. Someone has managed to ___ a tomato and a potato into one plant.

indispensable   4. A home computer, a telephone, and a fax machine are ___ tools for many self-employed people.

incentive   5. Airlines offer "frequent flier miles" toward free trips as a(n) ___ to get people to fly often.

rigor   6. Many teenagers don't foresee the ___s of parenthood, such as staying up all night with a sick child.

squander   7. By examining her last two months of spending, Coretta discovered that she had ___(e)d money on too many expensive meals.

curtail   8. The man on the street corner offered to sell me a watch, but he quickly ___(e)d his sales pitch when he saw a police officer approaching.

digress   9. Because our history teacher loved to talk, we often could get him to ___ from the lesson by asking him a question about sports or politics.

succumb   10. Carl tried hard to ignore the double-fudge chocolate cake on the menu, but he finally ___(e)d and ordered a slice.

NOTE: Now check your answers to these items by turning to page 178. Going over the answers carefully will help you prepare for the next two practices, for which answers are not given.

Sentence Check 2

Using the answer lines provided, complete each item below with **two** words from the box. Use each word once.

squander
rigor   1–2. Duane feels he ___(e)d too many years in inactivity, so now he welcomes the ___s of an exercise program.

curtail
incorporate   3–4. The company decided to ___ the construction of its new plant until the architects could decide on how to ___ an employee gym into the new building.

intermittent
succumb   5–6. My aunt has only ___ success in quitting smoking. Every few months she ___s to temptation, and then she has to quit all over again.

_____devastate_____   7–8. As Leo explained a failed business deal that had once ___(e)d him,
_____digress_____   he ___(e)d into the even more interesting tale of his romance with Molly, his
                                         business partner.

_____incentive_____   9–10. The infomercial offered free samples, ninety-day trials, and every other ___
_____indispensable_____   possible to get me to buy the "miracle medicine that would change my life."
                                          However, I found the sales pitch highly implausible°. I simply could not
                                          believe that this product was ___ to my well-being.

Final Check: *Learning to Study*

Here is a final opportunity for you to strengthen your knowledge of the ten words. First read the following selection carefully. Then fill in each blank with a word from the box at the top of the previous page. (Context clues will help you figure out which word goes in which blank.) Use each word once.

Linda never had to work very hard to make good grades in high school. But in college, where the (1)_____rigor_____s of course work were greater, she soon learned that her casual high-school study habits would no longer suffice°. Linda was also learning how easy it was to (2)_____squander_____ time on surfing the Web and partying. She didn't realize how badly she was doing until she saw her midterm grades, which (3)_____devastate_____(e)d her. She knew she had to make some changes right away and began to ponder° what they should be. As a(n) (4)_____incentive_____ to work harder, she tried studying with her friend Denise. But that didn't work; their conversation would (5)_____digress_____ from European history to personal topics, such as dates or favorite songs.

Linda decided she'd have to go it alone. She began to skip parties during the week and also to (6)_____curtail_____ the time she spent text-messaging or exchanging e-mails with friends. She discovered that a good place to study was (7)_____indispensable_____ to her new study habits. She found the library's silent third floor a sanctuary°, a place with no temptations to which she could (8)_____succumb_____. She also became more methodical° in her study habits, keeping an assignment book, writing due dates on a calendar, and setting up a study schedule. At first, Linda's performance fluctuated°, and so the improvement in her grades was (9)_____intermittent_____—A's and B's alternated with C's and D's. But little by little, she learned to (10)_____incorporate_____ a social life with serious study and earn grades she was proud of.

Scores	Sentence Check 2 _____%	Final Check _____%

alleviate	infamous
benefactor	intrinsic
covert	revulsion
cynic	speculate
demise	virile

Ten Words in Context

In the space provided, write the letter of the meaning closest to that of each **boldfaced** word. Use the context of the sentences to help you figure out each word's meaning.

1 alleviate
(ə-lē′vē-āt′)
-verb

● To **alleviate** his loneliness, the widower moved closer to his daughter and her family.

● After a long game in the August heat, the young baseball players **alleviated** their thirst with ice-cold lemonade.

_C_ *Alleviate* means

A. to consider.   B. to hide.   C. to ease.

2 benefactor
(běn′ə-făk′tər)
-noun

● The Second Street Bank is a long-time **benefactor** of the arts. This year it will sponsor a series of free jazz concerts in the parks.

● The wealthy **benefactor** who paid for the child's operation prefers to remain anonymous.

_A_ *Benefactor* means

A. a financial supporter.   B. a social critic.   C. a cooperative person.

3 covert
(kŭv′ərt)
-adjective

● Miriam and David's relationship is so **covert** that they never eat out. Even their best friends don't know they are seeing each other.

● If you enjoy **covert** activities, you should become a secret agent.

_B_ *Covert* means

A. obvious.   B. concealed.   C. easy to bear.

4 cynic
(sĭn′ĭk)
-noun

● Her parents' nasty divorce has made Libby a **cynic** about marriage.

● Mr. Bryant was a **cynic** about people until he fell down on a street corner and several strangers rushed to his aid.

_A_ *Cynic* means

A. someone who believes the worst.   B. someone who gives help.   C. someone with a bad reputation.

5 demise
(dĭ-mīz′)
-noun

● During my years in grade school and high school, the untimely **demise** of several of my classmates made me very aware of my mortality.

● In 1567, a beard caused a man's **demise**. Hans Steininger's beard was so long that he stepped on it while climbing stairs, lost his balance, fell down the steps, and died.

_C_ *Demise* means

A. popularity.   B. a secret.   C. dying.

6 infamous
(ĭn′fə-məs)
-adjective

● King Henry VIII of England was **infamous** throughout Europe for executing two of his six wives.

● Visitors to the dungeons of ancient castles always want to see the instruments of torture, including the **infamous** Iron Maiden—a body-shaped box with spikes inside.

_A_ *Infamous* means

A. known unfavorably.   B. thought to be annoying.   C. giving hope.

7 intrinsic
(ĭn-trĭn′sĭk)
-adjective

- Trust is **intrinsic** to any good friendship.
- Because Lian has an **intrinsic** desire to learn, she doesn't need the reward of good grades to motivate her studies.

B *Intrinsic* means   A. secret.   B. fundamental.   C. unnecessary.

8 revulsion
(rĭ-vŭl′shən)
-noun

- Whenever I read about child abuse in the newspaper, I am filled with such **revulsion** that I often cannot finish the article.
- When Sharon met the man who had cheated her father, she was overcome with **revulsion**.

B *Revulsion* means   A. interest.   B. hatred.   C. understanding.

9 speculate
(spĕk′yə-lāt′)
-verb

- It's interesting to **speculate** how history might have been different if Abraham Lincoln had lived a few years longer.
- The therapist asked Cassie to **speculate** about what might happen if she told Leon her true feelings.

C *Speculate* means   A. to remember.   B. to announce.   C. to guess.

10 virile
(vîr′əl)
-adjective

- Men who are unsure about their masculinity sometimes try to "prove" they are **virile** by being overly aggressive.
- When a male heron stamps his feet and sticks his neck out, and then drops his head and says "plop-buzz," the female finds him very **virile**. In fact, that behavior is how the male attracts a mate.

A *Virile* means   A. having attractive male qualities.   B. lacking in confidence.   C. unselfish.

Matching Words with Definitions

Following are definitions of the ten words. Clearly write or print each word next to its definition. The sentences above and on the previous page will help you decide on the meaning of each word.

1. _____covert_____ Secret; hidden

2. _____cynic_____ A person who believes the worst of people's behavior and motives; someone who believes people are motivated only by selfishness

3. _____intrinsic_____ Belonging to a person or thing by its very nature (and thus not dependent on circumstances); built-in

4. _____infamous_____ Having a very bad reputation; widely known for being vicious, criminal, or deserving of contempt

5. _____benefactor_____ A person or organization that gives help, especially financial aid

6. _____virile_____ Manly; masculine

7. _____demise_____ Death

8. _____speculate_____ To come up with ideas or theories about a subject; theorize

9. _____alleviate_____ To relieve; make easier to endure

10. _____revulsion_____ Great disgust or distaste

CAUTION: Do not go any further until you are sure the above answers are correct. Then you can use the definitions to help you in the following practices. Your goal is eventually to know the words well enough so that you don't need to check the definitions at all.

Sentence Check 1

Using the answer line provided, complete each item below with the correct word from the box. Use each word once.

A. alleviate	B. benefactor	C. covert	D. cynic	E. demise
F. infamous	G. intrinsic	H. revulsion	I. speculate	J. virile

intrinsic   1. Problems are ___ to life; they're unavoidable.

alleviate   2. My hunger isn't fully satisfied, but the apple ___(e)d it somewhat.

virile   3. Teenage guys usually welcome a deepening voice and a thickening beard as signs that they are becoming more ___.

cynic   4. The selfless work of the nuns in the slums of India is enough to touch the hearts of most hardened ___s.

infamous   5. Though she was tried and found not guilty, Lizzie Borden is still ___ for killing her parents with a hatchet.

covert   6. The children loved the ___ activities involved in preparing their mother's surprise party.

revulsion   7. The mass murderer's neighbors were overcome with ___ when they learned what their "friend" had been doing in his basement.

speculate   8. "As no group has claimed responsibility, we can only ___ on the motives for the bombing," said the newscaster.

benefactor   9. Roger Novak had been a well-known ___ of AIDS research, so it was no surprise that he left a lot of money for the research in his will.

demise   10. It's a good idea for married couples to discuss their funeral plans in case of each other's ___. For example, do they wish to be buried or cremated?

NOTE: Now check your answers to these items by turning to page 178. Going over the answers carefully will help you prepare for the next two practices, for which answers are not given.

Sentence Check 2

Using the answer lines provided, complete each item below with **two** words from the box. Use each word once.

intrinsic
alleviate
1–2. Nursing is a good career for Dee because it's a(n) ___ part of her personality to try to ___ people's pain. In addition, her physical and mental strength will help her handle the rigors° of nursing, such as intense stress and long hours.

revulsion
covert
3–4. Although everything about the Nazis filled the Dutch spy with ___, his ___ assignment was to make friends with top Nazi scientists. He had few qualms° about faking such friendships—he would have felt more guilty if he hadn't done everything in his power to fight the Nazis.

_____cynic_____

_____demise_____

5–6. The ___s in town said that Joyce's sorrow over her husband's ___ was much less than her joy in getting the money from his insurance policy.

_____virile_____

_____benefactor_____

7–8. Young men who are bullies usually think of themselves as ___, but a ___ of the weak is far more manly than someone who takes advantage of weakness.

_____infamous_____

_____speculate_____

9–10. With all the stories told about Jesse James, the Dalton Gang, and other ___ figures of the Wild West, we can only ___ as to how much is fact and how much is fiction.

Final Check: *The Mad Monk*

Here is a final opportunity for you to strengthen your knowledge of the ten words. First read the following selection carefully. Then fill in each blank with a word from the box at the top of the previous page. (Context clues will help you figure out which word goes in which blank.) Use each word once.

Shortly before the Russian Revolution, an eccentric° man named Rasputin became (1)_____infamous_____ as the "mad monk." Because he dressed like a peasant, drank heavily, and rarely bathed, the nobility often felt (2)_____revulsion_____ during their encounters° with him at the palace.

Yet despite his outward appearance, Rasputin possessed a(n) (3)_____intrinsic_____ charm that drew many to him, including the Russian empress. She thought him a great man of God and a special (4)_____benefactor_____ of her seriously ill son, whose condition she felt Rasputin (5)_____alleviate_____(e)d.

Many (6)_____cynic_____s believed otherwise. To them, Rasputin was no healer; instead, he was a man who exploited° his relationship with the empress for his own benefit. Rather than praise Rasputin, his enemies preferred to malign° him. In a pamphlet titled *The Holy Devil*, one of his critics described him as a sinister° man. This author even dared to (7)_____speculate_____ that the monk and the empress were romantically involved. This theory was strengthened by the fact that the empress's "holy man" pursued many women and boasted about how (8)_____virile_____ he was.

Finally, a group of Russian noblemen made (9)_____covert_____ plans to kill Rasputin. Somehow, the secret must have gotten out, for a Russian official warned Rasputin of a plot against him. He nevertheless accepted the noblemen's invitation to a dinner party, where they served him poisoned wine and cake. When Rasputin did not appear to succumb° to the poison, his enemies hastened his (10)_____demise_____ by shooting and stabbing him and then dumping him into an icy river. An autopsy revealed that he had died by drowning.

| Scores | Sentence Check 2 _____% | Final Check _____% |

CHAPTER 15

abstain	deficit
affiliate	dissent
agnostic	diversion
aspire	lucrative
benevolent	mandatory

Ten Words in Context

In the space provided, write the letter of the meaning closest to that of each **boldfaced** word. Use the context of the sentences to help you figure out each word's meaning.

1 abstain
(ăb-stān′)
-*verb*

● Although Luis has given up high-calorie desserts, he doesn't **abstain** completely from chocolate. He allows himself one small square of a Hershey bar a day.

● My sister called off her engagement to Clayton because he wouldn't **abstain** from dating other women.

__C__ *Abstain from* means   A. to desire.   B. to believe in.   C. to deny oneself.

2 affiliate
(ə-fĭl′ē-āt′)
-*verb*

● Diane is neither a Democrat nor a Republican. She isn't **affiliated** with any political party.

● The young singer could have earned more if she had been **affiliated** with the musicians' union, but she couldn't afford the membership dues.

__A__ *Affiliate* means   A. to join.   B. to study.   C. to hold back.

3 agnostic
(ăg-nŏs′tĭk)
-*noun*

● Iris believes there is a God, and Marcia feels sure there isn't. Jean, an **agnostic**, feels that we can't be certain one way or the other.

● My uncle, who was an **agnostic**, used to say, "Humans cannot understand a flower, let alone whether or not there's a God."

__B__ *Agnostic* means   A. one who denies God's existence.   B. one who feels we can't know if God exists.   C. one who is sure there is a God.

4 aspire
(ə-spīr′)
-*verb*

● Twelve-year-old Derek, who loves drawing buildings, **aspires** to be an architect.

● Millions of young people **aspire** to be professional athletes, but only a few will succeed.

__B__ *Aspire* means   A. to fear.   B. to wish.   C. to volunteer.

5 benevolent
(bə-nĕv′ə-lənt)
-*adjective*

● People are more **benevolent** at Christmas, the "season for giving."

● In 1878, William Booth founded a **benevolent** association to help the poor of London. He called it the Salvation Army.

__C__ *Benevolent* means   A. recreational.   B. profitable.   C. charitable.

6 deficit
(dĕf′ə-sĭt)
-*noun*

● Our club has spent much more money than it has taken in, so it now has a huge budget **deficit**.

● Residents are asked not to water their lawns because a **deficit** of rain has dangerously lowered the water supply.

__A__ *Deficit* means   A. a lack.   B. an overflow.   C. a collection.

7 dissent
(dĭ-sĕnt′)
-noun

- The committee was so torn by **dissent** that its members could not even agree on whether or not to schedule another meeting.
- The dictator permitted people to agree with his policies or keep silent about them, but not to express **dissent**.

B *Dissent* means   A. plans.   B. opposition.   C. relief.

8 diversion
(də-vûr′zhən)
-noun

- My history teacher says that one of her favorite **diversions** during summer vacation is reading mystery novels.
- Skip likes his job, but he also enjoys such **diversions** as playing video games, watching baseball, and reading humorous stories.

A *Diversion* means   A. a way to relax.   B. something easy.   C. an assignment.

9 lucrative
(lōō′krə-tĭv)
-adjective

- Investments in the stock market can be **lucrative**. However, they can also result in great financial loss.
- "Teaching at a small college isn't **lucrative**," Professor Baum admitted, "but I've never felt the need to make lots of money."

B *Lucrative* means   A. required.   B. financially rewarding.   C. risky.

10 mandatory
(măn′də-tôr′ē)
-adjective

- Members of the basketball team have to follow strict rules. For example, it's **mandatory** that each player attend at least 80 percent of the practices.
- "A research paper isn't **mandatory**," the instructor said, "but if you write one, you'll get extra credit."

C *Mandatory* means   A. unimportant.   B. helpful.   C. essential.

Matching Words with Definitions

Following are definitions of the ten words. Clearly write or print each word next to its definition. The sentences above and on the previous page will help you decide on the meaning of each word.

1. _____aspire_____ To strongly desire; to be ambitious (to do something or to get something)

2. _____lucrative_____ Profitable; well-paying

3. _____deficit_____ A shortage; a lack (in amount)

4. _____abstain_____ To hold oneself back from something; refrain

5. _____benevolent_____ Showing kindness; charitable

6. _____agnostic_____ A person who believes we cannot know whether or not there is a God

7. _____mandatory_____ Required

8. _____diversion_____ An amusement or pastime; anything that relaxes or amuses

9. _____affiliate_____ To associate; join

10. _____dissent_____ Disagreement

CAUTION: Do not go any further until you are sure the above answers are correct. Then you can use the definitions to help you in the following practices. Your goal is eventually to know the words well enough so that you don't need to check the definitions at all.

Sentence Check 1

Using the answer line provided, complete each item below with the correct word from the box. Use each word once.

A. **abstain**	B. **affiliate**	C. **agnostic**	D. **aspire**	E. **benevolent**
F. **deficit**	G. **dissent**	H. **diversion**	I. **lucrative**	J. **mandatory**

aspire   1. My kid brother ___s to become the video-game champion of the world.

benevolent   2. The ___ fund at my church collects money to help poor families in our parish.

diversion   3. My parents enjoy card games, but my sister and I prefer such ___s as computer games and music videos.

mandatory   4. An entrance fee wasn't ___, but a sign at the museum entrance suggested that visitors make a donation.

abstain   5. Because Hank needs to lose weight, his doctor recommended that he ___ from all sweets and fatty foods.

deficit   6. We could overcome a(n) ___ of organs for transplants if more people would agree to have their organs donated after they die.

dissent   7. There was no ___ in the family on whether or not to start a vegetable garden this year. We all agreed it was a great idea.

affiliate   8. Yong could have joined the all-male club, but he prefers to ___ with organizations that welcome both men and women.

agnostic   9. "When someone who believes in God marries someone who does not," the comic asked, "do they give birth to a(n) ___?"

lucrative   10. Acting is ___ for only a small percentage of performers. The rest need additional sources of income, such as waiting on tables or parking cars.

NOTE: Now check your answers to these items by turning to page 178. Going over the answers carefully will help you prepare for the next two practices, for which answers are not given.

Sentence Check 2

Using the answer lines provided, complete each item below with **two** words from the box. Use each word once.

affiliate
 diversion   1–2. My uncle decided to splurge and ___ with a country club because golf is his favorite ___.

abstain
 mandatory   3–4. Gail didn't ___ from smoking cigarettes until her employer made not smoking ___. Keeping her job was a very good incentive° to get her to quit.

agnostic
 benevolent   5–6. Some people think that since Stan is a(n) ___, he must be amoral°. It's true he's not sure if God exists, but that doesn't mean he lacks a moral sense. In fact, he recently founded a ___ society at work to raise money for disabled children in the area.

_____deficit_____   7–8. The ___ in the township treasury is causing a lot of ___ over whether or not
_____dissent_____   taxes should be raised.

_____aspire_____   9–10. Because my father ___s to make enough money to send his children to
_____lucrative_____   college, he's working hard to make his auto repair business as ___ as
                                        possible.

Final Check: *Conflict Over Holidays*

Here is a final opportunity for you to strengthen your knowledge of the ten words. First read the following selection carefully. Then fill in each blank with a word from the box at the top of the previous page. (Context clues will help you figure out which word goes in which blank.) Use each word once.

While Jeanne and Paul are generally a happily married couple, they do struggle over one point of (1)_____dissent_____. They disagree as to how their family should observe religious holidays.

"The emphasis on presents," says Jeanne, "has made the season (2)_____lucrative_____ for all those mercenary° retailers who overcharge at holiday time. Also, people who should be watching their expenses create unnecessary (3)_____deficit_____s in their budgets by squandering° money on unimportant gifts." She complains that exchanging presents at Christmas is practically (4)_____mandatory_____, whether or not one believes in the holiday's religious significance. Jeanne (5)_____aspire_____s to keep her home free of all such nonreligious customs and thus wants her children to (6)_____abstain_____ from traditions such as gift-giving and dyeing Easter eggs. She feels the family's money would be better spent if it were donated to a (7)_____benevolent_____ organization for helping the poor. Some of Jeanne's neighbors assume that she is a(n) (8)_____agnostic_____ because of her lack of holiday spirit. They are wrong, however. Jeanne believes deeply in God and is (9)_____affiliate_____(e)d with a church.

While Paul understands Jeanne's concerns, he prefers the conventional° way of celebrating holidays. "Children enjoy the customary (10)_____diversion_____s that are connected with the holidays," he says. "What would Christmas be without a visit to Santa and gifts under the tree? What would Easter be without colorful eggs and an Easter egg hunt? These are pleasant practices that enhance° the joy of the season."

Scores   Sentence Check 2 _____%   Final Check _____%

CHAPTER 16

charisma	poignant
contemporary	prevalent
contend	proponent
conversely	quest
extrovert	traumatic

Ten Words in Context

In the space provided, write the letter of the meaning closest to that of each **boldfaced** word. Use the context of the sentences to help you figure out each word's meaning.

1 charisma
(kə-rĭz′mə)
-noun

● Kamal has such **charisma** that when he ran for class president, almost every person in the tenth grade voted for him. His classmates couldn't resist Kamal's magnetic personality.

● Great Britain's Princess Diana obviously had great **charisma**. She continues to have numerous loyal fans—long after her death.

_B_ *Charisma* means   A. feelings.   B. personal appeal.   C. luck.

2 contemporary
(kən-těm′pə-rěr′ē)
-adjective

● Beth likes **contemporary** furniture, but her husband prefers antiques.

● My grandfather says that compared to kids in his day, **contemporary** youngsters are soft and lazy.

_C_ *Contemporary* means   A. common.   B. old-fashioned.   C. today's.

3 contend
(kən-těnd′)
-verb

● The defense attorney **contended** that his client was insane and therefore could not be held responsible for the murder.

● Scientists **contend** that no two snowflakes are identical, but how could they possibly prove it?

_C_ *Contend* means   A. to wish.   B. to deny.   C. to declare.

4 conversely
(kən-vûrs′lē)
-adverb

● Ron, who is basically bored by food, eats in order to live. **Conversely,** Nate loves food so much that he seems to live in order to eat.

● Mary drives her children to school whenever it rains. **Conversely,** Thea makes her kids walk because she thinks a little rain never hurt anyone.

_A_ *Conversely* means   A. in contrast.   B. in a modern way.   C. similarly.

5 extrovert
(ěk′strə-vûrt′)
-noun

● Surprisingly, not all performers are **extroverts**. Offstage, many are quiet and shy.

● Ms. Stein hired Roberto to greet and chat with her clients because he's such an **extrovert**.

_C_ *Extrovert* means   A. a supporter of causes.   B. a timid person.   C. a sociable person.

6 poignant
(poin′yənt)
-adjective

● The service honoring American soldiers missing in action was touching. A speech by a friend of one of the soldiers was particularly **poignant**.

● I cried when I read a **poignant** story about a dying girl who gave away all of her dolls to "poor children."

_A_ *Poignant* means   A. affecting the emotions.   B. correct.   C. lively.

7 prevalent
(prĕv′ə-lənt)
-*adjective*

● Unemployment was **prevalent** during America's Great Depression. By 1932, over twelve million people were out of work.

● Television sets are more **prevalent** in the United States than bathtubs. Over half of American homes have three or more TVs. Far fewer homes have more than one bathtub.

B *Prevalent* means   A. favorable.   B. found frequently.   C. unlikely.

8 proponent
(prō-pō′nənt)
-*noun*

● I voted for Senator Williams, a **proponent** of improved services for the elderly, because I feel that many older people need greater assistance.

● Although Elaine quit work to take care of her children, she is a **proponent** of employer-supported day care.

C *Proponent* means   A. a recipient.   B. an opponent.   C. a supporter.

9 quest
(kwĕst)
-*noun*

● During Carlo's **quest** for the perfect pizza, he sampled the cheese pizza at twenty-seven different restaurants.

● Ponce de Leon's **quest** was for the Fountain of Youth; what he found instead was Florida.

A *Quest* means   A. a hunt.   B. a question.   C. a design.

10 traumatic
(trô-măt′ĭk)
-*adjective*

● Divorce can be less **traumatic** for children if their fears and feelings are taken into account as the divorce takes place.

● My cousin has had nightmares ever since his **traumatic** experience of being trapped in a coal mine.

C *Traumatic* means   A. familiar.   B. reasonable.   C. extremely upsetting.

Matching Words with Definitions

Following are definitions of the ten words. Clearly write or print each word next to its definition. The sentences above and on the previous page will help you decide on the meaning of each word.

1. _____conversely_____   In an opposite manner; in an altogether different way

2. _____charisma_____   The quality of a leader which captures great popular devotion; personal magnetism; charm

3. _____quest_____   A search; pursuit

4. _____prevalent_____   Widespread; common

5. _____contend_____   To state to be so; claim; affirm

6. _____contemporary_____   Modern; up-to-date

7. _____proponent_____   Someone who supports a cause

8. _____poignant_____   Emotionally moving; touching

9. _____traumatic_____   Causing painful emotions, with possible long-lasting psychological effects

10. _____extrovert_____   An outgoing, sociable person

CAUTION: Do not go any further until you are sure the above answers are correct. Then you can use the definitions to help you in the following practices. Your goal is eventually to know the words well enough so that you don't need to check the definitions at all.

Sentence Check 1

Using the answer line provided, complete each item below with the correct word from the box. Use each word once.

A. charisma	B. contemporary	C. contend	D. conversely	E. extrovert
F. poignant	G. prevalent	H. proponent	I. quest	J. traumatic

Conversely   1. I study best in the morning. ___, my sister concentrates better at night.

extrovert   2. Nancy is a(n) ___ by nature, but since she's become depressed, she has avoided other people.

poignant   3. At the airport, I was very moved by the ___ reunion of family members who had been separated for years.

prevalent   4. Underage drinking was so ___ in the fraternity house that college officials ordered the house closed for a year.

contend   5. "This woman ___s that she was here before you," said the supermarket checkout clerk. "Is it her turn now?"

proponent   6. Felipe is a(n) ___ of exercising for good health. He even encourages his young children to swim or cycle every day.

charisma   7. Certain movie stars may not be great actors, but they have a(n) ___ that makes people want to see their films.

contemporary   8. Abby didn't like the apartment with the old-fashioned bathtub and radiators. She preferred a more ___ place.

traumatic   9. Repeating third grade was ___ for my brother. It still pains him to think about it, even though he's a successful businessman now.

quest   10. During the past three hundred years, several people have gone on a(n) ___ for Noah's ark. Some have looked for it in northeastern Turkey, on Mount Ararat, sixteen thousand feet above sea level.

NOTE: Now check your answers to these items by turning to page 178. Going over the answers carefully will help you prepare for the next two practices, for which answers are not given.

Sentence Check 2

Using the answer lines provided, complete each item below with **two** words from the box. Use each word once.

prevalent
contemporary   1–2. Many people are surprised to learn how ___ poverty is in ___ America. Today, millions live below the poverty line, and the number seems to escalate° daily.

extrovert
Conversely   3–4. Judy and Martin Reed exemplify° the old saying "Opposites attract." A(n) ___, Judy chooses work that brings her into constant contact with others. ___, Martin prefers jobs in which he mainly works alone.

_____traumatic_____
_____proponent_____

5–6. Ever since the ___ experience of finding her twelve-year-old son dead from a drug overdose, Sophie has been a strong ___ of mandatory° drug education in the public schools. If drug education isn't required, she says, schools may cut corners and omit it.

_____contend_____
_____poignant_____

7–8. My mother ___s that *Romeo and Juliet* is the most ___ story ever written, but my sister claims Erich Segal's *Love Story* is more moving.

_____charisma_____
_____quest_____

9–10. Mahatma Gandhi's ___ and vision inspired millions of fellow Indians to join him enthusiastically in the ___ for peaceful solutions to national problems. Gandhi incorporated° nonviolence and political activism into a highly effective method for social change: passive resistance.

Final Check: *Dr. Martin Luther King, Jr.*

Here is a final opportunity for you to strengthen your knowledge of the ten words. First read the following selection carefully. Then fill in each blank with a word from the box at the top of the previous page. (Context clues will help you figure out which word goes in which blank.) Use each word once.

(1)_____Contemporary_____ young people may be able to list the many accomplishments of the Reverend Dr. Martin Luther King, Jr. They may know that he was a civil rights leader who aspired° to achieve racial harmony and was a(n) (2)_____proponent_____ of peaceful but direct action. They may know that he fought the discrimination against blacks that was so (3)_____prevalent_____ in our country in the 1950s and 1960s. They may also know that he received a great deal of acclaim° for his work. For example, in 1964 he won the Nobel Peace Prize. They may even (4)_____contend_____ that he is the most important social reformer in the history of our nation.

But can the young really know the (5)_____charisma_____, the powerful personal magnetism of this man? He was a perfect blend of quiet, considerate thinker and bold, outspoken (6)_____extrovert_____. When Dr. King spoke, people listened. He had such a forceful yet (7)_____poignant_____ way of speaking that those who heard him felt his message deep within. For most, this meant a stronger belief in and respect for the man and his ideals. (8)_____Conversely_____, for bigots, it meant hatred and fear of what he stood for.

Dr. King's (9)_____quest_____ for equal rights for all was clear when he said, "I have a dream that this nation will rise up and live out the true meaning of its creed: 'We hold these truths to be self-evident; that all men are created equal.'" He gave his time, his leadership, and, in the end, his life. His murder was a (10)_____traumatic_____ event in the lives of many Americans, who never fully recovered from that awful day. But because of Martin Luther King, Americans live with greater dignity. And many have taken up his fight against the inequities° of racism.

| Scores | Sentence Check 2 _____% | Final Check _____% |

congenial	prone
flippant	rapport
impasse	rationale
perception	relentless
prompt	reprisal

Ten Words in Context

In the space provided, write the letter of the meaning closest to that of each **boldfaced** word. Use the context of the sentences to help you figure out each word's meaning.

1 congenial
(kən-jēn′yəl)
-adjective

- I was nervous being at a party where I didn't know anyone, but the other guests were so **congenial** that I soon felt at ease.
- Beware of friendships that begin in Internet chat rooms. People who seem **congenial** online may be anything but pleasant in real life.

_C_ *Congenial* means   A. persistent.   B. intelligent.   C. friendly.

2 flippant
(flĭp′ənt)
-adjective

- "Don't give me a **flippant** answer," George's father told him. "Your financial situation is a serious matter."
- When a teenage boy is asked to clean his room, he's likely to give a **flippant** response such as "Why should I? I just cleaned it last month."

_A_ *Flippant* means   A. rude.   B. serious.   C. incorrect.

3 impasse
(ĭm′păs)
-noun

- The jurors had reached an **impasse**. They couldn't agree on a verdict—some thought the defendant was the murderer, but others were sure he was innocent.
- If you think you've reached an **impasse** when trying to solve a problem, take a break. The solution may occur to you while you're doing something else.

_A_ *Impasse* means   A. a deadlock.   B. a relationship.   C. an opportunity.

4 perception
(pər-sĕp′shən)
-noun

- Brenda's **perceptions** of others are usually accurate. She is a good judge of character.
- "Our **perceptions** of our problem differ," Tonya explained. "Sam thinks money is the main issue, but I believe it's a question of who controls the purse strings."

_B_ *Perception* means   A. a memory.   B. a view.   C. a desire.

5 prompt
(prŏmpt)
-verb

- To **prompt** her son Byron to get a job, Mrs. Davis pinned the want ads to his pillow.
- Fast-food clerks **prompt** customers to spend more money by asking such questions as "Would you like cookies or apple pie with that?"

_C_ *Prompt* means   A. to allow.   B. to agree with.   C. to encourage.

6 prone
(prōn)
-adjective

- Mr. Walker is **prone** to sleep problems, so he limits his intake of caffeine.
- **Prone** to fits of laughter during class, Chris controls himself by chewing on his pen.

_A_ *Prone* means   A. tending.   B. immune.   C. attracted.

7 rapport
(ră-pŏr′)
-noun

● In high school, I had such good **rapport** with my gym teacher that our close relationship continues to this day.

● If no **rapport** develops between you and your therapist after a month or two, start looking for a counselor who makes you feel comfortable.

<u>B</u> *Rapport* means   A. a report.   B. a personal connection.   C. a financial situation.

8 rationale
(răsh′ə-năl′)
-noun

● Danielle's **rationale** for majoring in business was simple. She said, "I want to make a lot of money."

● The **rationale** for not lowering the drinking age to 18 is that self-control and good judgment are still being developed at that age.

<u>B</u> *Rationale* means   A. a situation.   B. an explanation.   C. a question.

9 relentless
(rĭ-lĕnt′lĭs)
-adjective

● The dog's **relentless** barking got on my nerves. He barked the entire two hours his owners were out.

● In a large city, the noise of crowds and heavy traffic is so **relentless** that it can be difficult to find peace and quiet.

<u>C</u> *Relentless* means   A. occasional.   B. exciting.   C. nonstop.

10 reprisal
(rĭ-prī′zəl)
-noun

● In **reprisal** for being fired, a troubled man shot several people at the factory where he used to work.

● Fear of **reprisal** may keep children from telling parents or teachers about a bully who has threatened them.

<u>B</u> *Reprisal* means   A. disrespect.   B. revenge.   C. delay.

Matching Words with Definitions

Following are definitions of the ten words. Clearly write or print each word next to its definition. The sentences above and on the previous page will help you decide on the meaning of each word.

1. ___perception___ Insight or understanding gained through observation; impression

2. ___prone___ Having a tendency; inclined (to do something)

3. ___relentless___ Persistent; continuous

4. ___rationale___ The underlying reasons for something; logical basis

5. ___flippant___ Disrespectful and not serious enough

6. ___congenial___ Agreeable or pleasant in character; friendly; sociable

7. ___prompt___ To urge into action; motivate

8. ___reprisal___ The paying back of one injury or bad deed with another

9. ___impasse___ A situation with no way out; dead end

10. ___rapport___ Relationship, especially one that is close, trusting, or sympathetic

CAUTION: Do not go any further until you are sure the above answers are correct. Then you can use the definitions to help you in the following practices. Your goal is eventually to know the words well enough so that you don't need to check the definitions at all.

Sentence Check 1

Using the answer line provided, complete each item below with the correct word from the box. Use each word once.

A. **congenial**	B. **flippant**	C. **impasse**	D. **perception**	E. **prompt**
F. **prone**	G. **rapport**	H. **rationale**	I. **relentless**	J. **reprisal**

_____prone_____   1. Raquel is ___ to accidents, so her car insurance rates are quite high.

_____congenial_____   2. You will get along better in life if you are ___ to other people, rather than unpleasant.

_____flippant_____   3. My brother hides his lack of confidence by being ___. He rarely treats anything seriously.

_____prompt_____   4. It took his best friend's heart attack to ___ my dad to start exercising and eating right.

_____rapport_____   5. There was instant ___ between Duke and Otis. They talked as if they'd known each other for years.

_____impasse_____   6. At the movie's turning point, the bad guys reached a(n) ___. On one side of them was the police; on the other was a steep cliff.

_____relentless_____   7. During April and May, the rain was so ___ that we thought we might have to start building an ark.

_____perception_____   8. Floyd's ___ of human nature is strongly colored by some bad experiences. He thinks everyone is basically selfish.

_____reprisal_____   9. When Lacey and John divorced, she tried to get over half his income. In ___, he tried not to give her any of his income at all.

_____rationale_____   10. The ___ behind encouraging pregnant women to gain about twenty-five pounds is that low weight gain can lead to dangerously low birth weights.

NOTE: Now check your answers to these items by turning to page 178. Going over the answers carefully will help you prepare for the next two practices, for which answers are not given.

Sentence Check 2

Using the answer lines provided, complete each item below with **two** words from the box. Use each word once.

_____congenial_____
_____rapport_____   1–2. Because Wade is so ___ and easy to talk to, we established a warm ___ the first day we met.

_____rationale_____
_____prompt_____   3–4. Although the company president explained the ___ behind the pay cuts, his announcement ___(e)d an employee protest. However, once it was learned that the president was also taking a big pay cut, the employees' dissent° died down.

_____ prone

_____ flippant

5–6. The waitresses in our local diner are ___ to be funny and not always polite. If a customer says, "I'm ready to order now," he may get a ___ response such as, "And I'm ready to retire, but you don't hear me making a big deal about it."

_____ perception

_____ impasse

7–8. My ___ of the situation is that talks between the factory management and union officials reached a(n) ___ because neither side would compromise on salary increases and health benefits. In such situations, flexibility is a prerequisite° to progress.

_____ relentless

_____ reprisal

9–10. Alma could put up with occasional kidding, but her brother's teasing was often ___, going on for weeks at a time. Sick of it all, she finally planned a(n) ___ that would embarrass him in front of his friends.

Final Check: *Relating to Parents*

Here is a final opportunity for you to strengthen your knowledge of the ten words. First read the following selection carefully. Then fill in each blank with a word from the box at the top of the previous page. (Context clues will help you figure out which word goes in which blank.) Use each word once.

How do you respond when your parents deny you permission to do something? For example, if you want to travel and work around the country for the summer, but your parents say you're too young, do you become irate° and angrily demand that they stop curtailing° your rights? Do you plan a(n) (1)_____ reprisal _____, vowing to sabotage° their summer plans because they've ruined yours? Or do you explain the (2)_____ rationale _____ behind your request, so that your parents will understand your reasoning?

The way you behave when you and your parents reach a(n) (3)_____ impasse _____ on an issue can have a big effect on how they view you. Sure, you could retort°, "Fine. I'll go buy a leash so you can really run my life." But if you are consistently (4)_____ flippant _____ like that, you'll just strengthen their (5)_____ perception _____ of you as being too immature to be on your own. Also, if you are (6)_____ relentless _____ in your begging, asking them three hundred times a day, "But *why* won't you let me travel alone?" you might elicit° this response: "You may do some traveling alone right now—go directly to your room."

Instead, approach your parents in a (7)_____ congenial _____ way and try to develop a strong, friendly (8)_____ rapport _____ with them. An amiable°, respectful relationship will make them more (9)_____ prone _____ to see things your way. Even if you can't (10)_____ prompt _____ them to change their minds about this summer's plans, your chances of getting their support will be better the next time you want to try something new.

Scores   Sentence Check 2 _____%   Final Check _____%

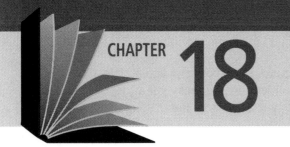

cor, cour	-ish
di-, du-	magni-, magn-
-dom	phob
-fy	pro-
il-, im-	psych-, psycho-

Ten Word Parts in Context

Figure out the meanings of the following ten word parts by looking *closely* and *carefully* at the context in which they appear. Then, in the space provided, write the letter of the meaning closest to that of each word part.

1 cor, cour

● I felt truly welcomed by my **cordial** hosts. Their kindness and generosity were heartfelt.

● Emmy was **courageous** enough to face the bully without backing down. I would have been too scared to do the same.

_C_ The word part *cor* or *cour* means   A. resembling.   B. double.   C. heart.

2 di-, du-

● When Tyrone and Verna got **divorced**, they had to spend a difficult day dividing their household possessions into two groups.

● One of the three band members didn't show up, so only a **duo** played at the dance.

_B_ The word part *di-* or *du-* means   A. make.   B. two.   C. great.

3 -dom

● A few actors achieve overnight success, but for most, the road to **stardom** is long and difficult.

● "One sure way to put my husband into a deep state of **boredom**," Jasmin said, "is to take him with me when I shop for shoes."

_B_ The word part *-dom* means   A. like.   B. state of being.   C. fear.

4 -fy

● Would it **simplify** matters if I held your baby while you go into the dressing room to try on the slacks?

● First **liquefy** the ice cream over heat. Then mix in the strawberry jam.

_A_ The word part *-fy* means   A. cause to become.   B. again.   C. dislike.

5 il-, im-

● Nita doesn't seem to care that it's **illegal** to park next to a fire hydrant.

● My brother-in-law is so **immature** that he often acts as if he is 16 instead of a married man of 26.

_A_ The word part *il-* or *im-* means   A. not.   B. double.   C. like.

6 -ish

● My **devilish** brother once videotaped me huffing and puffing my way through aerobics, and now he shows the tape to every new friend I bring home.

● Of all the girls at school, Jessie was the most **stylish**, wearing only the latest clothing featured in the fashion magazines.

_B_ The word part *-ish* means   A. forth.   B. characteristic of.   C. mind.

7 magni-, magn-

- My grandmother uses a **magnifying** glass to make the small print in the newspaper appear larger.
- Eight years after starting Standard Oil in 1870, oil **magnate** John D. Rockefeller controlled about 85 percent of the country's oil industry.

<u>C</u> The word part *magni-* or *magn-* means

    A. forward.   B. fear.   C. large.

8 phob

- One of the most unusual **phobias** is the fear of peanut butter sticking to the roof of one's mouth.
- Marilyn's mother has developed **agoraphobia** to the point that she is afraid even of going to the mailbox at the end of the driveway.

<u>C</u> The word part *phob* means

    A. forth.   B. quality.   C. fear.

9 pro-

- **Proceed** down to the end of this hallway, make a left, and you will see the x-ray department.
- One scientist **propels** his car with a fuel he gets by burning garbage.

<u>A</u> The word part *pro-* means

    A. forward.   B. resembling.   C. dislike.

10 psych-, psycho-

- To treat her depression, Lee takes medication and also sees a **psychiatrist** once a week.
- A **psychoactive** drug is one that affects mental processes.

<u>A</u> The word part *psych-* or *psycho-* means

    A. mind.   B. make.   C. again.

Matching Word Parts with Definitions

Following are definitions of the ten word parts. Clearly write or print each word part next to its definition. The sentences above and on the previous page will help you decide on the meaning of each word part.

1. ___magni-, magn-___ Great; large

2. ___-fy___ Cause to be or become; make

3. ___pro-___ Forward; forth

4. ___phob___ Fear

5. ___di-, du-___ Two; double

6. ___-ish___ Resembling; like; characteristic of

7. ___cor, cour___ Heart

8. ___psych-, psycho___ Mental processes; mind

9. ___-dom___ State of being; condition

10. ___il-, im-___ Not

CAUTION: Do not go any further until you are sure the above answers are correct. Then you can use the definitions to help you in the following practices. Your goal is eventually to know the word parts well enough so that you don't need to check the definitions at all.

Sentence Check 1

Using the answer line provided, complete each *italicized* word below with the correct word part from the box. Use each word part once.

A. cour	B. di-, du-	C. -dom	D. -fy	E. il-, im-
F. -ish	G. magni-	H. phob	I. pro-	J. psycho-

__boyish__ 1. Despite her (*boy* . . .) ___ hairstyle, Paula looks very feminine.

__Wisdom__ 2. (*Wis* . . .) ___ is what we gain when we learn from our mistakes.

__discouraged__ 3. The parents were greatly (*dis . . . aged*) ___ when every attempt to find their son failed.

__immobile__ 4. To keep the accident victim (. . . *mobile*) ___, the paramedics tied her to a stretcher.

__produced__ 5. The reason these life-size dolls are so expensive is that only one hundred are (. . . *duced*) ___ each year.

__magnified__ 6. The funhouse mirror (. . . *fied*) ___ my reflection so that I looked fifty pounds heavier.

__duplicate__ 7. I always (. . . *plicate*) ___ important papers and letters so that if the original gets lost, I still have the copy.

__psychoanalyst__ 8. Barb's (. . . *analyst*) ___ asked her to write down her dreams, as they might be helpful in understanding her problems.

__intensify__ 9. If you want to find a job before all the graduates start looking for employment next month, you'd better (*intensi* . . .) ___ your search.

__claustrophobia__ 10. It's lucky Santa Claus doesn't have (*claustro* . . . *ia*) ___. Otherwise, he would be too frightened of confined spaces to come down the chimney.

NOTE: Now check your answers to these items by turning to page 178. Going over the answers carefully will help you prepare for the next two practices, for which answers are not given.

Sentence Check 2

Using the answer line provided, complete each *italicized* word in the sentences below with the correct word part from the box. Use each word part once.

__magnificent__
__impractical__ 1–2. The apartment the realtor showed us was (. . . *ficent*) ___, but it was (. . . *practical*) ___ for us. Not only was it too large, but it would also make an uncomfortable dent in our budget.

__phobic__
__freedom__ 3–4. Everyone has fears, but (. . . *ic*) ___ people need to gain (*free* . . .) __ from the extreme fears that devastate° them and their families.

__psychotherapy__
__promote__ 5–6. The purpose of (. . . *therapy*) ___ is to (. . . *mote*) ___ mental health.

_____ foolish   7–8. Florence and I felt (*fool . . .*) ___ when we sang "The Star-Spangled Banner"
_____ duet   as a (. . . *et*) ___ and forgot the words halfway through.

_____ discourage 9–10. The mayor didn't allow racial tensions to (*dis . . . age*) ___ him. He just made
_____ unify   more of an effort to (*uni . . .*) ___ the city.

Final Check: *Held Back by Fears*

Here is a final opportunity for you to strengthen your knowledge of the ten word parts. First read the following selection carefully. Then complete each *italicized* word in the parentheses below with a word part from the box at the top of the previous page. (Context clues will help you figure out which word part goes in which blank.) Use each word part once.

At age 24, Gina is facing a major (. . . *lemma*°)
(1)_____ dilemma _____. She desperately wants
to live and work outside her hometown, but she
is prevented from traveling by her (. . . *ias*)
(2)_____ phobias _____. She suffers from
(. . . *logical*) (3)_____ illogical _____ but intense
fears of bridges and airplanes that are so traumatic°
that they cause nightmares and breathing problems.
Gina is convinced that if she doesn't fall off a bridge
or crash in an airplane, the mere possibility of such a
calamity° will so (*terri . . .*) (4)_____ terrify _____ her that she'll succumb° to a heart attack.

For some time now, Gina's friends have tried to persuade her to start seeing a (. . . *logist*)
(5)_____ psychologist _____. They believe her problem will only increase in (. . . *tude*)
(6)_____ magnitude _____ if she doesn't get help. But her relatives often make flippant° remarks
about Gina's condition, saying that she is just too cheap to travel. Accusing her of being (*child . . .*)
(7)_____ childish _____, her brothers call her "baby" and "chicken." They say if she only had a little
more (. . . *age*) (8)_____ courage _____, she would be able to go places. They don't realize that if
she could have controlled her fears by now, she would have.

Gina is seriously considering her friends' advice because she feels she has squandered° too much
of her time and energy on her fears. She hopes she will make rapid (. . . *gress*) (9)_____ progress _____
in gaining (*free . . .*) (10)_____ freedom _____ from her fears so that she can start to live a full life.

| Scores | Sentence Check 2 _____% | Final Check _____% |

The box at the right lists twenty-five words from Unit Three. Using the clues at the bottom of the page, fill in these words to complete the puzzle that follows.

The completed crossword puzzle:

- 2 Across: INTRINSIC
- 4 Across: REPRISAL
- 6 Across: ASPIRE
- 8 Across: ALLEVIATE
- 9 Across: SUCCUMB
- 10 Across: LUCRATIVE
- 11 Across: QUEST
- 15 Across: RIGOR
- 20 Across: INCORPORATE
- 23 Across: DISSENT
- 24 Across: DEMISE
- 25 Across: POIGNANT
- 1 Down: CONGENIAL
- 3 Down: CONTEND
- 5 Down: IMPASSE
- 7 Down: PROMPT
- 12 Down: EXTROVERT
- 13 Down: DIGRESS
- 14 Down: CURTAIL
- 16 Down: ABSTAIN
- 17 Down: VIRILE
- 18 Down: DEFICIT
- 19 Down: PRONE
- 21 Down: CHARISMA
- 22 Down: CYNIC

Word box:

abstain
alleviate
aspire
charisma
congenial
contend
curtail
cynic
deficit
demise
digress
dissent
extrovert
impasse
incorporate
intrinsic
lucrative
poignant
prompt
prone
quest
reprisal
rigor
succumb
virile

ACROSS

2. Belonging to a person or thing by its very nature (and thus not dependent on circumstances)

4. The paying back of one injury or bad deed with another

6. To strongly desire; to be ambitious (to do something or to get something)

8. To relieve; make easier to endure

9. To give in; stop resisting

10. Profitable; well paying

11. A search; pursuit

15. Great hardship or difficulty

20. To unite into a single whole; combine

23. Disagreement

24. Death

25. Emotionally moving; touching

DOWN

1. Agreeable or pleasant in character; friendly

3. To state to be so; claim

5. A situation with no way out; dead end

7. To urge into action

12. An outgoing, sociable person

13. To turn aside, or stray, especially from the main topic in speaking or writing

14. To cut short or reduce

16. To hold oneself back from something; refrain

17. Manly; masculine

18. A shortage; a lack (in amount)

19. Having a tendency; inclined

21. The quality of a leader which captures great popular devotion; personal magnetism

22. A person who believes the worst of people's behavior and motives

PART A

Choose the word that best completes each item and write it in the space provided.

_____intermittent_____ 1. In irregular bursts of energy, dying stars give off ___ radio signals.

A. virile   B. intermittent   C. congenial   D. flippant

_____speculate_____ 2. Scientists ___ that the average life span of a dinosaur was probably 100 to 120 years.

A. speculate   B. digress   C. detract   D. squander

_____demise_____ 3. The ___ of a Connecticut man was strange indeed. He died when his five-hundred-pound wife sat on him.

A. diversion   B. charisma   C. perception   D. demise

_____curtailed_____ 4. A power failure ___ our viewing of the TV mystery, so we never found out who had committed the murder.

A. prompted   B. curtailed   C. contended   D. dissented

_____covert_____ 5. The CIA's ___ activities often include "bugging" people's telephone lines with tiny hidden microphones.

A. covert   B. traumatic   C. virile   D. congenial

_____Proponents_____ 6. ___ of gun control point out that gun accidents in American homes result in over a thousand deaths each year.

A. Quests   B. Incentives   C. Proponents   D. Rigors

_____impasse_____ 7. The talks between the two countries reached a(n) ___ when each side claimed the oil-rich border area as its own.

A. benefactor   B. rapport   C. diversion   D. impasse

_____Prone_____ 8. ___ to oversleeping, Rashid keeps his alarm clock across the room so he has to get out of bed to turn it off.

A. Intrinsic   B. Lucrative   C. Prone   D. Covert

_____abstain_____ 9. Alcohol is involved in nearly half of all traffic deaths in the United States, so people should ___ from drinking and driving.

A. affiliate   B. abstain   C. contend   D. aspire

_____deficit_____ 10. When I realized that I didn't have enough money for holiday gifts, I decided to overcome the ___ by taking an extra part-time job in December.

A. charisma   B. perception   C. dissent   D. deficit

(Continues on next page)

PART B

On the answer line, write the letter of the choice that best completes each item.

_B_ 11. If you **aspire** to be an Olympic swimmer,
     A. then find a sport you prefer.   C. become a coach instead.
     B. you must be ready to practice continually.   D. you may have a fear of water.

_C_ 12. A child with **relentless** questions is probably
     A. ill.   C. curious.
     B. angry.   D. too shy to ask.

_C_ 13. The enormously successful movie *Titanic* **incorporated**
     A. many millions of dollars.   C. elements of romance, adventure, and tragedy.
     B. an ocean liner which struck an iceberg.   D. Leonardo DiCaprio.

_D_ 14. Many men try to make themselves look more **virile** by
     A. eating more fruits and vegetables.   C. making quilts.
     B. learning to play a musical instrument.   D. lifting weights.

_B_ 15. The boss's **perception** of Cory was
     A. the comment "Good morning."   C. the afternoon shift.
     B. that Cory was a hard worker.   D. eight dollars an hour.

_A_ 16. Joel seems to believe that his friends exist in order to serve him. **Conversely**, Julie
     A. believes she exists to serve her friends.   C. has far fewer friends than Joel.
     B. agrees with Joel's point of view.   D. is not a friend of Joel's.

_C_ 17. In his lecture about television, the speaker **digressed** by
     A. mentioning a game-show series.
     B. saying, "Good morning. My topic today is television."
     C. discussing a soccer game he had seen the night before.
     D. examining television ads aimed at children.

_A_ 18. Carmen's face showed **revulsion** as she listened to the speaker talk about
     A. exactly what happens to a person's body as he is electrocuted.
     B. the gourmet appetizers, meals, and desserts served on the cruise ship.
     C. advances in spinal-cord research that hold great promise for accident victims.
     D. financial-aid packages available to incoming college freshmen.

_B_ 19. Elaine works hard at her job as a lawyer. For **diversion**, she
     A. reads all the latest law journals to keep up with recent developments.
     B. gardens and plays field hockey.
     C. writes briefs, attends hearings, and meets with clients.
     D. attended college and law school.

_B_ 20. Knowing that her auto accident had been a **traumatic** experience, Beverly's friends
     A. expected her to heal soon.
     B. were hesitant to make her talk about the horrible event.
     C. wondered why she was making such a big deal of it.
     D. knew she would be joking about it soon.

Score   (Number correct) _____ x 5 = _____ %

Enter your score above and in the **Vocabulary Performance Chart** on the inside back cover of the book.

PART A

Complete each item with a word from the box. Use each word once.

A. **benefactor**	B. **contend**	C. **devastate**	D. **extrovert**	E. **flippant**
F. **lucrative**	G. **poignant**	H. **quest**	I. **rapport**	J. **rationale**
K. **reprisal**	L. **rigor**	M. **succumb**		

_____devastate_____ 1. Jill was ____(e)d when she lost her job and, with it, her hopes of affording a house.

_____rapport_____ 2. I have excellent ___ with my brother, but I haven't spoken to my older sister for years.

_____extrovert_____ 3. Rudy is such a(n) ___ that he makes friends with most of the customers at his beauty salon.

_____rigor_____ 4. Before the turn of the century, the ___s of prizefighting included boxing without gloves.

_____succumb_____ 5. City Council ___(e)d to public pressure and passed a law that made smoking in restaurants illegal.

_____rationale_____ 6. My ___ for using cloth napkins is that they result in fewer trees being cut down to make paper napkins.

_____poignant_____ 7. It was ___ to see the bear immediately adopt the orphaned cub.

_____lucrative_____ 8. Halloween is ___ for candy manufacturers. The holiday earns them about a billion dollars a year.

_____quest_____ 9. In some fairy tales, the hero searches far and wide, on a(n) ___ for some precious object or missing person.

_____benefactor_____ 10. The high school's chief ___ has offered to pay all college costs for any low-income student who graduates from the school.

_____reprisal_____ 11. When her brother kept taking her bike without asking, Meg's ___ was simply not to warn him that one of the tires was going flat.

_____contend_____ 12. The street's residents ___ that they complained for months about the huge pothole before the city government did anything about it.

_____flippant_____ 13. When the principal asked Randy why he had spilled milk on some girls in the lunchroom, his ___ response was "Because they were thirsty."

(Continues on next page)

PART B

Write **C** if the italicized word is used **correctly**. Write **I** if the word is used **incorrectly**.

_C_ 14. For two weeks, the newspapers reported on the crimes of the *infamous* serial killer.

_I_ 15. Fran often *squanders* her money by walking through rain or snow instead of paying for a cab.

_I_ 16. Priests, rabbis, and other *agnostics* signed the petition asking for aid to the homeless.

_C_ 17. The comedian Groucho Marx once joked that he wouldn't want to *affiliate* himself with any club that would accept him as a member.

_C_ 18. The desire to aid others seems *intrinsic* to many animals. Baboons, for example, will try to free other baboons that are caged.

_I_ 19. Halloween has *contemporary* roots. Each year, the ancient Irish would dress as demons and witches to frighten away ghosts who might otherwise claim their bodies.

PART C

On the answer line, write the letter of the word that is the **synonym** of the boldfaced word.

Example: _A_ **traumatic**   A. upsetting   B. surprising   C. comforting

_C_ 20. **benevolent**   A. cruel   B. gifted   C. kind

_A_ 21. **alleviate**   A. relieve   B. worsen   C. raise

_A_ 22. **indispensable**   A. essential   B. expensive   C. unnecessary

PART D

On the answer line, write the letter of the word that is the **antonym** of the boldfaced word.

Example: _C_ **traumatic**   A. upsetting   B. surprising   C. comforting

_B_ 23. **prevalent**   A. heavy   B. rare   C. common

_A_ 24. **congenial**   A. disagreeable   B. clever   C. pleasant

_B_ 25. **mandatory**   A. required   B. optional   C. noisy

Score   (Number correct) _____ x 4 = _____%

Enter your score above and in the **Vocabulary Performance Chart** on the inside back cover of the book.

Each item below starts with a pair of words in CAPITAL LETTERS. For each item, figure out the relationship between these two words. Then decide which of the choices (A, B, C, or D) expresses a similar relationship. Write the letter of your choice on the answer line.

D___ 1. CURTAIL : SHORTEN ::
    A. seek : find   C. silence : conversation
    B. depart : arrive   D. ask : inquire

B___ 2. DEVASTATE : DISASTER ::
    A. harm : nurse   C. bore : surprise
    B. amaze : miracle   D. cold : snow

C___ 3. INCENTIVE : MONEY ::
    A. youth : adulthood   C. vehicle : motorcycle
    B. cash : poverty   D. sanitation worker : garbage

A___ 4. BENEFACTOR : SUPPORTS ::
    A. surgeon : operates   C. soldier : helmet
    B. leader : follows   D. waiter : waitress

B___ 5. CYNIC : OPTIMISTIC ::
    A. cucumber : vegetable C. outcast : excluded
    B. criminal : law-abiding D. ballerina : graceful

D___ 6. VIRILE : FEMININE ::
    A. manly : macho   C. popular : celebrity
    B. apartment : dwelling D. fashionable : outmoded

C___ 7. AGNOSTIC : RELIGIOUS ::
    A. salesperson : persuasive C. hermit : sociable
    B. secretary : telephone   D. corn : crop

A___ 8. DISSENT : DISAGREEMENT ::
    A. remedy : solution   C. discord : harmony
    B. chemist : scientist   D. rival : helpful

B___ 9. DEFICIT : SURPLUS ::
    A. debt : poverty   C. clouds : rain
    B. border : interior   D. race car : speedy

B___ 10. CONTEMPORARY : OLD-FASHIONED ::
    A. outdated : old   C. thoughtful : gift
    B. copy : original   D. handlebar : bicycle

(Continues on next page)

C   11. EXTROVERT : FRIENDLINESS ::
    A. performer : shyness   C. artist : creativity
    B. victor : defeated   D. clown : circus

D   12. POIGNANT : TRAGEDY ::
    A. mobile : motionless   C. giggle : baby
    B. depressing : comedy   D. noisy : riot

A   13. PROMPT : DISCOURAGE ::
    A. careful : careless   C. fragrant : flower
    B. book : library   D. late : tardy

B   14. FLIPPANT : REMARK ::
    A. runner : sprint   C. modest : humble
    B. insulting : gesture   D. singer : chorus

B   15. REPRISAL : ENEMY ::
    A. tears : joke   C. revenge : ally
    B. cooperation : teammate   D. terror : fear

A   16. INTERMITTENT : STEADY ::
    A. fortunate : unlucky   C. wise : advice
    B. treacherous : dishonest   D. instrument : violin

C   17. SPECULATE : THEORY ::
    A. speak : silent   C. draw : picture
    B. primary : secondary   D. manual : electronic

D   18. DIVERSION : FISHING ::
    A. work : play   C. guitar : drum
    B. fun : exciting   D. dessert : apple pie

B   19. CHARISMA : BLAND ::
    A. honest : trustworthy   C. premature : early
    B. modesty : boastful   D. emergency : rush

B   20. IMPASSE : PROBLEMATIC ::
    A. round : corners   C. alien : native
    B. success : satisfying   D. traitor : betrayal

Score   (Number correct) _____ x 5 = _____ %

PART A

Listed in the left-hand column below are ten common word parts, followed by words in which the parts are used. In each blank, write in the letter of the correct definition on the right.

Word Parts		Examples	Definitions
E	1. **cor, cour**	cordial, courageous	A. Two; double
A	2. **di-, du-**	divorced, duo	B. Mental processes; mind
H	3. **-dom**	stardom, boredom	C. Not
I	4. **-fy**	simplify, liquefy	D. Fear
C	5. **il-, im-**	illegal, immature	E. Heart
J	6. **-ish**	devilish, stylish	F. Forward; forth
G	7. **magni-, magn-**	magnifying, magnate	G. Great; large
D	8. **phob**	phobia, agoraphobia	H. State of being; condition
F	9. **pro-**	proceed, propel	I. Cause to be or become; make
B	10. **psych-, psycho-**	psychiatrist, psychologist	J. Resembling; like; characteristic of

PART B

Using the answer line provided, complete each *italicized* word in the sentences below with the correct word part from the box. Not every word part will be used.

A. **-cour**	B. **-dom**	C. **du-**	D. **-fy**	E. **il-**
F. **-ish**	G. **magni-**	H. **phob**	I. **pro-**	J. **psycho-**

__boredom__ 11. Considering all the books, movies, and TV programs in everyday life, there's no reason for (*bore . . .*) ___.

__dual__ 12. The car that is used for driving instruction has (*. . . al*) ___ controls, one set for the student and one for the teacher.

__purifying__ 13. A filter added to the kitchen faucet will remove chemicals, thereby (*puri . . . ing*) ___ the water and making it taste better.

__nightmarish__ 14. The (*nightmar . . .*) ___ experience of constantly hiccuping can be stopped with drugs.

__acrophobia__ 15. A victim of (*acro . . . ia*) ___, a fear of heights, Diane refused any job that required working higher than the second floor.

(Continues on next page)

PART C

Use your knowledge of word parts to determine the meaning of the **boldfaced** words. On the answer line, write the letter of each meaning.

__C__ 16. "Go through the red double doors," said the secretary, "and then **proceed** down the hallway."

    A. go quickly   B. go fearfully   C. go forward

__B__ 17. A blue moon is **improbable**.

    A. shocking   B. unlikely   C. beautiful

__A__ 18. Our parents received a **magnum** of champagne as an anniversary gift.

    A. a large bottle   B. a medium-sized bottle   C. a small bottle

__C__ 19. Ken's report emphasized the **core** of the plan.

    A. the details   B. the background   C. the central part

__B__ 20. Belle suffered from a **psychosis**.

    A. a physical disease   B. a mental disorder   C. a heart problem

Score   (Number correct) _____ x 5 = _____%

Unit Four

CHAPTER 19

benign	glib
blasé	haughty
comprise	libel
condescend	pseudonym
facade	redundant

Ten Words in Context

In the space provided, write the letter of the meaning closest to that of each **boldfaced** word. Use the context of the sentences to help you figure out each word's meaning.

1 benign
(bǐ-nīn′)
-adjective

- Finding a stranger on our doorstep startled me, but the **benign** expression on his face told me not to worry.
- Gorilla mothers, usually loving and **benign**, have been known to attack their babies if they are put in the same cage.

<u>B</u> *Benign* means   A. realistic.   B. kindhearted.   C. bored.

2 blasé
(blă-zā′)
-adjective

- The new staff members were enthusiastic at the weekly meetings, but the old-timers were pretty **blasé**.
- No matter how many games I see, I will never become **blasé** about baseball. Each game is new and exciting to me.

<u>A</u> *Blasé* means   A. unexcited.   B. obvious.   C. repetitive.

3 comprise
(kŏm-prīz′)
-verb

- The United Kingdom **comprises** England, Scotland, Wales, and Northern Ireland.
- Saliva **comprises** about sixty ingredients, including minerals that help repair tooth enamel.

<u>C</u> *Comprise* means   A. to cause.   B. to reveal.   C. to be made up of.

4 condescend
(kŏn′dǐ-sěnd′)
-verb

- The snobby millionaire wouldn't **condescend** to associate with anyone who wasn't also rich.
- Although everyone else in the office took turns making coffee, Bill would not **condescend** to perform "such a lowly task."

<u>A</u> *Condescend* means   A. to lower oneself.   B. to dare something frightening.   C. to remember.

5 facade
(fə-sŏd′)
-noun

- The **facade** of the old department store was cleaned this summer. Now the store's brick front is an inviting bright orange-red.
- The **facade** of the hotel—facing Main Street—was marble, but the sides and back were made of steel.

<u>C</u> *Facade* means   A. an inside.   B. a top.   C. a front.

6 glib
(glĭb)
-adjective

- Always ready with a slick promise, the **glib** politician smoothly talked his way into being re-elected.
- Jerome thought his conversation would impress Sofia, but she found it **glib** and insincere.

<u>C</u> *Glib* means   A. bored.   B. strict.   C. smooth.

7 haughty
(hô′tē)
-adjective

● The Smiths acted as though they were better than anybody else. Not surprisingly, their **haughty** manner made them unpopular with their neighbors.

● After being promoted to manager, Gil was **haughty** with his old office buddies, saying he now had more important things to do than waste time with them.

A *Haughty* means   A. snobbish.   B. angry.   C. wordy.

8 libel
(lī′bəl)
-noun

● When Nick saw his name listed in the article as a gang member, he was furious. "That's **libel**!" he yelled. "How dare they print such a lie about me?"

● Many magazine editors double-check the facts they publish about a person. Then, if they are accused of **libel**, they can prove that they stated the truth.

B *Libel* means   A. a false name.   B. a printed falsehood.   C. a repeated expression.

9 pseudonym
(sōō′də-nĭm′)
-noun

● When writing a personal story for a family magazine, Bev used a **pseudonym**. She didn't want everyone in town to know about her problems.

● The author Stephen King uses a **pseudonym** on some of his books so readers won't be aware that so many of the horror novels on the market are his.

C *Pseudonym* means   A. a weak vocabulary.   B. a personal experience.   C. a false name.

10 redundant
(rĭ-dŭn′dənt)
-adjective

● The TV ad for a headache medicine was so **redundant** that it gave me a headache! The name of the product was repeated at least a dozen times.

● The teacher wrote "**redundant**" in several spots in the essay where Eric had repeated a point or used extra, unneeded words.

C *Redundant* means   A. grammatical.   B. proud.   C. repetitious.

Matching Words with Definitions

Following are definitions of the ten words. Clearly write or print each word next to its definition. The sentences above and on the previous page will help you decide on the meaning of each word.

1. _____pseudonym_____   A false name used by an author; a pen name

2. _____condescend_____   To do something one feels is beneath oneself

3. _____blasé_____   Unexcited or bored about something already experienced repeatedly

4. _____facade_____   The front of a building

5. _____redundant_____   Wordy or needlessly repetitive

6. _____benign_____   Kindly; gentle

7. _____libel_____   The publishing of false information that harms a person's reputation

8. _____haughty_____   Proud of one's appearance or accomplishments to the point of looking down on others; arrogant

9. _____comprise_____   To consist of; include

10. _____glib_____   Characterized by a smooth, easy manner of speaking that often suggests insincerity or thoughtlessness

CAUTION: Do not go any further until you are sure the above answers are correct. Then you can use the definitions to help you in the following practices. Your goal is eventually to know the words well enough so that you don't need to check the definitions at all.

Sentence Check 1

Using the answer line provided, complete each item below with the correct word from the box. Use each word once.

| A. **benign** | B. **blasé** | C. **comprise** | D. **condescend** | E. **facade** |
| F. **glib** | G. **haughty** | H. **libel** | I. **pseudonym** | J. **redundant** |

comprise   1. A receptionist's job ___s answering the phone, greeting customers, opening the mail, dealing with messengers, and smiling.

redundant   2. My aunt's e-mails are annoyingly ___, repeating "news" she has already given us by telephone.

haughty   3. Since becoming a fashion model, Nora has been very ___, even snubbing some of her old, unglamorous friends.

libel   4. One actress sued a magazine for ___ because it printed a false and damaging story about her being drunk in public.

glib   5. Harry, always ready with some made-up excuse, is ___ enough to talk himself out of any difficulty at the snap of a finger.

benign   6. In his usual ___ manner, my neighbor carefully picked up the ant in his kitchen, brought it outside, and gently put it down on the sidewalk.

blasé   7. When my sister first got her job at the recording studio, she was thrilled to go to work each day. Now, after ten years, she's ___ about her work and wants to change jobs.

facade   8. Lidia's grandfather made her a dollhouse with a ___ just like the front of her family's house: black shutters, a red front door, and even the same address.

condescend   9. The conceited young baseball player wouldn't ___ to talk to his fans until an old-timer reminded him that the fans were the ones who had made him a star.

pseudonym   10. Samuel Langhorne Clemens wasn't the first author to use the ___ Mark Twain. A newspaper writer of the time used the same pen name.

NOTE: Now check your answers to these items by turning to page 178. Going over the answers carefully will help you prepare for the next two practices, for which answers are not given.

Sentence Check 2

Using the answer lines provided, complete each item below with **two** words from the box. Use each word once.

haughty
condescend   1–2. Believing he was better than everyone else at the supermarket, Dan was so ___ that he would rarely ___ to speak to the other cashiers.

libel
pseudonym   3–4. One author was accused of ___ when he wrote a damaging article about the governor's wife. Subsequently°, he used a ___ so people wouldn't know he was the author whose facts were in doubt.

_____glib_____

_____benign_____

5–6. At first Joanne thought Barry was too ___, that his smooth talk was all show. As she got to know him better, however, her perception° of him changed. She found that his easy manner reflected a friendly and ___ nature.

_____comprise_____

_____facade_____

7–8. The scenery crew for the summer theatre ___(e)d three artists and a set designer. They created an intricate° ___ of a medieval castle, complete with a carved door, a drawbridge, and a moat.

_____blasé_____

_____redundant_____

9–10. The writing teacher had become ___ from repeatedly seeing the same problems: careless organization, lack of focus, and writing so ___ that many sentences said the same thing. In addition, students often turned to plagiarism° rather than use their own words.

Final Check: *Interview with a Rude Star*

Here is a final opportunity for you to strengthen your knowledge of the ten words. First read the following selection carefully. Then fill in each blank with a word from the box at the top of the previous page. (Context clues will help you figure out which word goes in which blank.) Use each word once.

When a famous actress arrived in town to work on a movie, an editor asked me to interview her. Because this was my first interview assignment, I felt far from (1)_____blasé_____ about it. Instead, I was both excited and scared. Would a star (2)_____condescend_____ to see me, an unknown, inexperienced reporter?

When I arrived at the movie set, I saw the actress standing in front of the painted (3)_____facade_____ of a mansion. During a break in the filming, I approached her and introduced myself. Trying to be as congenial° as possible, I smiled and told her I was pleased to meet her. "Well, let's get this over with," she said, clearly annoyed.

The interview went terribly. My dream of establishing a comfortable rapport° with the star soon vanished as the interview degenerated° into an awkward, demoralizing° situation that I just wanted to end. Although it (4)_____comprise_____(e)d carefully thought-out questions, she sighed or rolled her eyes at every one of them. And no matter how (5)_____benign_____ my manner, she seemed to view me as some sort of threat. At one point, she became irate° and yelled, "That's (6)_____redundant_____! I don't have time to answer the same question twice." When I asked her about serious issues, her answers were totally (7)_____glib_____—insincere and shallow.

Now I have to write about her. Here's my dilemma°: Should I hide my revulsion° and say good things about her? Or should I tell the truth—that she's a (8)_____haughty_____, rude woman who thinks only of herself and expects others to do the same? If I do, she might accuse me of maligning° her and sue me for (9)_____libel_____. Maybe the editor will let me use a (10)_____pseudonym_____, so my real name won't appear on an article about this miserable woman.

| Scores | Sentence Check 2 _____% | Final Check _____% |

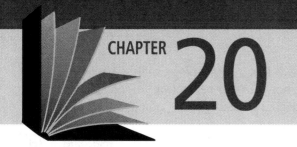

averse	endow
detract	expulsion
disdain	mortify
divulge	nullify
elation	ominous

Ten Words in Context

In the space provided, write the letter of the meaning closest to that of each **boldfaced** word. Use the context of the sentences to help you figure out each word's meaning.

1 averse
(ə-vûrs′)
-adjective

- That little boy was once so **averse** to tomatoes that the very sight of them made him gag.
- Being **averse** to screaming crowds, I'd rather just listen to my iPod than go to a rock concert.

A *Averse* means
 A. opposed. B. accustomed. C. open.

2 detract
(dĭ-trăkt′)
-verb

- Julius thinks the scar on his cheek **detracts** from his good looks, but it's barely noticeable.
- All of the litter in the park certainly **detracts** from the beauty of the trees and flowers.

C *Detract* means
 A. to result. B. to benefit. C. to take away.

3 disdain
(dĭs-dān′)
-noun

- The snobby server in the French restaurant viewed Tanya with **disdain** because she couldn't pronounce anything on the menu.
- I was afraid my request to see the state senator would be treated with **disdain**. Instead, the senator's secretary politely made an appointment for me.

B *Disdain* means
 A. pride. B. disrespect. C. sorrow.

4 divulge
(dĭ-vŭlj′)
-verb

- My father wouldn't **divulge** the type of car he had bought, saying only, "It's a surprise."
- It's against the law to ask people to **divulge** their age at a job interview.

C *Divulge* means
 A. to hide. B. to recall. C. to tell.

5 elation
(ĭ-lā′shən)
-noun

- The principal shouted with **elation** when the football team scored the winning touchdown.
- Roy had expected to feel **elation** at his graduation. Instead, he felt sadness at the thought of not seeing his high-school friends every day.

C *Elation* means
 A. anger. B. confusion. C. happiness.

6 endow
(ĕn-dou′)
-verb

- Nature has **endowed** hummingbirds with the ability to fly backward.
- The author Oscar Wilde was **endowed** with the ability to find humor in any situation. While dying, he said of the ugly wallpaper in his hotel room, "One of us had to go."

A *Endow* means
 A. to equip. B. to curse. C. to threaten.

7 expulsion
(ĕks-pŭl′shən)
-noun

- The manager told us we risked **expulsion** from the theater if we continued to talk on our cell phones during the movie.
- **Expulsion** from school is supposed to be a punishment, but some students may consider not being allowed to attend classes a reward.

_B_ *Expulsion* means   A. being canceled.   B. being forced out.   C. being embarrassed.

8 mortify
(môr′tə-fī′)
-verb

- It would **mortify** me if my voice cracked during my choir solo.
- I doubt anything will ever **mortify** me more than the streamer of toilet paper that clung to my shoe as I returned from the ladies' room to rejoin my date in a fancy restaurant.

_A_ *Mortify* means   A. to shame.   B. to insult.   C. to delay.

9 nullify
(nŭl′ə-fī′)
-verb

- The college will **nullify** my student ID at the end of the term unless I update it with a new sticker.
- A soft-drink company decided to **nullify** its contract with a well-known athlete because he was convicted of drunken driving.

_C_ *Nullify* means   A. to renew.   B. to reveal.   C. to cancel.

10 ominous
(ŏm′ə-nəs)
-adjective

- To many, cemeteries have an **ominous** quality, particularly at night or on Halloween, when the threat of ghosts can seem very real.
- The sore's failure to heal was **ominous**, a possible sign of cancer.

_B_ *Ominous* means   A. embarrassing.   B. threatening.   C. unworthy.

Matching Words with Definitions

Following are definitions of the ten words. Clearly write or print each word next to its definition. The sentences above and on the previous page will help you decide on the meaning of each word.

1. _____endow_____ To provide with a talent or quality

2. _____disdain_____ An attitude or feeling of contempt; scorn

3. _____expulsion_____ The act or condition of being forced to leave

4. _____ominous_____ Threatening harm or evil; menacing

5. _____divulge_____ To reveal; make known

6. _____averse_____ Having a feeling of dislike or distaste for something

7. _____mortify_____ To humiliate or embarrass

8. _____detract_____ To lessen what is admirable or worthwhile about something

9. _____elation_____ A feeling of great joy or pride

10. _____nullify_____ To make legally ineffective; cancel

CAUTION: Do not go any further until you are sure the above answers are correct. Then you can use the definitions to help you in the following practices. Your goal is eventually to know the words well enough so that you don't need to check the definitions at all.

Sentence Check 1

Using the answer line provided, complete each item below with the correct word from the box. Use each word once.

A. **averse**	B. **detract**	C. **disdain**	D. **divulge**	E. **elation**
F. **endow**	G. **expulsion**	H. **mortified**	I. **nullified**	J. **ominous**

_____detract_____ 1. People talking in a movie theater greatly ___ from the enjoyment of watching a film.

_____ominous_____ 2. Because of the dark, ___ storm clouds, we canceled the softball game.

_____averse_____ 3. I'm ___ to speaking in public because I don't enjoy making a fool of myself.

_____elation_____ 4. When he received the college scholarship, my brother felt such ___ that he wept with joy.

_____nullified_____ 5. The results of the mayoral election were ___ after the townspeople found evidence of voting fraud.

_____endow_____ 6. The American water shrew is ___(e)d with feet that have air pockets, enabling the small animal to walk on water.

_____expulsion_____ 7. Some people want a law calling for the ___ of illegal immigrants. Others want them to be forgiven and allowed to stay in the United States permanently.

_____disdain_____ 8. Vinnie's repeated boasts about his muscle-building backfired. They caused his date to look at him with ___, not admiration.

_____divulge_____ 9. Never trust Esta with a secret. She'll ___ it the minute you turn your back.

_____mortified_____ 10. The reporter was ___ when he learned that he had delivered much of his news story facing away from the TV camera.

NOTE: Now check your answers to these items by turning to page 178. Going over the answers carefully will help you prepare for the next two practices, for which answers are not given.

Sentence Check 2

Using the answer lines provided, complete each item below with **two** words from the box. Use each word once.

_____averse_____
_____nullified_____
1–2. Some people are so ___ to living near a nuclear plant that they want the plant's license to be ___. They say the plant infringes° on every homeowner's right to safety.

_____endow_____
_____detract_____
3–4. Shannon is ___(e)d with beautiful curly red hair, but her self-image is so low that she feels her hair ___s from her looks. However, others find her hair to be one of her many attractive physical attributes°.

_____divulge_____
_____expulsion_____
5–6. When someone ___(e)d to a counselor that a certain student was selling drugs, an investigation began that led to that student's ___ from school.

_____ mortified

_____ disdain

7–8. Amy was ___ by the low grade she received for her speech, a grade she considered a sign of the teacher's ___ for her. However, the teacher's rationale° for the grade was that the speech was incoherent°.

_____ ominous

_____ elation

9–10. Marty had believed his headaches and blurred vision were ___ signs of some terrible syndrome°, so he felt ___ when he learned that he simply needed glasses.

Final Check: *The Nightmare of Gym*

Here is a final opportunity for you to strengthen your knowledge of the ten words. First read the following selection carefully. Then fill in each blank with a word from the box at the top of the previous page. (Context clues will help you figure out which word goes in which blank.) Use each word once.

I was not (1)_____ endow _____(e)d with athletic ability. In a frequent nightmare, I'm still trying to pass my mandatory° gym class so that I can graduate from high school. The situation always looks grim. For one thing, the teacher has threatened me with (2)_____ expulsion _____ from school if I don't pass. Also appearing in my dream is the terrifying vault horse, the very sight of which (3)_____ detract _____s from my mental health. I run toward the horse, leap, and nose-dive into the mat. Ignoring my despair, the rest of the gym class laughs. Once again, I am (4)_____ mortified _____ by my athletic performance.

Next, a single (5)_____ ominous _____ rope threatens overhead, where it hangs from the ceiling. I try to contrive° some excuse to get out of climbing it. However, my excuses are so incoherent° that my teacher says, "I don't understand anything you're saying. Get started." Wondering if anyone has ever died from rope burn, I struggle to climb it. Almost to the top, I sweat so much that I slide back to the floor, landing at the gym teacher's feet. "What a loser," the teacher mutters with an expression of total (6)_____ disdain _____.

Because I've always been (7)_____ averse _____ to square-dancing, that too appears in the nightmare. Having forgotten my sneakers, I'm forced to dance in my socks. I slip, rather than dance, around the polished floor. During one high-speed turn, I go sliding—right into the men's locker room, where the smell causes me to pass out.

The only pleasant part of the dream comes near the end. With amazement and (8)_____ elation _____, I learn that I will graduate after all. I smile, thinking I'll never have to face the rigors° of gym class again.

But then, the principal (9)_____ divulge _____s the terrible truth. I haven't managed to pass gym. My graduation depends on my agreeing to take four more years of gym when I get to college. If I don't, my high school diploma will be (10)_____ nullified _____.

| Scores | Sentence Check 2 _____ % | Final Check _____ % |

Enter your scores above and in the **Vocabulary Performance Chart** on the inside back cover of the book.

credible	interim
cursory	latent
designate	secular
deviate	shun
improvise	simulate

Ten Words in Context

In the space provided, write the letter of the meaning closest to that of each **boldfaced** word. Use the context of the sentences to help you figure out each word's meaning.

1 credible
(krĕd′ə-bəl)
-adjective

- Some jurors doubted the witness's testimony, but most of them found it **credible**.
- As **credible** as Mr. Bower's resumé may seem, I don't think you should hire him without checking his references.

C *Credible* means A. long. B. boring. C. believable.

2 cursory
(kûr′sə-rē)
-adjective

- Most people do only a **cursory** job of brushing their teeth. To avoid cavities, however, you must brush for at least two minutes.
- Because James had to work late, he had only enough time to give his apartment a **cursory** cleaning before his parents arrived.

C *Cursory* means A. careful. B. consistent. C. quick.

3 designate
(dĕz′ĭg-nāt′)
-verb

- At the party, Isabel drank soda rather than beer because her friends had **designated** her as the driver for the trip home.
- A coworker was **designated** to present Vonnie with the "Employee of the Year" award at the company banquet.

B *Designate* means A. to forbid. B. to assign. C. to hire.

4 deviate
(dē′vē-āt′)
-verb

- Having taken the wrong exit off the highway, we had to **deviate** somewhat from the route marked on the map.
- If you **deviate** even a little from the directions when you write your paper, you might hurt your grade.

B *Deviate* means A. to follow. B. to depart. C. to gain.

5 improvise
(ĭm′prə-vīz′)
-verb

- Nadia can **improvise** accompaniments on the piano to songs she's never heard before. How can she play so well without any preparation or sheet music?
- When I rang the doorbell, I wasn't expecting Ellen's father to come to the door, so I had to quickly **improvise** an explanation for my visit.

C *Improvise* means A. to remember. B. to keep away from. C. to make up.

6 interim
(ĭn′tər-ĭm)
-noun

- Cassie hadn't seen her nephews for years. In the **interim**, they had grown from troubled boys into serious young men.
- After the secretary left, it took two weeks for her replacement to arrive at the real-estate office. In the **interim**, the agents had to do their own typing.

A *Interim* means A. the time between. B. the future. C. the place.

7 latent
(lāt′ənt)
-adjective

- Certain viruses, such as the one for AIDS, can be **latent** in the body for years before symptoms appear.
- After he retired, my father discovered his **latent** artistic talent. He took up oil painting and now sells much of his work.

_B_ _Latent_ means   A. partial.   B. inactive.   C. absent.

8 secular
(sĕk′yə-lər)
-adjective

- While our government is **secular**, some countries are governed according to religious laws.
- Devoting himself to a deeply religious life, the Hindu holy man denied himself most **secular** pleasures.

_C_ _Secular_ means   A. spiritual.   B. reliable.   C. nonreligious.

9 shun
(shŭn)
-verb

- I used to see a lot of Tracy, but since our argument, she **shuns** me whenever possible.
- The Amish live without many modern conveniences. For example, they **shun** automobiles and electric lights.

_A_ _Shun_ means   A. to keep away from.   B. to recognize.   C. to observe.

10 simulate
(sĭm′yoo-lāt′)
-verb

- The tan plastic of our kitchen table, with its wood-grain design, **simulates** oak.
- Equipment that **simulates** a human heart can keep someone alive only for a short time, until an actual heart can be substituted.

_B_ _Simulate_ means   A. to contrast with.   B. to imitate.   C. to be made of.

Matching Words with Definitions

Following are definitions of the ten words. Clearly write or print each word next to its definition. The sentences above and on the previous page will help you decide on the meaning of each word.

1. _____improvise_____ To compose, perform, or provide without preparation; invent

2. _____credible_____ Believable

3. _____interim_____ The period of time in between; meantime

4. _____designate_____ To name to an office or duty; appoint

5. _____simulate_____ To act or look like; imitate

6. _____secular_____ Not directly related to religion; not spiritual; worldly

7. _____cursory_____ Done quickly and without attention to detail

8. _____shun_____ To keep away from; avoid consistently

9. _____latent_____ Present but hidden or inactive

10. _____deviate_____ To turn aside or stray, as from a path, direction, or standard

CAUTION: Do not go any further until you are sure the above answers are correct. Then you can use the definitions to help you in the following practices. Your goal is eventually to know the words well enough so that you don't need to check the definitions at all.

Sentence Check 1

Using the answer line provided, complete each item below with the correct word from the box. Use each word once.

A. **credible**	B. **cursory**	C. **designate**	D. **deviate**	E. **improvise**
F. **interim**	G. **latent**	H. **secular**	I. **shun**	J. **simulate**

latent   1. Nikki's ___ ability in basketball became apparent when she turned 12. Her movements had once been clumsy, but now they were smooth and controlled.

designate   2. Presidents ___ as Supreme Court justices people who share their political views.

deviate   3. I hear Andy dropped out of college. What caused him to ___ from his plan of getting his degree?

credible   4. Because his story about a flat tire sounded ___, my parents allowed the stranger to use our telephone.

interim   5. In the ___ between applying to college and getting the letter of acceptance, I spent a lot of time worrying.

cursory   6. Margo couldn't identify the driver of the car that had hit her. She'd given him only a(n) ___ glance at the time of the accident.

secular   7. The chorus is known for its gospel music, but it also performs ___ compositions, including show tunes.

improvise   8. When the actor forgot his lines, he was forced to ___ some dialog until the stage manager whispered to him from offstage.

shun   9. Tony found the hardest part of overcoming his addiction was learning to ___ people and places that would tempt him to use drugs again.

simulate   10. The zoo's exhibits ___ the natural environments of animals. The orangutans, for example, live in a space that looks much like an Asian rain forest.

> **NOTE:** Now check your answers to these items by turning to page 179. Going over the answers carefully will help you prepare for the next two practices, for which answers are not given.

Sentence Check 2

Using the answer lines provided, complete each item below with **two** words from the box. Use each word once.

interim
latent   1–2. In seventh grade, Jack looked upon girls with great disdain°. Then, in the ___ between seventh and eighth grades, his ___ interest in them suddenly surfaced.

cursory
secular   3–4. In looking for a college, Luke gave only ___ attention to ___ schools. He was quite sure he wanted to attend a Catholic school.

__credible__   5–6. Matt told his mother he was late because he had fallen while running home. To make his story more ___, he had scratched his knee with a rock to ___ an injury from a fall.

__simulate__

__deviate__   7–8. Della wanted to be a cheerleader, but she willingly ___(e)d from that goal when she was ___(e)d class mascot and got to wear a polar bear costume to all the games.

__designate__

__shun__   9–10. Proud of his ability to create new dishes, Franco tended to ___ cookbooks. He preferred to ___ meals, using whatever ingredients happened to be on hand. In fact, cooking was one of his favorite diversions°.

__improvise__

Final Check: *Skipping Church*

Here is a final opportunity for you to strengthen your knowledge of the ten words. First read the following selection carefully. Then fill in each blank with a word from the box at the top of the previous page. (Context clues will help you figure out which word goes in which blank.) Use each word once.

I remember so well the time my mother's back injury prevented her from going to church with my brother and me. For five weeks, we were supposed to go by ourselves. Zack and I back then preferred (1)__secular__ activities to religious ones, so we decided to (2)__shun__ church while Mom was recovering. We (3)__simulate__(e)d the churchgoers she wanted us to be by getting dressed every Sunday in our good clothes and leaving home and returning at the right times. We spent the (4)__interim__ at a restaurant or at the movies. Of course, we knew Mom would question us about the service. Each week one of us was (5)__designate__(e)d to invent a sermon. I thought Zack's sermons sounded not only (6)__credible__, but also inspiring. I, conversely°, tended to (7)__improvise__ on the spot and didn't sound so believable. But Mom never seemed to notice how weak my sermons were or how (8)__cursory__ our answers were when she asked whom we'd seen and what news we'd heard.

Finally, she was ready to attend church again. Over dinner Saturday evening, she began what seemed to be an innocent conversation. Gently, but showing a previously (9)__latent__ talent for cross-examination that could have made her a star attorney, she questioned us in a quiet but relentless° manner about our "church-going." The more she persisted, the more Zack and I stumbled and (10)__deviate__(e)d from our official story. We eventually concluded we were caught, and the realization mortified° us. Looking downward in shame, we divulged° all the details of our "secret" scheme. We felt pretty foolish when we learned she'd known all along that we had never set foot in church.

Scores   Sentence Check 2 _____ %   Final Check _____ %

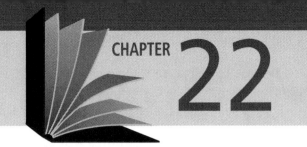

commemorate	empathy
complacent	menial
consensus	niche
deplete	transcend
diligent	waive

Ten Words in Context

In the space provided, write the letter of the meaning closest to that of each **boldfaced** word. Use the context of the sentences to help you figure out each word's meaning.

1 commemorate
(kə-mĕm′ə-rāt′)
-*verb*

● Thomas devoted himself to feeding the hungry. So on the anniversary of his death, it seems wrong to **commemorate** his life with a fancy dinner party that only the rich can attend.

● Each year, my parents **commemorate** their first date by having dinner at McDonalds, the place where they first met.

<u>B</u> *Commemorate* means
    A. to share.   B. to celebrate.   C. to believe.

2 complacent
(kəm-plā′sənt)
-*adjective*

● Elected officials cannot afford to be **complacent** about winning an election. Before long, they'll have to campaign again for the voters' support.

● Getting all A's hasn't made Ivy **complacent**. She continues to work hard at school.

<u>C</u> *Complacent* means
    A. very eager.   B. reasonable.   C. too much at ease.

3 consensus
(kən-sen′səs)
-*noun*

● A vote revealed strong agreement among the teachers. The **consensus** was that they would strike if the school board did not act quickly to raise their pay.

● The family **consensus** was that we should go camping again this summer. Ray was the only one who wanted to do something else for a change.

<u>A</u> *Consensus* means
    A. a majority view.   B. an unusual idea.   C. a question.

4 deplete
(dĭ-plēt′)
-*verb*

● I'd like to help you out with a loan, but unexpected car repairs have managed to **deplete** my bank account.

● In order not to **deplete** their small supply of canned food, the shipwreck survivors searched the island for plants they could eat.

<u>A</u> *Deplete* means
    A. to use up.   B. to forget.   C. to find.

5 diligent
(dĭl′ə-jənt)
-*adjective*

● I wish I had been more **diligent** about practicing piano when I was younger. It would be nice to be able to play well now.

● Diane was lazy when she first joined the family business, but she soon became so **diligent** that she inspired others to work harder.

<u>C</u> *Diligent* means
    A. self-satisfied.   B. lucky.   C. hard-working.

6 empathy
(ĕm′pə-thē)
-*noun*

● Families who lost loved ones in the attacks on the World Trade Center and the Pentagon have **empathy** for one another because of their shared grief.

● Ms. Allan is an excellent career counselor partly because of her great **empathy**. She understands each student's feelings and point of view.

<u>B</u> *Empathy* means
    A. a common opinion.   B. a sympathetic understanding.   C. an efficiency.

7 menial
(mē′nē-əl)
-adjective

- Julio seems to think my summer job delivering pizza is **menial** work, but I've found that it requires some skills.
- Every job can be done with pride. Even **menial** jobs such as washing windows or scrubbing floors can be performed with care.

<u>A</u> *Menial* means   A. unskilled.   B. steady.   C. satisfying.

8 niche
(nĭch)
-noun

- Although her degree was in accounting, Kendra decided her **niche** was really in business management, so she went back to school for more training.
- Dom spent the years after college moving restlessly from job to job, never finding a comfortable **niche** for himself.

<u>B</u> *Niche* means   A. a shared opinion.   B. a suitable place.   C. an education.

9 transcend
(trăn-sĕnd′)
-verb

- The psychic convinced her clients that she could **transcend** time and space and talk directly with the dead.
- Yoga can help one **transcend** the cares of the world and reach a state of relaxation.

<u>B</u> *Transcend* means   A. to participate in.   B. to go past.   C. to use up.

10 waive
(wāv)
-verb

- The defendant decided to **waive** his right to an attorney and, instead, speak for himself in court.
- Since Lin had studied so much math on her own, the school **waived** the requirement that she take high school algebra.

<u>C</u> *Waive* means   A. to lose.   B. to honor.   C. to give up.

Matching Words with Definitions

Following are definitions of the ten words. Clearly write or print each word next to its definition. The sentences above and on the previous page will help you decide on the meaning of each word.

1. _____menial_____ Not requiring special skills or higher intellectual abilities

2. _____empathy_____ The ability to share in someone else's feelings or thoughts

3. _____transcend_____ To rise above or go beyond the limits of; exceed

4. _____commemorate_____ To honor the memory of someone or something, as with a ceremony; celebrate; observe

5. _____waive_____ To willingly give up (as a claim, privilege, or right); do without

6. _____consensus_____ An opinion held by everyone (or almost everyone) involved

7. _____complacent_____ Self-satisfied; feeling too much satisfaction with oneself or one's accomplishments

8. _____diligent_____ Steady, determined, and careful in work

9. _____niche_____ An activity or situation especially suited to a person

10. _____deplete_____ To use up

CAUTION: Do not go any further until you are sure the above answers are correct. Then you can use the definitions to help you in the following practices. Your goal is eventually to know the words well enough so that you don't need to check the definitions at all.

Sentence Check 1

Using the answer line provided, complete each item below with the correct word from the box. Use each word once.

A. commemorate	B. complacent	C. consensus	D. deplete	E. diligent
F. empathy	G. menial	H. niche	I. transcend	J. waive

_____waive_____ 1. The old man decided to ___ any claim he had to the family fortune, preferring to see the money go to the younger generation.

_____commemorate_____ 2. The American Inventors' Association gathered at a banquet to ___ Thomas Edison.

_____deplete_____ 3. My grandfather, who's recovering from heart surgery, is weak, so it doesn't take much effort for him to ___ the little energy he has.

_____transcend_____ 4. Many people believe that Shakespeare's works ___ those of all other authors.

_____complacent_____ 5. The hair salon got off to a good start, but then the owners became ___ about their success and stopped trying to attract new customers.

_____niche_____ 6. Several sessions with a career counselor helped Suzanne consider what her ___ in the working world might be.

_____menial_____ 7. The children like to help out at the family restaurant, but they are able to perform only ___ tasks, such as mopping floors and cleaning tables.

_____diligent_____ 8. Arnie has been ___ in his study of German because he hopes to speak the language with his relatives from Germany when they visit next summer.

_____consensus_____ 9. I had hoped the restaurant would be good, but our group's ___ was that the food was only so-so, and the service was even worse.

_____empathy_____ 10. Dr. Grange is a brilliant mathematician, but she lacks ___ for her students. She doesn't understand how they can find some problems so difficult.

NOTE: Now check your answers to these items by turning to page 179. Going over the answers carefully will help you prepare for the next two practices, for which answers are not given.

Sentence Check 2

Using the answer lines provided, complete each item below with **two** words from the box. Use each word once.

_____waive_____
_____deplete_____ 1–2. Lynn begged the bank to ___ the overdraft charge of thirty dollars, telling them that it would entirely ___ her savings.

_____consensus_____
_____empathy_____ 3–4. In high school, Julio was voted "Most Likely to Become a Psychologist." It was the ___ of his classmates that he was the student endowed° with the most ___ for other people.

_____niche_____
_____transcend_____ 5–6. My mother could have stayed in her comfortable ___ as part of the secretarial pool, but she was averse° to remaining there. She wanted to ___ the limits of that job and become an executive herself.

_____commemorate_____
_____menial_____

7–8. "On this, our hundredth anniversary celebration," said the company president, "I'd like to ___ our founder with a toast. He ran the company from top to bottom, doing even such ___ jobs as emptying garbage cans. He truly exemplified° the values of dedication and hard work."

_____diligent_____
_____complacent_____

9–10. Dr. Roberts and Dr. Krill practice medicine very differently. Dr. Roberts is ___ about reading journals and learning new techniques. Conversely°, Dr. Krill is more ___ and never tries anything new.

Final Check: *A Model Teacher*

Here is a final opportunity for you to strengthen your knowledge of the ten words. First read the following selection carefully. Then fill in each blank with a word from the box at the top of the previous page. (Context clues will help you figure out which word goes in which blank.) Use each word once.

At Eastman High School reunions, the conversation usually gets around to the question "Who was our best teacher?" And year after year, the (1)_____consensus_____ of the graduates has been that Mr. MacDonald was the best. Many remember Joe MacDonald as the epitome° of teaching—the teacher against whom they measured all others.

He had started his professional life as a highly paid attorney. However, never at home with the law, he left his lucrative° practice and found his (2)_____niche_____ as an English teacher in the shabby classrooms at Eastman. Mr. MacDonald somehow helped his students (3)_____transcend_____ their broken-down surroundings and experience the magic in the words of Shakespeare, Dickinson, or Frost. Even those who tended to shun° reading began to think there might be something to this literature stuff after all.

Mr. MacDonald's enthusiasm for his work was never (4)_____deplete_____(e)d. In fact, instead of being used up, his zeal° actually increased through the years. Other teachers became (5)_____complacent_____ about their work and did only cursory° lesson preparation. But Mr. MacDonald never became blasé°; he was as (6)_____diligent_____ as an eager first-year teacher. He could often be found talking with students after school, as his great (7)_____empathy_____ for students—he had good rapport° with them and understood their problems—was well known. He was fun, too. On the first really beautiful spring day of each year, he'd (8)_____waive_____ his lesson plan and take the class outdoors to sit in the sunshine and talk about literature. And no task was too (9)_____menial_____ for him. He was often seen picking up trash from the grounds—something other teachers would never condescend° to do.

After Mr. MacDonald's retirement, his former students wanted to honor him in some way. They thought about a statue, but decided to (10)_____commemorate_____ his teaching in the way that he'd like best, with a college scholarship for an Eastman student, which was established in his name.

Scores   Sentence Check 2 _____%   Final Check _____%

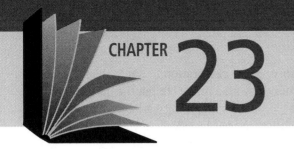

bizarre	gist
conducive	hamper
falter	paradox
flaunt	repertoire
frenzy	viable

Ten Words in Context

In the space provided, write the letter of the meaning closest to that of each **boldfaced** word. Use the context of the sentences to help you figure out each word's meaning.

1 bizarre
(bĭ-zär′)
-adjective

- Some mentally ill people have **bizarre** ideas. For example, they may think that the TV is talking to them or that others can steal their thoughts.
- Wally's outfits may seem **bizarre**, but when you see him with his even stranger-looking friends, his clothing looks quite ordinary.

_C_ *Bizarre* means   A. limited.   B. ordinary.   C. odd.

2 conducive
(kən-dōo′sĭv)
-adjective

- A deliciously warm and sunny April day is **conducive** to a bad case of spring fever.
- Learning to budget an allowance at a young age is **conducive** to good spending habits later in life.

_A_ *Conducive* means   A. favorable.   B. similar.   C. damaging.

3 falter
(fôl′tər)
-verb

- Vince **faltered** on the first few notes of his piano piece but then played the rest without pausing.
- Even public speakers who now sound smooth and confident must have **faltered** when giving their first speeches.

_B_ *Falter* means   A. to show off.   B. to hesitate.   C. to succeed.

4 flaunt
(flônt)
-verb

- Instead of enjoying their wealth quietly, the Stewarts **flaunt** every new thing they buy in front of their poor relatives.
- Tamika never **flaunted** her high grades. In fact, I didn't know that she was first in her class until she received the highest academic award at graduation.

_C_ *Flaunt* means   A. to interfere with.   B. to approve of.   C. to exhibit.

5 frenzy
(frĕn′zē)
-noun

- When Grace couldn't find her little son in the department store, she went into a **frenzy** and didn't calm down until she knew he was safe.
- The holiday season always includes a **frenzy** of last-minute shopping.

_C_ *Frenzy* means   A. a calm condition.   B. an angry condition.   C. an excited condition.

6 gist
(jĭst)
-noun

- We asked Alex to skip the details and get right to the **gist** of the argument.
- The **gist** of Joan Didion's book *The Year of Magical Thinking* is that life as you know it can change in a second.

_B_ *Gist* means   A. the small parts.   B. the main idea.   C. the benefit.

7 hamper
(hăm′pər)
-verb

- "We never meant to **hamper** your struggle for independence," Tom's parents said. "From now on, we'll let you handle your own life, including your laundry and meals."

- A series of major computer crashes **hampered** business all along the West Coast today.

A *Hamper* means   A. to restrict.   B. to show off.   C. to promote.

8 paradox
(păr′ə-dŏx′)
-noun

- When Della kept postponing her decision about whether or not to go back to school, I reminded her of the **paradox** "No decision is also a decision."

- The story of King Midas illustrates a famous **paradox**: "When the gods wish to punish us, they answer our prayers." The king gets what he thinks will be the best thing in the world—the golden touch—and then discovers that it is the worst thing when he accidentally turns his daughter into a golden statue.

C *Paradox* means   A. an outburst.   B. a simple statement.   C. a seeming contradiction.

9 repertoire
(rĕp′ər-twŏr′)
-noun

- The actor's **repertoire** includes drama, storytelling, song, and dance.

- In order to be successful in school, it's important to have a **repertoire** of study strategies from which to choose.

A *Repertoire* means   A. a variety of skills.   B. a reason to do something.   C. a statement of intent.

10 viable
(vī′ə-bəl)
-adjective

- The parties in the labor dispute can reach a **viable** agreement only if both sides benefit equally.

- The little boy quickly learned that using plastic tape is not a **viable** solution to mending a broken vase.

A *Viable* means   A. practical.   B. attractive.   C. expensive.

Matching Words with Definitions

Following are definitions of the ten words. Clearly write or print each word next to its definition. The sentences above and on the previous page will help you decide on the meaning of each word.

1. _____gist_____ The main point or essential part of a matter; central idea

2. _____falter_____ To act or speak with uncertainty; hesitate

3. _____hamper_____ To limit, interfere with, or restrict

4. _____frenzy_____ A wild outburst of excited feelings or actions

5. _____viable_____ Workable; capable of being successful or effective

6. _____paradox_____ A statement that seems contradictory yet may be true

7. _____repertoire_____ A range or collection of skills or accomplishments

8. _____bizarre_____ Dramatically unusual, as in manner or appearance; strange

9. _____conducive_____ Tending to promote or bring about

10. _____flaunt_____ To show off (something)

CAUTION: Do not go any further until you are sure the above answers are correct. Then you can use the definitions to help you in the following practices. Your goal is eventually to know the words well enough so that you don't need to check the definitions at all.

Sentence Check 1

Using the answer line provided, complete each item below with the correct word from the box. Use each word once.

A. **bizarre**	B. **conducive**	C. **falter**	D. **flaunt**	E. **frenzy**
F. **gist**	G. **hamper**	H. **paradox**	I. **repertoire**	J. **viable**

_____bizarre_____ 1. Halloween offers everyone the chance to look as ___ as possible.

_____repertoire_____ 2. Al Pacino's ___ includes both modern dramas and Shakespearean plays.

_____falter_____ 3. When a reporter asked Senator Drake a difficult question, the senator ___(e)d for a moment before answering.

_____conducive_____ 4. For snails, heat is ___ to sleep. In fact, desert snails may sleep three or four years at a time.

_____gist_____ 5. The ___ of Kelly's essay was that school should be open only four days a week, from 8 a.m. to 6 p.m.

_____hamper_____ 6. Since ordinary clothes may ___ movement, sweatpants and loose T-shirts are recommended for the exercise class.

_____viable_____ 7. This morning, the staff could not come up with a ___ plan to improve business. Every suggestion had a drawback.

_____paradox_____ 8. When Chun's parents said they worried when he didn't call home, he said, "Remember that well-known ___—no news is good news."

_____frenzy_____ 9. Delia was in a ___ because she had locked her keys in the car and she was already twenty minutes late for work.

_____flaunt_____ 10. Lucas believed the only way he could get a date was to ___ his wealth by wearing a gold watch and driving an expensive sports car.

NOTE: Now check your answers to these items by turning to page 179. Going over the answers carefully will help you prepare for the next two practices, for which answers are not given.

Sentence Check 2

Using the answer lines provided, complete each item below with **two** words from the box. Use each word once.

_____repertoire_____
_____falter_____   1–2. Although Jenny chose the songs from her ___ that she knew best, she wasn't complacent° about being prepared. Afraid she would ___ the night of the concert, she practiced the songs over and over.

_____gist_____
_____hamper_____   3–4. The ___ of the lecture was that although the United States encourages free trade, some other countries ___ it.

conducive   5–6. Unfortunately, forming a committee wasn't ___ to alleviating° the company's
viable   parking problem. No one could think of a ___ plan to increase the number of
                 parking spaces.

frenzy   7–8. Bruno is so prone° to changing his mind that his rapid shifts of opinion
paradox   sometimes make me irate°. Once, in a ___ of anger, I shouted this ___:
                 "You're always the same—always changing your mind!"

bizarre   9–10. My mother took me aside at the party and said, "That looks more like a
flaunt   strange costume than a dress. It's bad enough your clothing looks so ___, but
                 do you have to mortify° me and ___ it in front of all my friends?"

Final Check: My Talented Roommate

Here is a final opportunity for you to strengthen your knowledge of the ten words. First read the following selection carefully. Then fill in each blank with a word from the box at the top of the previous page. (Context clues will help you figure out which word goes in which blank.) Use each word once.

"If you've got it, (1)_____flaunt_____ it!" That's the (2)_____gist_____ of Georgia's philosophy. Georgia is my dorm roommate. A dance and theater major, she is a true extrovert°—always showing off, always "onstage." It seems she is in constant motion, going from graceful leaps down the hall to such (3)_____bizarre_____ acrobatics as swinging by her knees from the clothes rod in her closet. Some days Georgia performs her entire (4)_____repertoire_____ right in our room. The (5)_____paradox_____ "less is more" doesn't apply to her on those occasions, when she delights by acting, singing, and dancing everything she's ever learned. Attracted by her talent and charisma°, an audience always gathers to watch. The lack of space in our room never seems to (6)_____hamper_____ her movements. Since Georgia's shows are not very (7)_____conducive_____ to good studying on my part, I join the crowd drawn by her magnetism. She is so smooth and confident—I have never seen her (8)_____falter_____. She moves easily from ballet to tap to jazz. She'll tell jokes, sing part of an opera, and perform a scene from _A Chorus Line_. Not knowing all the words never stops her—she simply improvises° lines as she goes along. When she finishes, her audience breaks into a (9)_____frenzy_____ of applause. It's difficult to break into show business, which is why most drama students give up on this quest° and settle for a more conventional° career. But I contend° Georgia is talented enough to build a (10)_____viable_____ career in show business.

| Scores | Sentence Check 2 _____% | Final Check _____% |

Enter your scores above and in the **Vocabulary Performance Chart** on the inside back cover of the book.

aster-, astro-	mis-
contra-	omni-
-er, -or	pop
-gamy	rect
geo-	the, theo-

Ten Word Parts in Context

Figure out the meanings of the following ten word parts by looking *closely* and *carefully* at the context in which they appear. Then, in the space provided, write the letter of the meaning closest to that of each word part.

1 aster-, astro-

- The **aster** is a lovely flower named for its starlike shape: its petals point outward from a yellow disk.
- **Astrologers** claim to interpret the influence of the stars and planets on our lives.

B The word part *aster-* or *astro-* means

    A. someone who does something.   B. star.   C. marriage.

2 contra-

- **Contrary** to his campaign promise, the governor is going to raise gasoline taxes.
- The warning label on the bottle of arthritis medicine contained this **contraindication**: "We recommend against taking this product if you are already using aspirin or similar painkillers."

C The word part *contra-* means

    A. all.   B. straight.   C. against.

3 -er, -or

- When the young **singer** at an NBA game forgot the words to the National Anthem, the coach came over and sang along with her.
- American **visitors** to Canadian cities are often amazed by how clean the streets are.

C The word part *-er* or *-or* means

    A. god.   B. wrong.   C. someone who does something.

4 -gamy

- Jackson brought charges of **bigamy** against his wife after he learned that she was still legally married to her first husband.
- King Mongut of Siam, whose story was told in the musical *The King and I*, practiced **polygamy**. He was reported to have had 9,000 wives.

A The word part *-gamy* means

    A. marriage.   B. opposite.   C. god.

5 geo-

- Pierce County, North Dakota, has the distinction of being the **geographic** center of North America.
- **Geophysics** is the science of the matter and forces of the Earth, including oceans, volcanoes, and earthquakes.

A The word part *geo-* means

    A. earth.   B. people.   C. outer space.

6 mis-

- I think there is something wrong with a child who never **misbehaves**.
- The telephone caller **misrepresented** herself. She said she was doing a survey, but she really wanted to sell me life insurance.

C The word part *mis-* means

    A. for.   B. straight.   C. badly.

7 omni-

- Until they lost to the Giants in the Super Bowl, the 2007–2008 New England Patriots seemed **omnipotent**. They defeated all their opponents, completing the first 18–0 season in NFL history.
- Some dinosaurs ate only plants, and others ate only meat. Still others were **omnivorous**—they ate all kinds of food.

B   The word part *omni-* means   A. right.   B. all.   C. wrong.

8 pop

- In 1770, the United States was not very **populous**. Only about two million people lived here then.
- In order to **populate** the West, the government gave free land to people who would build on it.

A   The word part *pop* means   A. people.   B. everywhere.   C. opposite.

9 rect

- Every time I play Monopoly, I seem to pick the card that reads, "Go **directly** to jail. Do not pass Go. Do not collect $200."
- "Suck in those stomachs!" yelled the coach. "Pull back those shoulders, and stand **erect**!"

B   The word part *rect* means   A. opposite.   B. straight.   C. wrong.

10 the, theo-

- **Monotheism** is the belief that there is only one God.
- **Theology** is the study of the nature of God and religious truth.

A   The word part *the* or *theo-* means   A. god.   B. everywhere.   C. for.

Matching Word Parts with Definitions

Following are definitions of the ten word parts. Clearly write or print each word part next to its definition. The sentences above and on the previous page will help you decide on the meaning of each word part.

1. _____mis-_____ Wrong; badly

2. _____rect_____ Straight

3. _____aster-, astro-_____ Star, outer space

4. _____pop_____ People

5. _____-er, -or_____ Someone who (does something)

6. _____geo-_____ Earth; geography

7. _____the, theo-_____ God or a god

8. _____omni-_____ All; everywhere

9. _____-gamy_____ Marriage

10. _____contra-_____ Against; contrasting; opposite

CAUTION: Do not go any further until you are sure the above answers are correct. Then you can use the definitions to help you in the following practices. Your goal is eventually to know the word parts well enough so that you don't need to check the definitions at all.

Sentence Check 1

Using the answer line provided, complete each *italicized* word below with the correct word part from the box. Use each word part once.

A. aster-, astro-	B. contra-	C. -er, -or	D. -gamy	E. geo-
F. mis-	G. omni-	H. pop	I. rect	J. the, theo-

_____actor_____ 1. Wade, a professional (*act . . .*) ___, seems to be playing a part even when he's offstage.

_____geochemistry_____ 2. The study of the chemical makeup of the Earth's crust is called (. . . *chemistry*) ___.

_____omnipresent_____ 3. Poverty is (. . . *present*) ___ in large cities in India, where people beg on every street.

_____asterisk_____ 4. A small starlike figure called an (. . . *isk*) ___ (*) is often used in books and magazines to indicate a footnote.

_____director_____ 5. On a movie set, the (*di . . . or*) ___ is the person who keeps everyone and everything running on course.

_____theologian_____ 6. John Wesley was the eighteenth-century British (. . . *logian*) ___ who founded Methodism.

_____misplace_____ 7. If I don't hang my house key on a special hook in the kitchen as soon as I get home, I'll (. . . *place*) ___ it.

_____contradict_____ 8. Young children go through a stage in which they (. . . *dict*) ___ everything a parent says. If the parent says yes, the child will usually say no.

_____Monogamy_____ 9. (*Mono . . .*) ___ doesn't stop people from having more than one husband or wife. It only requires them to have one at a time.

_____populated_____ 10. The few places on Earth that have not yet been (. . . *ulated*) ___ by humans probably would not appeal to many. Who wants to live on the snowcapped peak of a mountain?

NOTE: Now check your answers to these items by turning to page 179. Going over the answers carefully will help you prepare for the next two practices, for which answers are not given.

Sentence Check 2

Using the answer line provided, complete each *italicized* word in the sentences below with the correct word part from the box. Use each word part once.

_____rectangle_____
_____mistake_____ 1–2. The kindergartners were asked to draw a (. . . *angle*) ___, but several made a (. . . *take*) ___ and drew a circle instead.

_____Pantheists_____
_____omnipresent_____ 3–4. (*Pan . . . ists*) ___ believe that God is not a personality but an (. . . *present*) ___ force of nature, present throughout the universe.

_____ Doctor _____   5–6. (*Doct . . .*) ___ Fisher was very (*. . . ular*) ___ with the townspeople because
_____ popular _____   she always took the time to answer their questions and had great empathy°
                                for her patients' suffering.

_____ contrary _____   7–8. The two Mayfield brothers made (*. . . ry*) career decisions. One is an
_____ astronaut _____   archaeologist who speculates° about what our past might have been like. The
                               other is an (*. . . naut*) who thinks about our future in space.

_____ geography _____ 9–10. In (*. . . graphy*) ___ class, we learned not only about the location and climate
_____ exogamy _____   of various countries but also about customs. For example, in some African
                               nations, (*exo . . .*) ___, or marrying outside the tribe, is customary; those who
                               refuse risk expulsion° from their native community.

Final Check: *Fascinating Courses*

Here is a final opportunity for you to strengthen your knowledge of the ten word parts. First read the following selection carefully. Then complete each *italicized* word in the parentheses below with a word part from the box at the top of the previous page. (Context clues will help you figure out which word part goes in which blank.) Use each word part once.

Each semester, I like to choose one fascinating course unrelated to my major. Last fall, for example, I took a(n) (*. . . logy*) (1) _____ geology _____ course that focused on the remarkable changes in the Earth's surface over time. Then in the spring, I took (*. . . nomy*) (2) _____ astronomy _____. When I looked at the stars through a telescope, I felt tiny and insignificant in (*. . . st*) (3) _____ contrast _____ to the enormous sizes and distances of outer space. This experience made me ponder° the nature of God and prompted° me to look for a class on religion.

So this semester I'm taking a course in (*. . . logy*) (4) _____ theology _____. One day we spent three hours discussing this question: If God is (*. . . potent*) (5) _____ omnipotent _____, then why hasn't He or She alleviated° all of humanity's suffering? We've also talked about how much (*. . . understanding*) (6) _____ misunderstanding _____ arises when people do not know about each other's beliefs. This confusion hampers° the pursuit of unity in the world. For example, I've long heard my (*minist . . .*) (7) _____ minister _____ preach that we should be true to one partner, but I never knew that in some other religions, (*poly . . .*) (8) _____ polygamy _____ is quite acceptable. Conversely°, in Catholicism, priests and nuns have to abstain° from marrying. It seems there's no clear consensus° on this subject.

If we were to take a survey of the world's (*. . . ulation*) (9) _____ population _____, many people would probably say they look to their church for (*di . . . ion*) (10) _____ direction _____ in their lives. I've learned that there's a rationale° for understanding other religions as well.

| Scores | Sentence Check 2 _____% | Final Check _____% |

The box at the right lists twenty-five words from Unit Four. Using the clues at the bottom of the page, fill in these words to complete the puzzle that follows.

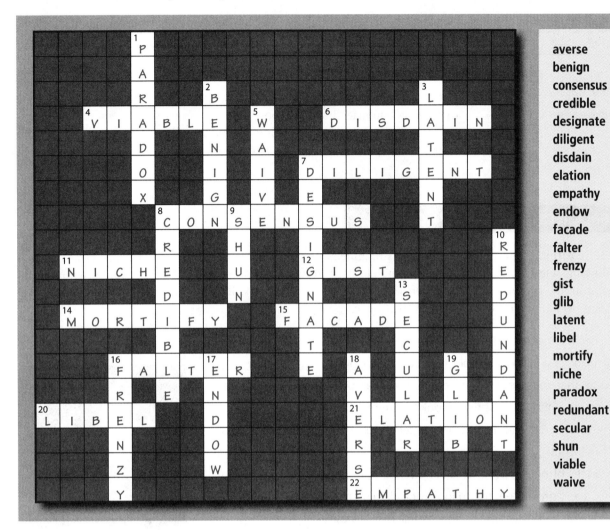

averse
benign
consensus
credible
designate
diligent
disdain
elation
empathy
endow
facade
falter
frenzy
gist
glib
latent
libel
mortify
niche
paradox
redundant
secular
shun
viable
waive

ACROSS

4. Workable; capable of being successful or effective

6. An attitude of contempt; scorn

7. Steady, determined, and careful in work

8. An opinion held by most or all involved

11. An activity or situation especially suited to a person

12. The main point or essential part of a matter; central idea

14. To humiliate or embarrass

15. The front of a building

16. To act or speak with uncertainty; hesitate

20. The publishing of false information that harms a person's reputation

21. A feeling of great joy or pride

22. The ability to share in another's feelings or thoughts

DOWN

1. A statement that seems contradictory yet may be true

2. Kindly; gentle

3. Present but hidden or inactive

5. To willingly give up; do without

7. To name to an office or duty; appoint

8. Believable

9. To keep away from; avoid consistently

10. Wordy or needlessly repetitive

13. Not directly related to religion; not spiritual; worldly

16. A wild outburst of excited feelings or actions

17. To provide with a talent or quality

18. Having a feeling of dislike or distaste for something

19. Characterized by a smooth, easy manner of speaking that often suggests insincerity

PART A

Choose the word that best completes each item and write it in the space provided.

hampered   1. The rain ___ the work of the road construction crew.

         A. hampered   B. improvised   C. flaunted   D. designated

faltered   2. Suddenly dizzy from the heat, the speaker ___ and covered his eyes.

         A. transcended   B. simulated   C. faltered   D. waived

blasé   3. It's hard to become ___ about great music. No matter how often you hear it, you never tire of it.

         A. viable   B. haughty   C. blasé   D. secular

deviated   4. When he decided to become a teacher, Brian certainly ___ from his plan to become a stockbroker.

         A. improvised   B. deviated   C. simulated   D. divulged

complacent   5. Though pleased with the A on her last English paper, Lee was careful not to become ___—she began work on the next assignment immediately.

         A. complacent   B. secular   C. ominous   D. menial

pseudonym   6. We were amazed to learn that gentle, soft-spoken Dr. Geyer writes horror novels under the ___ of Trent Paterson.

         A. interim   B. pseudonym   C. consensus   D. expulsion

elation   7. When Scott won the gymnastics competition, his parents' ___ was as great as his own joy and pride.

         A. elation   B. facade   C. niche   D. libel

repertoire   8. My nephew's ___ of tricks for getting his own way includes pouting, crying, and throwing tantrums.

         A. interim   B. empathy   C. consensus   D. repertoire

diligent   9. I'm not quick with home repairs, but I'm ___. I work steadily and carefully until I get the job done.

         A. diligent   B. glib   C. haughty   D. cursory

libel   10. Because the article made unproven accusations against the mayor, the editors wouldn't print it for fear of being sued for ___.

         A. paradox   B. expulsion   C. empathy   D. libel

(Continues on next page)

PART B

On the answer line, write the letter of the choice that best completes each item.

B   11. Among Beverly's many pets, the most **bizarre** is her
    A. green parrot.
    B. hissing cockroach.
    C. miniature poodle.
    D. goldfish.

C   12. According to cartoons, situation comedies, and the like, which of the following job types is most likely to attract **glib** characters?
    A. Cowboy
    B. Accountant
    C. Used-car salesperson
    D. Plumber

D   13. A person **endowed** with an honest nature
    A. wishes he had an honest nature.
    B. is lacking an honest nature.
    C. pretends to have an honest nature.
    D. possesses an honest nature.

B   14. **Ominous** music in a movie score generally means that
    A. a love scene is about to happen.
    B. something scary or evil is about to happen.
    C. an exciting action scene is about to happen.
    D. the opening credits are about to be shown.

D   15. Napoleon Bonaparte was so **averse** to cats that he
    A. insisted one live in every room of his palace.
    B. stroked one for luck every morning.
    C. sneezed and itched whenever one was near.
    D. left the room in disgust if one entered.

D   16. Concerning fish, the term "feeding **frenzy**" refers to
    A. the period after eating when fish are relaxed.
    B. a period of starvation when food is scarce.
    C. a quiet, methodical search for food.
    D. a wild, excited period of feeding.

C   17. New England **comprises**
    A. the Atlantic Ocean.
    B. clam chowder, lobster, and lighthouses.
    C. Maine, New Hampshire, Massachusetts, Rhode Island, Connecticut, and Vermont.
    D. shipbuilding, fishing, and manufacturing.

B   18. Our cat has tested positive for the disease feline leukemia. But since the virus can be **latent**,
    A. we are having her put to sleep because she is suffering so much.
    B. she may not develop any symptoms for a long time.
    C. we know she will die very soon.
    D. we are sure she doesn't have the virus.

C   19. Marissa told her employer that she felt dizzy and feverish and needed to see a doctor. Her boss answered, with great **empathy**,
    A. "Well, don't let your personal problems interfere with your work."
    B. "Sorry to hear that. Can you work overtime tonight?"
    C. "You must be feeling terrible. Is there anything I can do?"
    D. "Do you think you have the flu? Don't give it to me!"

A   20. A frequent dream of mine always **mortifies** me. In it,
    A. I am in public and suddenly realize I'm naked.
    B. I can fly as easily as a bird.
    C. I am in my childhood home talking with my father, who is young and healthy again.
    D. I am in a furious argument with a coworker whom I dislike.

Score   (Number correct) _____ x 5 = _____%

PART A

Complete each item with a word from the box. Use each word once.

A. **commemorate**	B. **consensus**	C. **credible**	D. **designate**	E. **divulge**
F. **flaunt**	G. **gist**	H. **improvise**	I. **interim**	J. **paradox**
K. **secular**	L. **simulate**	M. **viable**		

paradox   1. It's a(n) ___ that we can sometimes be more generous by giving less.

gist   2. Authors often state the ___ of an article in the introductory paragraph.

flaunt   3. Alonso ___s his good voice by singing louder than anyone else in the choir.

secular   4. More and more nuns are wearing ___ clothes rather than traditional religious dress.

commemorate   5. On Presidents' Day, the nation ___s George Washington and Abraham Lincoln.

divulge   6. I think it's selfish of Dolly not to ___ her secret recipe for poppyseed salad dressing.

simulate   7. Films that ___ the experience of riding on a roller coaster give me a genuine feeling of nausea.

improvise   8. I don't mind speaking before a group if I have time to prepare, but I'd be scared to death if I had to ___ a speech on the spot.

viable   9. The only ___ plan for making enough money to keep up the payments on the house is to rent out some of its rooms.

credible   10. Although the businessman at first seemed to be a ___ witness, the police started doubting him once he began to change the details of his story.

consensus   11. The ___ among the city's sportswriters is that Bridgewater High will win the basketball championship this year.

interim   12. When the church's pastor resigned, a retired minister stepped in for the ___ until a permanent replacement was found.

designate   13. The boys ___(e)d my little brother the treasurer of their tree-house club because he's the only one who receives a regular allowance.

(Continues on next page)

PART B

Write **C** if the italicized word is used **correctly**. Write **I** if the word is used **incorrectly**.

I   14. In a democracy, it's important for people to *waive* their right to vote.

C   15. "That bow tie *detracts* from Alan's appearance," said Paloma. "He looks strangled and gift-wrapped."

I   16. Wayne has *transcended* his usual good grades by failing three of his four classes this semester.

C   17. Because *menial* tasks require little thought, I was able to plan some of my essay while cleaning my apartment yesterday.

C   18. The host's famous sister remained in her room for most of the party, although she did *condescend* to come downstairs and say good night to the other guests before they left.

I   19. By careful saving, I managed to *deplete* my bank account from $80 to almost $1,200 by the summer's end.

PART C

On the answer line, write the letter of the word that is the **synonym** of the boldfaced word.

Example: __A__ **bizarre**   A. strange   B. ordinary   C. expensive

A   20. **haughty**   A. proud   B. humble   C. tall

B   21. **disdain**   A. loss   B. contempt   C. admiration

C   22. **benign**   A. cruel   B. broken   C. kindly

PART D

On the answer line, write the letter of the word that is the **antonym** of the boldfaced word.

Example: __B__ **bizarre**   A. strange   B. ordinary   C. expensive

B   23. **shun**   A. owe   B. seek   C. avoid

A   24. **facade**   A. back   B. light   C. front

B   25. **nullify**   A. ignore   B. approve   C. cancel

Score   (Number correct) _____ x 4 = _____%

Each item below starts with a pair of words in CAPITAL LETTERS. For each item, figure out the relationship between these two words. Then decide which of the choices (A, B, C, or D) expresses a similar relationship. Write the letter of your choice on the answer line.

D 1. PSEUDONYM : AUTHOR ::
   A. address : map
   B. story : true
   C. word : dictionary
   D. costume : actor

B 2. FACADE : BUILDING ::
   A. house : cellar
   B. face : head
   C. street : sign
   D. neighborhood : town

C 3. HAUGHTY : ARROGANCE ::
   A. thirsty : water
   B. brave : fear
   C. clever : intelligence
   D. muscle : strength

A 4. REDUNDANT : WORDY ::
   A. error : mistake
   B. paper : book
   C. word : repeat
   D. paper : read

D 5. DETRACT : IMPROVE ::
   A. blame : error
   B. open : door
   C. criticize : scold
   D. ascend : descend

A 6. ELATION : WONDERFUL NEWS ::
   A. pain : injury
   B. wisdom : ignorance
   C. satisfaction : failure
   D. football : sport

B 7. OMINOUS : STORM CLOUDS ::
   A. bright : fog
   B. fragrant : flowers
   C. flock : seagull
   D. sophomore : grade

D 8. CURSORY : CAREFUL ::
   A. sharp : blade
   B. quick : rapid
   C. wild : untamed
   D. plentiful : scarce

C 9. IMPROVISE : REHEARSE ::
   A. schedule : roster
   B. attempt : try
   C. restore : destroy
   D. comedian : joke

A 10. SHUN : OUTCAST ::
   A. celebrate : hero
   B. triangle : shape
   C. poem : poet
   D. welcome : foe

(Continues on next page)

_D_ 11. COMMEMORATE : ANNIVERSARY ::
    A. trophy : winner   C. break : diamond
    B. horn : bull   D. regret : mistake

_B_ 12. DILIGENT : HARD-WORKING ::
    A. presence : absence   C. frightful : comforting
    B. dirty : unclean   D. silk : torn

_C_ 13. EMPATHY : UNCARING ::
    A. liberty : free   C. reliability : irresponsible
    B. sympathy : compassionate   D. clarity : clear

_C_ 14. CONDUCIVE : HELPFUL ::
    A. nervous : calm   C. lazy : idle
    B. actor : actress   D. prepared : unready

_B_ 15. HAMPER : OBSTACLE ::
    A. forest : trees   C. gift : present
    B. assist : instruction   D. darken : bleach

_D_ 16. VIABLE : IMPOSSIBLE ::
    A. sneaky : sly   C. applause : approval
    B. probable : likely   D. accidental : intentional

_A_ 17. EXPULSION : SCHOOL ::
    A. eviction : apartment   C. celebration : funeral
    B. graduation : college   D. exercise : gym

_D_ 18. COMPLACENT : SELF-DOUBT ::
    A. tired : exhaustion   C. transparent : clearness
    B. uninterested : indifference   D. rigid : flexibility

_C_ 19. NICHE : SUITABLE ::
    A. kitchen cabinet : cereal   C. haunted house : scary
    B. high school : classroom   D. doctor's office : chilly

_A_ 20. BIZARRE : ODDITY ::
    A. treacherous : traitor   C. unknown : celebrity
    B. strange : ordinary   D. landlord : tenant

Score   (Number correct) _____ x 5 = _____ %

PART A

Listed in the left-hand column below are ten common word parts, followed by words in which the parts are used. In each blank, write in the letter of the correct definition on the right.

Word Parts	Examples	Definitions
B 1. **aster-, astro-**	aster, astrologer	A. Someone who (does something)
F 2. **contra-**	contrary, contraindication	B. Star, outer space
A 3. **-er, -or**	singer, visitor	C. All; everywhere
G 4. **-gamy**	bigamy, polygamy	D. Straight
H 5. **geo-**	geographic, geophysics	E. God or a god
J 6. **mis-**	misbehave, misrepresent	F. Against; contrasting; opposite
C 7. **omni-**	omnipotent, omnivorous	G. Marriage
I 8. **pop**	populous, populate	H. Earth
D 9. **rect**	directly, erect	I. People
E 10. **the, theo-**	monotheism, theology	J. Wrong; badly

PART B

Using the answer line provided, complete each *italicized* word in the sentences below with the correct word part from the box. Not every word part will be used.

A. **aster-**	B. **contra-**	C. **-er**	D. **-gamy**	E. **geo-**
F. **mis-**	G. **omni-**	H. **pop**	I. **rect**	J. **theo-**

popular _____ 11. Vanilla ice cream is even more (. . . *ular*) ___ among Americans than chocolate is.

Contrary _____ 12. (. . . *ry*) ___ to what many suppose, Shakespeare made his living by acting as well as by writing.

asteroids _____ 13. Circling the sun between the paths of Mars and Jupiter are thousands of (. . . *oids*) ___, or small planets.

bigamy _____ 14. The movie was about a woman who, thinking her husband was dead, married again. Later, husband #1 showed up, making her guilty of (*bi* . . .) ___.

geographic _____ 15. An interesting (. . . *graphic*) ___ fact is that Mount Everest, the highest mountain in the world, has grown a foot taller over the last century.

(Continues on next page)

PART C

Use your knowledge of word parts to determine the meaning of the **boldfaced** words. On the answer line, write the letter of each meaning.

_C_ 16. Mr. Nolan is a man of many **misdeeds**.

    A. religious feelings   B. girlfriends   C. immoral acts

_B_ 17. Houses are usually **rectilinear**; that is, they are characterized by

    A. opposing forces.   B. straight lines.   C. great cost.

_B_ 18. There will be many **exhibitors** at the state fair this year.

    A. farm exhibits   B. people who exhibit   C. exhibit fees

_C_ 19. Throughout history, a common form of government has been **theocracy**, in which the government is considered to be based on

    A. laws voted on by everyone.   B. immoral laws.   C. religious authority.

_B_ 20. There's too much knowledge in the world today for any one person to claim **omniscience**.

    A. knowledge of biology   B. complete knowledge   C. partial knowledge

Score   (Number correct) _____ x 5 = _____%

Enter your score above and in the **Vocabulary Performance Chart** on the inside back cover of the book.

Unit Five

Chapter 25

devoid	jeopardize
implore	sibling
infuriate	smug
intimidate	sneer
introvert	vivacious

Chapter 26

condone	furtive
contemplate	gape
feasible	pathetic
feign	precedent
fiscal	punitive

Chapter 27

cryptic	inhibition
deficient	ironic
depict	rupture
detrimental	saturate
implicit	vindictive

Chapter 28

constrict	habitat
exhaustive	pragmatic
fallible	pretentious
formulate	reconcile
genial	vile

Chapter 29

avid	mediate
dwindle	muted
esteem	nurture
evoke	pacify
legacy	transient

Chapter 30

aloof	longevity
ambivalent	magnitude
augment	mundane
dispel	obscure
explicit	render

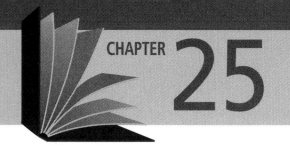

devoid	jeopardize
implore	sibling
infuriate	smug
intimidate	sneer
introvert	vivacious

Ten Words in Context

In the space provided, write the letter of the meaning closest to that of each **boldfaced** word. Use the context of the sentences to help you figure out each word's meaning.

1 devoid
(dĭ-void′)
-adjective

● The French fries were so thin, dry, and **devoid** of taste that they seemed like toothpicks.

● Sometimes Carl is totally **devoid** of common sense. Once he went on vacation leaving his front door unlocked and the newspaper delivery service uncanceled.

A *Devoid of* means   A. without.   B. equal to.   C. possessing.

2 implore
(ĭm-plôr′)
-verb

● Please hide all the candy bars, and don't tell me where they are no matter how much I **implore** you.

● The princess **implored** the evil magician to spare the handsome prince's life.

C *Implore* means   A. to educate.   B. to deny.   C. to urge.

3 infuriate
(ĭn-fyoŏr′ē-āt′)
-verb

● Peter so **infuriated** Sheila that she shut off her cell phone while he was still talking.

● At the grocery store, it **infuriates** me when people with a cartload of food get in the express line.

A *Infuriate* means   A. to anger.   B. to encourage.   C. to frighten.

4 intimidate
(ĭn-tĭm′ə-dāt′)
-verb

● Will's huge size **intimidates** strangers, but anyone who knows him realizes that he's a very gentle man.

● Public speaking so **intimidates** Midori that she would rather write four term papers than give a single oral report.

B *Intimidate* means   A. to calm.   B. to scare.   C. to annoy.

5 introvert
(ĭn′trə-vûrt′)
-noun

● Pearl is a very outgoing person, but her boyfriend Larry is such an **introvert** that he seldom socializes at all.

● It could be difficult for an **introvert** to succeed in a sales career, which involves a great deal of contact with the public.

B *Introvert* means   A. a conceited person.   B. a shy person.   C. a busy person.

6 jeopardize
(jĕp′ər-dīz′)
-verb

● Molly is so clumsy that she **jeopardizes** every fragile item she touches. Whatever she picks up is liable to get broken.

● Pregnant women who take drugs **jeopardize** their babies' health.

C *Jeopardize* means   A. to play with.   B. to take into account.   C. to put in danger.

7 sibling
(sĭb′lĭng)
-noun

- Do you think twins are more similar in personality than other **siblings**?
- It's hard enough for children to move to foster homes; it's even worse when **siblings** have to be separated.

A *Sibling* means   A. a brother or sister.   B. a cousin.   C. a friend.

8 smug
(smŭg)
-adjective

- Self-confidence is a virtue, but being **smug** is carrying self-confidence too far.
- I avoid **smug** people. They are very generous in judging themselves while viewing others narrow-mindedly.

C *Smug* means   A. full of life.   B. dishonest.   C. too self-satisfied.

9 sneer
(snēr)
-verb

- Sarita is terrific with little children. No matter how silly their questions are, she never **sneers** at them.
- Instead of encouraging us when we make a mistake, our biology teacher **sneers** at us with a scornful smile or a put-down.

B *Sneer at* means   A. to leave.   B. to mock.   C. to ignore.

10 vivacious
(vĭ-vā′shəs)
-adjective

- My father is such a **vivacious** host that he makes his guests feel bright and lively too.
- Between scenes, the actors might appear tired and dull, but they become **vivacious** once the camera is running.

B *Vivacious* means   A. good-looking.   B. peppy.   C. irritable.

Matching Words with Definitions

Following are definitions of the ten words. Clearly write or print each word next to its definition. The sentences above and on the previous page will help you decide on the meaning of each word.

1. _____introvert_____ A shy or inwardly directed person

2. _____devoid_____ Completely lacking

3. _____sibling_____ A sister or brother

4. _____infuriate_____ To anger greatly

5. _____vivacious_____ Lively; full of life and enthusiasm

6. _____implore_____ To beg; plead

7. _____sneer_____ To show or express contempt or ridicule

8. _____intimidate_____ To make timid or afraid; frighten

9. _____smug_____ Overly pleased with one's own cleverness, goodness, etc.; too self-satisfied

10. _____jeopardize_____ To endanger; put at risk of loss or injury

CAUTION: Do not go any further until you are sure the above answers are correct. Then you can use the definitions to help you in the following practices. Your goal is eventually to know the words well enough so that you don't need to check the definitions at all.

Sentence Check 1

Using the answer line provided, complete each item below with the correct word from the box. Use each word once.

A. **devoid**	B. **implore**	C. **infuriate**	D. **intimidate**	E. **introvert**
F. **jeopardize**	G. **sibling**	H. **smug**	I. **sneer**	J. **vivacious**

_____vivacious_____ 1. You may call Linda charming and ___, but to me, she's just an irritating chatterbox.

_____implore_____ 2. I ___ you not to mention the DVD player to Hakim. I want to surprise him with it.

_____devoid_____ 3. The genius who invents a chocolate ice cream that's ___ of calories should win a medal.

_____introvert_____ 4. Working with computers all day suits my brother. He's too much of a(n) ___ to enjoy working much with other people.

_____jeopardize_____ 5. I don't understand why Eileen enjoys activities that ___ her life, like skydiving and mountain climbing.

_____sibling_____ 6. Christmas is the one time of year when my grandparents, parents, and three ___s are able to get together.

_____infuriate_____ 7. There used to be little that angered my father, but since he got laid off, it seems that everything we kids do ___s him.

_____sneer_____ 8. When he found Art selling drugs near the elementary school, the arresting officer ___(e)d at him, snarling, "You scum."

_____intimidate_____ 9. It's better to get children's cooperation by setting shared goals than by trying to ___ them with threats of punishment.

_____smug_____ 10. Jenny would be more popular if she didn't get that ___ look on her face every time she answers the teacher's question correctly.

NOTE: Now check your answers to these items by turning to page 179. Going over the answers carefully will help you prepare for the next two practices, for which answers are not given.

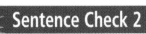

Sentence Check 2

Using the answer lines provided, complete each item below with **two** words from the box. Use each word once.

_____infuriate_____
_____sibling_____
1–2. The people I love best can ___ me the most. No one can make me as angry as my parents and ___s can. I guess close relationships are conducive° to strong feelings, both positive and negative.

_____implore_____
_____devoid_____
3–4. Please don't ___ me to help you with your term paper. Since you delayed working on it for so long, I'm ___ of sympathy. I don't mean to gloat°, but why should I give up my evening when I was diligent° about getting the paper done and you were playing video games all week?

_____sneer_____   5–6. I think Marvin only pretends to look down on the weightlifters in school. He
_____intimidate_____   ___s at them to hide the fact that they ___ him.

_____vivacious_____   7–8. Among her close friends, my sister is known as a really ___ woman,
_____introvert_____   energetic and bubbly. But she often seems like a(n) ___ around people she
                             doesn't know well.

_____jeopardize_____   9–10. I told Seth he would ___ his chances of getting a date for the dance if he
_____smug_____   waited until the last minute to ask someone. But he was ___ enough to think
                             that any girl he asked would be happy to break a date with someone else to
                             go to the dance with him.

Final Check: *Cal and His Sisters*

Here is a final opportunity for you to strengthen your knowledge of the ten words. First read the following
selection carefully. Then fill in each blank with a word from the box at the top of the previous page.
(Context clues will help you figure out which word goes in which blank.) Use each word once.

I've never met (1)_____sibling_____s who are less alike
than Cal and his sisters, Margo and Tina. First, they are different
in their approach to school. All of them get good grades, but
while Margo and Tina don't brag about their intelligence, Cal
does. When he gets straight A's, he flaunts° his report card and
(2)_____sneer_____s at classmates who haven't done
as well. Naturally, being so (3)_____smug_____ about his
grades (4)_____jeopardize_____s his chances of having many
friends, and he's often by himself. Margo is a true extrovert°—
she's completely (5)_____devoid_____ of shyness. She's so
(6)_____vivacious_____ that people naturally flock around
her, and she's constantly busy with movie dates, study sessions with
friends, and parties. Nothing seems to (7)_____intimidate_____
Margo. She will walk into a room full of strangers, boldly strike up a
conversation, and leave an hour later with several new best friends. Conversely°, Tina is usually so quiet that
people barely notice she is in the room. However, Tina is not a complete (8)_____introvert_____.
She's not shy; she just puts her energy into having a few close friends, rather than a crowd of acquaintances.
I actually think Tina is the most interesting of the three. While Cal is devoted mostly to himself and his
intelligence, and Margo is busy being popular, Tina is altruistic° and cares deeply about other people. It
(9)_____infuriate_____s her to know that there are hungry, homeless people living in her own city,
and she quietly volunteers some of her time to helping them. She once (10)_____implore_____(e)d
Cal and Margo to get involved in the same kind of work, but neither of them had any interest in becoming
affiliated° with her project.

Scores   Sentence Check 2 _____%   Final Check _____%

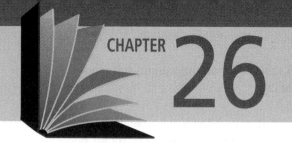

condone	furtive
contemplate	gape
feasible	pathetic
feign	precedent
fiscal	punitive

Ten Words in Context

In the space provided, write the letter of the meaning closest to that of each **boldfaced** word. Use the context of the sentences to help you figure out each word's meaning.

1 condone
(kən-dōn′)
-*verb*

- I cannot **condone** Elaine's smoking in public. It threatens other people's health.
- Teachers may overlook it when you're three minutes late. But they are not going to **condone** your walking into class a half hour late.

_A_ *Condone* means   A. to excuse.   B. to recall.   C. to punish.

2 contemplate
(kŏn′təm-plāt′)
-*verb*

- Because Ben hadn't studied for the test, he **contemplated** cheating. He quickly realized, however, that the eagle-eyed teacher would spot him.
- Whenever Anne's husband drank too much, she would **contemplate** separation, but then she would feel guilty for thinking about leaving a sick man.

_A_ *Contemplate* means   A. to consider.   B. to pretend.   C. to avoid.

3 feasible
(fē′zə-bəl)
-*adjective*

- It isn't **feasible** for me to work full time and keep the house clean unless someone helps me with the cleaning chores.
- Maya told her supervisor, "It just isn't **feasible** for this staff to do the work of the two people who were fired. You need to hire more people."

_C_ *Feasible* means   A. wrong.   B. legal.   C. possible.

4 feign
(fān)
-*verb*

- Since I had heard about my surprise party, I had to **feign** shock when everyone yelled, "Surprise!"
- You can **feign** a head cold by pretending you're too stuffed up to pronounce an *l, n,* or *m.* Try it by saying, "I have a code id by dose."

_C_ *Feign* means   A. to wish for.   B. to prove.   C. to fake.

5 fiscal
(fĭs′kəl)
-*adjective*

- The gift shop closed because of **fiscal** problems. It simply didn't make enough money to cover its expenses.
- Some states have passed laws allowing child-support payments to be taken directly from the paychecks of divorced parents who ignore their **fiscal** responsibility to their children.

_B_ *Fiscal* means   A. emotional.   B. financial.   C. unfair.

6 furtive
(fûr′tĭv)
-*adjective*

- At the football game, a guard in the stands noticed the **furtive** movement of a thief's hand toward a spectator's pocket.
- According to experts, teenagers who are **furtive** about where they are going and with whom may be involved with drugs.

_A_ *Furtive* means   A. sneaky.   B. dependable.   C. serious.

7 gape
(gāp)
-verb

● Everyone stopped to **gape** at the odd-looking sculpture in front of the library.

● Because drivers slowed down to **gape** at an accident in the southbound lanes, northbound traffic was backed up for miles.

_C_ *Gape* means   A. to yell.   B. to appreciate.   C. to stare.

8 pathetic
(pə-thĕt′ĭk)
-adjective

● That plumber's work was **pathetic**. Not only does the faucet still drip, but now the pipe is leaking.

● Health care in some areas of the world is **pathetic**. People are dying of diseases that are easily treatable with modern medicine.

_B_ *Pathetic* means   A. ordinary.   B. miserable.   C. expensive.

9 precedent
(prĕs′ĭ-dĕnt)
-noun

● When Jean's employer gave her three months off after her baby was born, a **precedent** was set for anyone else in the company who became a parent.

● To set a **precedent**, the teacher gave the student who stole the exam an F for the entire course. "Others will think twice before they do the same," he explained.

_C_ *Precedent* means   A. a question.   B. a delay.   C. a model.

10 punitive
(pyōō′nĭ-tĭv)
-adjective

● Judge Starn is especially **punitive** with drunken drivers, giving every one of them a jail term.

● Many parents find that reward is a better basis for teaching children than **punitive** action is.

_A_ *Punitive* means   A. punishing.   B. forgiving.   C. uneven.

Matching Words with Definitions

Following are definitions of the ten words. Clearly write or print each word next to its definition. The sentences above and on the previous page will help you decide on the meaning of each word.

1. _____feasible_____   Possible; able to be done

2. _____furtive_____   Done or behaving so as not to be noticed; secret

3. _____gape_____   To stare in wonder or amazement, often with one's mouth wide open

4. _____precedent_____   Anything that may serve as an example in dealing with later similar circumstances

5. _____condone_____   To forgive or overlook

6. _____punitive_____   Giving or involving punishment; punishing

7. _____fiscal_____   Financial

8. _____contemplate_____   To think about seriously

9. _____pathetic_____   Pitifully inadequate or unsuccessful

10. _____feign_____   To pretend; give a false show of

CAUTION: Do not go any further until you are sure the above answers are correct. Then you can use the definitions to help you in the following practices. Your goal is eventually to know the words well enough so that you don't need to check the definitions at all.

Sentence Check 1

Using the answer line provided, complete each item below with the correct word from the box. Use each word once.

A. condone	B. contemplate	C. feasible	D. feign	E. fiscal
F. furtive	G. gape	H. pathetic	I. precedent	J. punitive

___gape___   1. Disabled people don't like others to ___ at them. Instead of a stare, a simple smile would be appreciated.

___contemplate___   2. From time to time, I ___ attending business school, but so far I've made no firm decision.

___precedent___   3. Lawyers can strengthen a case by finding a useful ___ among previous similar cases.

___feasible___   4. It's not ___ for me to attend two weddings in the same afternoon, so I'll have to choose between them.

___condone___   5. The principal does not ___ hitting students. He believes that every problem has a nonviolent solution.

___fiscal___   6. At the low-cost clinic, Clayton had to give evidence of his ___ situation, such as a tax form or current pay stub, before he could receive treatment.

___furtive___   7. The people on the elevator didn't want to stare at the patch on my eye, but several took ___ glances.

___pathetic___   8. Mr. Hall's living conditions were ___. There was no heat or electricity in his apartment, and the walls were crumbling.

___feign___   9. When I gave my oral report in class, I tried to ___ confidence, but my shaking legs revealed my nervousness.

___punitive___   10. My mother wasn't usually ___, but one day I pushed her too far, and she said, "If you do that one more time, I will send you to your room for the rest of your adolescence."

NOTE: Now check your answers to these items by turning to page 179. Going over the answers carefully will help you prepare for the next two practices, for which answers are not given.

Sentence Check 2

Using the answer lines provided, complete each item below with **two** words from the box. Use each word once.

___feasible___
___fiscal___   1–2. "Would it be ___ for us to buy a new copy machine?" Hal asked at the office budget meeting. The boss replied, "Unfortunately, our ___ situation is too tight. That purchase would deplete° our funds and create a deficit° in our budget."

___punitive___
___contemplate___   3–4. Some parents take only ___ measures when children misbehave. They never take time to ___ the benefits of a gentler approach. However, benign° encouragement is often more effective than punishment.

gape
pathetic

5–6. Several passersby stopped to ___ at the homeless man and his ___ shelter, made of cardboard and a torn blanket. The poignant° sight moved one woman to go to a restaurant and buy a meal for the man.

condone
furtive

7–8. The fourth-grade teacher said, "I will not ___ any ___ behavior in my class. Rita, please stop passing notes under your desk to Ellen."

precedent
feign

9–10. The ___ was set many years ago: When the winner of a beauty contest is announced, the runner-up ___s happiness for the winner, despite the fact that she is quite devoid° of happiness at the moment.

Final Check: *Shoplifter*

Here is a final opportunity for you to strengthen your knowledge of the ten words. First read the following selection carefully. Then fill in each blank with a word from the box at the top of the previous page. (Context clues will help you figure out which word goes in which blank.) Use each word once.

Valerie took a (1)_____ _furtive_ _____ glance around her. When it seemed that no one was watching, she stuffed a blue shirt into the bottom of her purse and darted out of the women's department. She walked slowly around the shoe department for a while and then left the store.

"Stop! You! Stop!" shouted a guard, who seemed to appear from nowhere. Then another man in street clothes grabbed her purse and pulled out the shirt.

"But . . . but . . . it's not mine. I don't know how it got there," Valerie cried.

The two men just looked at each other and laughed at the blatant° lie. The guard said, "That's what all shoplifters say. People steal without taking time to (2)_____ _contemplate_ _____ the possible results. Then when they're caught, they loudly (3)_____ _feign_ _____ innocence."

As the guard began to phone the police, Valerie implored° the men, "Please don't press charges. Please. This is the first time I've ever done anything like this, and I'll never do it again."

The men laughed again. "Your argument is (4)_____ _pathetic_ _____," the man in street clothes sneered°. "It's everyone's first time. Our store has a policy on shoplifters: It's mandatory° for us to press charges, even if it's the first offense. We can't set a bad (5)_____ _precedent_ _____ by letting a shoplifter go, as if we (6)_____ _condone_ _____(e)d such crimes."

"That's right," said the guard. "Shoplifting is all too prevalent° in our store. This shirt costs only twenty dollars, but the twenties add up. Our (7)_____ _fiscal_ _____ officer reported a loss of about $150,000 worth of merchandise to shoplifters last year. So it simply isn't (8)_____ _feasible_ _____ to let you walk away. Unfortunately, we have no choice but to take (9)_____ _punitive_ _____ action."

Soon Valerie was led to the police car. She covered her face as other shoppers stopped to (10)_____ _gape_ _____ at the lovely young woman, an unlikely-looking criminal.

Scores	Sentence Check 2 _____%	Final Check _____%

cryptic	inhibition
deficient	ironic
depict	rupture
detrimental	saturate
implicit	vindictive

Ten Words in Context

In the space provided, write the letter of the meaning closest to that of each **boldfaced** word. Use the context of the sentences to help you figure out each word's meaning.

1 cryptic
(krĭp′tĭk)
-adjective

- Whenever I ask Tomas what's happening in his life, he always gives the same **cryptic** reply: "It's a green world, my friend."
- Next to the dead woman's body was a **cryptic** note that said, "Not now."

_B_ *Cryptic* means   A. cruel.   B. puzzling.   C. humorous.

2 deficient
(dĭ-fĭsh′ənt)
-adjective

- When people have too little iron in their blood, it sometimes means that their diet is also **deficient** in iron.
- Gil's manners are **deficient**. For example, I've never heard him thank anyone for anything.

_A_ *Deficient* means   A. lacking.   B. sensitive.   C. increasing.

3 depict
(dĭ-pĭkt′)
-verb

- The painting **depicts** a typical nineteenth-century summer day in the park.
- Harriet Beecher Stowe's novel *Uncle Tom's Cabin* **depicted** the cruelty of slavery so forcefully that the book helped to begin the Civil War.

_B_ *Depict* means   A. to hide.   B. to show.   C. to predict.

4 detrimental
(dĕ′trə-mĕn′təl)
-adjective

- Do you think all television is **detrimental** to children, or are some programs a positive influence on them?
- The gases from automobiles and factories have been so **detrimental** to the environment that some of the damage may be permanent.

_C_ *Detrimental* means   A. useful.   B. new.   C. damaging.

5 implicit
(ĭm-plĭs′ĭt)
-adjective

- When the gangster growled, "I'm sure you want your family to stay healthy," Harris understood the **implicit** threat.
- Although it's never been said, there's an **implicit** understanding that Carla will be promoted when Earl finally retires.

_C_ *Implicit* means   A. playful.   B. modern.   C. unspoken.

6 inhibition
(ĭn′hə-bĭsh′ən)
-noun

- A two-year-old has no **inhibitions** about running around naked.
- Sarah's family is openly affectionate, with no **inhibitions** about hugging or kissing in public.

_A_ *Inhibition* means   A. an inner block.   B. a habit.   C. a purpose.

7 ironic
(ī-rŏn′ĭk)
-adjective

● It's **ironic** that Loretta is such a strict mother, because she was certainly wild in her youth.

● "The Gift of the Magi" is a short story with an **ironic** twist: A woman sells her long hair to buy a chain for her husband's watch, while her husband sells his watch to buy ornaments for her hair.

A *Ironic* means   A. unexpected.   B. inadequate.   C. reasonable.

8 rupture
(rŭp′chər)
-verb

● If the dam were to **rupture**, the town would disappear under many feet of water.

● The bulge in the baby's stomach was caused by a muscle wall that had **ruptured** and would have to be repaired.

C *Rupture* means   A. to heal.   B. to exist.   C. to come apart.

9 saturate
(săch′ə-rāt′)
-verb

● Most people like their cereal crunchy, but Teresa lets hers sit until the milk has **saturated** every piece.

● Studying history for three hours **saturated** my brain—I couldn't have absorbed one more bit of information.

C *Saturate* means   A. to protect.   B. to empty.   C. to fill.

10 vindictive
(vĭn-dĭk′tĭv)
-adjective

● If a woman refuses to date my older brother, he becomes **vindictive**. One way he takes revenge is to forward her all his junk e-mail.

● After she was given two weeks' notice, the **vindictive** employee intentionally infected all the office computers with a virus.

B *Vindictive* means   A. sympathetic.   B. spiteful.   C. puzzling.

Matching Words with Definitions

Following are definitions of the ten words. Clearly write or print each word next to its definition. The sentences above and on the previous page will help you decide on the meaning of each word.

1. _____inhibition_____ A holding back or blocking of some action, feeling, or thought

2. _____cryptic_____ Having a vague or hidden meaning; mysterious

3. _____implicit_____ Suggested but not directly expressed; unstated, but able to be understood

4. _____vindictive_____ Inclined to seek revenge; vengeful

5. _____depict_____ To represent in pictures or words; describe

6. _____rupture_____ To burst or break apart

7. _____deficient_____ Lacking something essential; inadequate; insufficient

8. _____saturate_____ To soak or fill as much as possible

9. _____detrimental_____ Harmful; causing damage

10. _____ironic_____ Opposite to what might be expected

CAUTION: Do not go any further until you are sure the above answers are correct. Then you can use the definitions to help you in the following practices. Your goal is eventually to know the words well enough so that you don't need to check the definitions at all.

Sentence Check 1

Using the answer line provided, complete each item below with the correct word from the box. Use each word once.

A. cryptic	B. deficient	C. depict	D. detrimental	E. implicit
F. inhibition	G. ironic	H. rupture	I. saturate	J. vindictive

deficient   1. A person can be intelligent and yet be ___ in common sense.

rupture   2. When the pressure in the gas pipe became too great, the pipe ___(e)d.

ironic   3. Isn't it ___ that the richest man in town won the million-dollar lottery?

detrimental   4. Even something as healthful as vitamins can be ___ to your health when taken in very large amounts.

inhibition   5. Becky's usual lack of ___ was evident the day she came to class barefoot.

depict   6. In the novel *Oliver Twist*, Charles Dickens ___s life in an English orphanage as truly pathetic°, with little food and no love.

vindictive   7. The clans, or families, of ancient Scotland were extremely ___. If anyone from another clan harmed one of their members, the others would take full revenge.

cryptic   8. The fifth-grade assignment was written in double talk. Everyone laughed as the students tried to make out the teacher's ___ message.

saturate   9. The aroma of Gretchen's perfume so ___(e)d the air in the car that Steve coughed and rolled down a window.

implicit   10. Although it's not written in teachers' contracts, there is a(n) ___ understanding that teachers will spend time preparing lessons and responding to students' work.

NOTE: Now check your answers to these items by turning to page 179. Going over the answers carefully will help you prepare for the next two practices, for which answers are not given.

Sentence Check 2

Using the answer lines provided, complete each item below with **two** words from the box. Use each word once.

rupture
saturate   1–2. Water-balloon fights are fun until a balloon ___s against your clothes, and they get ___(e)d with cold water.

cryptic
depict   3–4. Most viewers find the painting, with its dozens of dots on a white background, to be ___. However, it's possible to figure out what the painting ___s by mentally connecting the dots.

vindictive
detrimental   5–6. I feel it's a waste of energy to retaliate° when someone has injured me, but my sister is always trying to get even with people. Her ___ attitude is ___ to her relationships with family and friends.

_____ ironic _____

_____ implicit _____

7–8. It's ___ that the book *Live Simply on Little Money* has made the author wealthy, since a(n) ___ message of the book is that the author himself requires little money.

_____ inhibition _____

_____ deficient _____

9–10. Gerry feels people should "lose their ___s" and do whatever they feel like doing, but I think people who are totally ___ in self-control have poor manners.

Final Check: *A Nutty Newspaper Office*

Here is a final opportunity for you to strengthen your knowledge of the ten words. First read the following selection carefully. Then fill in each blank with a word from the box at the top of the previous page. (Context clues will help you figure out which word goes in which blank.) Use each word once.

My therapist says it's (1)_____ detrimental _____ to my mental health to keep my thoughts bottled up inside of me, so I'll drop all (2)_____ inhibition _____s and tell you about the newspaper office where I work.

Let me attempt to describe my managing editor first. It's sort of (3)_____ ironic _____ that Ed is in communications because I've never met anyone harder to talk to. Although he's a proponent° of clear expression, Ed communicates as unclearly as anyone I know. For example, if I say, "How are you doing today, Ed?" he'll give me some (4)_____ cryptic _____ response such as "The tidal pools of time are catching up with me." I used to think there might be some deep wisdom (5)_____ implicit _____ in Ed's incoherent° statements, but now I just think he's a little eccentric°.

Then there's Seymour, our sportswriter. Seymour is perfectly normal except that he has unexplained fits of crying two or three times a week. In the middle of a conversation about the baseball playoffs or the next heavyweight title fight, Seymour suddenly goes into a frenzy° of crying and (6)_____ saturate _____s handfuls of Kleenex with his tears.

Now, I don't mean to (7)_____ depict _____ our office as a totally depressing place. It is not entirely (8)_____ deficient _____ in excitement, but even our excitement is bizarre°. It is usually provided by Jan, a (9)_____ vindictive _____ typesetter who, whenever she feels injured by Ed, takes revenge in some horrible but entertaining way. One of her favorite types of reprisal° is sneaking fictional items about him into the society column. I'll never forget the time Ed was in the hospital after his appendix (10)_____ rupture _____(e)d. He almost broke his stitches when he read that he was taking a vacation at a nudist colony. The article infuriated° him so much that he probably would have sued the newspaper for libel°—if he didn't work there himself.

| Scores | Sentence Check 2 _____% | Final Check _____% |

CHAPTER 28

constrict	habitat
exhaustive	pragmatic
fallible	pretentious
formulate	reconcile
genial	vile

Ten Words in Context

In the space provided, write the letter of the meaning closest to that of each **boldfaced** word. Use the context of the sentences to help you figure out each word's meaning.

1 constrict
(kən-strĭkt′)
-verb

- The summer highway construction will **constrict** traffic by confining it to only two lanes.
- For centuries in China, girls' feet were **constricted** with binding to keep them from growing to normal size. Women's feet were considered most attractive if they were less than four inches long.

_C_ *Constrict* means   A. to expand.   B. to repair.   C. to squeeze.

2 exhaustive
(ĭg-zô′stĭv)
-adjective

- Don't buy a used car without putting it through an **exhaustive** inspection. Check every detail, from hood to trunk.
- My teacher recommended an **exhaustive** thousand-page biography of Freud, but who has time to read such a thorough account?

_B_ *Exhaustive* means   A. smooth.   B. detailed.   C. narrow.

3 fallible
(făl′ə-bəl)
-adjective

- "I know we all are **fallible**," the boss told his workers. "But do you have to make so many of your mistakes on company time?"
- When they are little, kids think their parents can do no wrong; but when they become **teenagers**, their parents suddenly seem fallible.

_C_ *Fallible* means   A. optimistic.   B. friendly.   C. imperfect.

4 formulate
(fôr′myə-lāt′)
-verb

- The author first **formulated** an outline of his plot and then began writing his mystery.
- Before stepping into his boss's office, Toshio had carefully **formulated** his case for a raise.

_A_ *Formulate* means   A. to develop.   B. to question.   C. to accept.

5 genial
(jēn′yəl)
-adjective

- I was worried that my grandmother's treatment at the nursing home might be harsh, so I was relieved when the nurses and aides turned out to be very **genial**.
- Stacey found her first dance instructor so rude and unpleasant that she changed to a more **genial** one.

_C_ *Genial* means   A. good-looking.   B. practical.   C. good-natured.

6 habitat
(hăb′ĭ-tăt)
-noun

- Many people believe that wild animals should be allowed to remain in their natural **habitats** and not be captured and put in zoos.
- Mosses can live in a large variety of humid **habitats**, from very cold to very hot.

_C_ *Habitat* means   A. a pattern.   B. a plan.   C. a territory.

7 pragmatic
(prăg-măt′ĭk)
-adjective

- We always called my sister "Practical Polly" because she was the most **pragmatic** member of the family.
- When Vince was single, he spent most of his money on travel. Now that he has a family to support, he must spend his money in more **pragmatic** ways.

A *Pragmatic* means   A. sensible.   B. patient.   C. pleasant.

8 pretentious
(prē-tĕn′shəs)
-adjective

- Dana's classmates don't like her because she's so **pretentious**. It's hard to like someone who acts as if she knows it all.
- My aunt marked her husband's grave with a large, **pretentious** monument, as though he were a member of a royal family.

B *Pretentious* means   A. overly imaginative.   B. important-seeming.   C. cruel.

9 reconcile
(rĕk′ən-sīl′)
-verb

- When my grandfather died, we worked hard to **reconcile** Grandma to the fact that he was really gone.
- After his third wreck in six months, Ahmed **reconciled** himself to living somewhere along a bus line and doing without a car.

A *Reconcile to* means   A. to bring to accept.   B. to frighten about.   C. to hide from.

10 vile
(vīl)
-adjective

- My sister loves a certain cheese that has the **vile** odor of something that fell off a garbage truck.
- When I finally get around to cleaning out the refrigerator, I always find some **vile** moldy leftovers at the back of a shelf.

C *Vile* means   A. threatening.   B. natural.   C. nasty.

Matching Words with Definitions

Following are definitions of the ten words. Clearly write or print each word next to its definition. The sentences above and on the previous page will help you decide on the meaning of each word.

1. _____reconcile_____ To bring (oneself or someone else) to accept

2. _____habitat_____ The natural environment of an animal or a plant

3. _____pretentious_____ Making a show of excellence or importance, especially when undeserved

4. _____fallible_____ Capable of making an error

5. _____constrict_____ To make smaller or narrower, as by squeezing or shrinking

6. _____exhaustive_____ Covering all possible details; complete; thorough

7. _____genial_____ Friendly, pleasant, and kindly

8. _____vile_____ Offensive to the senses, feelings, or thoughts; disgusting

9. _____formulate_____ To plan or express in an orderly way

10. _____pragmatic_____ Practical

CAUTION: Do not go any further until you are sure the above answers are correct. Then you can use the definitions to help you in the following practices. Your goal is eventually to know the words well enough so that you don't need to check the definitions at all.

Sentence Check 1

Using the answer line provided, complete each item below with the correct word from the box. Use each word once.

A. **constrict**	B. **exhaustive**	C. **fallible**	D. **formulate**	E. **genial**
F. **habitat**	G. **pragmatic**	H. **pretentious**	I. **reconcile**	J. **vile**

_____vile_____ 1. The local diner serves the world's most ___ beef stew, full of big globs of fat.

_____genial_____ 2. Why is Debra acting so unfriendly today? She's usually so ___.

_____reconcile_____ 3. My mother was forced to ___ herself to my independence when I moved into my own apartment.

_____constrict_____ 4. Bright light ___s the pupils of our eyes, letting in less light. Darkness makes them wider, letting in more light.

_____formulate_____ 5. My supervisor told me that if I wished to work on an independent project, I should first ___ a detailed plan of my idea.

_____exhaustive_____ 6. For her term paper on orchids, Waneta did ___ research, covering every aspect of the flower's growth and marketing.

_____Pretentious_____ 7. ___ about his intelligence, Norm tries to impress people by using big words.

_____habitat_____ 8. Children's stories sometimes mistakenly show penguins at the North Pole. The birds' ___ is actually near the South Pole.

_____pragmatic_____ 9. "It would be more ___," my brother said, "if you went to the grocery once a week for a larger order rather than going daily for just a few items."

_____fallible_____ 10. When the auto mechanic said, "Well, I'm ___ like everyone else," I responded, "Yes, but your mistake almost got me flattened by a truck."

NOTE: Now check your answers to these items by turning to page 179. Going over the answers carefully will help you prepare for the next two practices, for which answers are not given.

Sentence Check 2

Using the answer lines provided, complete each item below with **two** words from the box. Use each word once.

_____Reconcile_____
_____fallible_____
1–2. "You want me to be perfect, but that's impossible!" I cried. "___ yourself to the fact that every one of us is ___." It wasn't until then that my mother realized how detrimental° her criticism had been to our relationship.

_____formulate_____
_____habitat_____
3–4. Wildlife experts ___(e)d a plan to preserve what little remains of the gorilla's natural ___. Continued loss of that territory will jeopardize° these magnificent animals and could even result in the demise° of the species.

_____pragmatic_____
_____vile_____
5–6. My uncle was not at all ___ about fiscal° matters. He would spend household money on videotapes and ___-smelling cigars and leave the family without any extra cash.

_____exhaustive_____   7–8. When our pet python escaped, we quickly made a(n) ___ search throughout
_____constrict_____   the house and grounds. We found him wrapped around our dog, about to ___
                            the poor mutt to death.

_____genial_____   9–10. At the sales seminar, employees were taught to be ___ with customers and
_____pretentious_____   never to seem ___, no matter how much they knew. Customers like warm,
                             amiable° salespeople, not ones who show off.

Final Check: *Roughing It*

Here is a final opportunity for you to strengthen your knowledge of the ten words. First read the following selection carefully. Then fill in each blank with a word from the box at the top of the previous page. (Context clues will help you figure out which word goes in which blank.) Use each word once.

"Whose brilliant idea was this, anyway?" Sara asked. "If people were intended to sleep on the ground and cook over a fire, we wouldn't have beds and microwave ovens."

"Stop complaining," Emily said. "At least *you've* got on dry clothes. You didn't end up walking through some (1)_____vile_____ mud because your canoe overturned. And you didn't have a(n) (2)_____pretentious_____ partner who claimed to know everything about canoeing but actually didn't know enough to steer around a rock."

"So I made a mistake," George said. "We're all (3)_____fallible_____."

"Well," Emily responded, "your mistake has lost us our tent. And our sleeping bags and clothes are saturated° with muddy water."

Then Doug spoke up. "It's no big deal. We didn't plan for this, so let's improvise°. Sara and I will lend you clothes, and you two can squeeze into our tent."

"Squeeze is right, " said Emily. "Four in one tent won't work—it just isn't feasible°. We'll be so (4)_____constrict_____(e)d that we won't be able to exhale."

"It's your choice," said Doug. "Decide if you want to be in a crowded tent or sleep out in this wild-animal (5)_____habitat_____."

Sara couldn't resist adding, "If you had just listened to me this time and had been a bit more (6)_____pragmatic_____ when planning for this trip, we wouldn't be in such a mess. You would have written a(n) (7)_____exhaustive_____ list of what we would need, from A to Z. Then you would have (8)_____formulate_____(e)d a clear plan for who would take what. Then we wouldn't be out here with two corkscrews but no plastic to wrap our belongings in."

"Let's just stop complaining before this degenerates° into a shouting match. Instead, let's try to be a little more (9)_____genial_____ with one another," said Doug. "Right now, we need to (10)_____reconcile_____ ourselves to our imperfect situation and not let it detract° so much from our vacation that we forget to have a good time."

Scores	Sentence Check 2 _____%	Final Check _____%

Enter your scores above and in the **Vocabulary Performance Chart** on the inside back cover of the book.

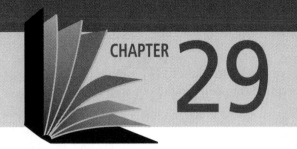

avid	mediate
dwindle	muted
esteem	nurture
evoke	pacify
legacy	transient

Ten Words in Context

In the space provided, write the letter of the meaning closest to that of each **boldfaced** word. Use the context of the sentences to help you figure out each word's meaning.

1 avid
(ăv'ĭd)
-*adjective*

● Suki, an **avid** reader, enjoys nothing more than a good science-fiction novel.

● Artie is such an **avid** sports fan that he has two televisions tuned to different sporting events so he doesn't miss any action.

B *Avid* means   A. likable.   B. devoted.   C. helpful.

2 dwindle
(dwĭn'dəl)
-*verb*

● As the number of leaves on the tree **dwindled**, the number on the ground increased.

● Chewing nicotine gum helped Doreen's craving for cigarettes to **dwindle**. She smoked fewer and fewer cigarettes each day until she quit altogether.

C *Dwindle* means   A. to make sense.   B. to drop suddenly.   C. to decrease.

3 esteem
(ĕ-stēm')
-*noun*

● When Mr. Bauer retired after coaching basketball for thirty years, his admiring students gave him a gold whistle as a sign of their **esteem**.

● The critics had such **esteem** for the play that they voted it "Best Drama of the Year."

B *Esteem* means   A. concern.   B. admiration.   C. curiosity.

4 evoke
(ē-vōk')
-*verb*

● Music can **evoke** powerful feelings. A sweet violin solo often moves its listeners to tears.

● The smells of cider and pumpkin pie **evoke** thoughts of autumn.

A *Evoke* means   A. to bring out.   B. to shelter.   C. to follow.

5 legacy
(lĕg'ə-sē)
-*noun*

● Ana's great-grandfather, grandmother, and mother were all musicians. She must have inherited their **legacy** of musical talent because she's an excellent piano and guitar player.

● One of the richest **legacies** that my mother handed down to me is the love of nature. I've inherited her interests in growing flowers and in hiking.

C *Legacy* means   A. a memory.   B. a high hope.   C. an inherited gift.

6 mediate
(mē'dē-āt')
-*verb*

● My father refused to **mediate** quarrels between my sister and me. He would say, "Settle your own fights."

● Each of the farmers claimed the stream was part of his property. Finally, they agreed to let the town council **mediate** their conflict.

B *Mediate* means   A. to avoid.   B. to settle.   C. to observe.

7 muted
(myoo'təd)
-adjective

- When I put in my earplugs, the yelling from the next apartment becomes **muted** enough so that it no longer disturbs me.
- The artist used **muted** rather than bright colors, giving the painting a quiet, peaceful tone.

A *Muted* means   A. soft.   B. temporary.   C. boring.

8 nurture
(nûr'chər)
-verb

- Although I often forget to water or feed my plants, my sister carefully **nurtures** her many ferns and violets.
- Many animals feed and protect their babies, but female fish, in general, do not **nurture** their young. The female only lays the eggs, which are guarded by the male until they hatch.

C *Nurture* means   A. to inspect.   B. to seek out.   C. to care for.

9 pacify
(păs'ə-fī')
-verb

- When I'm feeling nervous or upset, I often **pacify** myself with a soothing cup of mint tea.
- Not only did I anger Roberta by calling her boyfriend "a creep," but I failed to **pacify** her with my note of apology: "I'm sorry I called Mel a creep. It's not always wise to tell the truth."

C *Pacify* means   A. to amuse.   B. to encourage.   C. to soothe.

10 transient
(trăn'shənt)
-adjective

- The drug's dangers include both permanent brain damage and **transient** side effects, such as temporarily blurred vision.
- Julia wants a lasting relationship, but Rico seems interested in only a **transient** one.

B *Transient* means   A. dull.   B. short-lived.   C. hard to notice.

Matching Words with Definitions

Following are definitions of the ten words. Clearly write or print each word next to its definition. The sentences above and on the previous page will help you decide on the meaning of each word.

1. _____muted_____ Softened; toned down; made less intense

2. _____transient_____ Temporary; passing soon or quickly

3. _____avid_____ Enthusiastic, devoted; eager

4. _____pacify_____ To make calm or peaceful

5. _____evoke_____ To draw forth, as a mental image or a feeling

6. _____dwindle_____ To gradually lessen or shrink

7. _____mediate_____ To settle (a conflict) by acting as a go-between

8. _____esteem_____ High regard; respect; favorable opinion

9. _____nurture_____ To promote development by providing nourishment, support, and protection

10. _____legacy_____ Something handed down from people who have come before

CAUTION: Do not go any further until you are sure the above answers are correct. Then you can use the definitions to help you in the following practices. Your goal is eventually to know the words well enough so that you don't need to check the definitions at all.

Sentence Check 1

Using the answer line provided, complete each item below with the correct word from the box. Use each word once.

A. avid	B. dwindle	C. esteem	D. evoke	E. legacy
F. mediate	G. muted	H. nurture	I. pacify	J. transient

_____pacify_____ 1. When my newborn nephew starts to scream, his parents ___ him by rocking him and singing softly.

_____evoke_____ 2. The photos in my album ___ many fond memories of my high-school friends.

_____dwindle_____ 3. If you study too long at one sitting, your concentration will eventually begin to ___.

_____muted_____ 4. At the party, Cara and I kept our conversation ___ so that no one would overhear us.

_____nurture_____ 5. You must ___ a child with love and respect as well as with food and shelter.

_____transient_____ 6. Part of the charm of spring is that it's ___. It comes and goes so quickly that we can't wait for its return.

_____esteem_____ 7. To show his ___ for her singing, the talent agent sent Mary flowers after she performed in a local theater.

_____avid_____ 8. My cousin Bobby is the most ___ collector I know. He collects almost anything, from baseball cards to beer cans.

_____legacy_____ 9. Shakespeare's plays, a priceless ___ from the sixteenth and seventeenth centuries, have been enjoyed by generation after generation.

_____mediate_____ 10. Rather than go to court, Mr. Hillman and the owner of the gas station agreed to have a lawyer ___ their disagreement.

NOTE: Now check your answers to these items by turning to page 179. Going over the answers carefully will help you prepare for the next two practices, for which answers are not given.

Sentence Check 2

Using the answer lines provided, complete each item below with **two** words from the box. Use each word once.

_____esteem_____
_____transient_____ 1–2. Becky's ___ for Gerald turned out to be ___. She discovered that he used drugs and could not condone° his habit, so she broke up with him.

_____avid_____
_____dwindle_____ 3–4. Leo is such a(n) ___ chef that his enthusiasm for cooking never ___s. He's been known to cook with great zeal° for ten straight hours.

_____muted_____
_____pacify_____ 5–6. Loud music upsets our canary, but ___ tones ___ her.

_____nurture_____   7–8. It is necessary to ___ a human infant because it is the biological ___ of
_____legacy_____   newborn mammals to be unable to survive on their own. Parental care is
                                  indispensable°.

_____mediate_____   9–10. In the Bible, King Solomon ___s a dispute between two women, each of
_____evoke_____   whom contends° that a child is her own. To end the impasse°, the king
                                  suggests that the child be cut in two. This thought ___s horror in one of the
                                  women. The king then knows she is the real mother.

Final Check: *Getting Scared*

Here is a final opportunity for you to strengthen your knowledge of the ten words. First read the following selection carefully. Then fill in each blank with a word from the box at the top of the previous page. (Context clues will help you figure out which word goes in which blank.) Use each word once.

Do you remember trying to scare yourself and everybody else when you were a kid? For instance, maybe you were a(n) (1)_____avid_____ roller-coaster rider, closing your eyes and screaming and loving every minute. Afterward, you would (2)_____pacify_____ your still nervous stomach by quietly sipping an ice-cold Coke. If a short roller-coaster ride gave you too (3)_____transient_____ a thrill, there was always the long-term fear of a horror movie. If the horrors it depicted° were vile° enough, you might be scared about going to bed for the next three months.

And remember popping out from behind corners and yelling "Boo!" at your brother? The fight that followed ("You didn't scare me one bit." "Did too." "Did not." "Did too.") would go on until a grown-up (4)_____mediate_____(e)d the conflict. (Parents always seemed to be there to settle disputes among siblings° or to (5)_____nurture_____ and reassure you at times when you needed support.)

At other times, you and your friends probably sat around a campfire late at night, engaging in your favorite nocturnal° activity—telling ghost stories. Thrilled with the horror of it all, you spoke in voices so (6)_____muted_____ they were almost whispers. The storyteller who gained the most (7)_____esteem_____ was the one who could (8)_____evoke_____ the greatest terror in others. If anybody's fear started to (9)_____dwindle_____, this expert would build it up again with the most effective story in the campfire repertoire°, the story of the ghost in the outhouse, a (10)_____legacy_____ handed down from older brothers and sisters to younger ones. This traumatic° story always made you so scared that you needed to go to the outhouse. But fearing the ghost there, how could you?

Scores	Sentence Check 2 _____%	Final Check _____%

Enter your scores above and in the **Vocabulary Performance Chart** on the inside back cover of the book.

aloof	longevity
ambivalent	magnitude
augment	mundane
dispel	obscure
explicit	render

Ten Words in Context

In the space provided, write the letter of the meaning closest to that of each **boldfaced** word. Use the context of the sentences to help you figure out each word's meaning.

1 aloof
(ə-lōof′)
-adjective

● Some people say that the British are **aloof**, but the British people I've met seem warm and open.

● I knew that Tyrell was upset with me about something because he was **aloof** even when I tried to be friendly.

_C_ *Aloof* means   A. motivated.   B. lazy.   C. cold.

2 ambivalent
(ăm-bĭv′ə-lənt)
-adjective

● "Because I'm **ambivalent** about marriage," Earl said, "I keep swinging back and forth between wanting to set the date and wanting to break off my engagement."

● I'm **ambivalent** about my counselor. I appreciate her desire to be helpful, but I dislike her efforts to interfere in my life.

_B_ *Ambivalent* means   A. meaning well.   B. having mixed feelings.   C. experienced.

3 augment
(ôg-mĕnt′)
-verb

● Why are women so willing to **augment** their height by wearing high heels when this kind of footwear is so bad for their feet?

● Because Jamila needed additional money, she **augmented** her salary by typing term papers for college students.

_A_ *Augment* means   A. to add to.   B. to risk.   C. to cover up.

4 dispel
(dĭ-spĕl′)
-verb

● Vickie's sweet note of apology was enough to **dispel** the slight anger Rex still felt toward her.

● I tried to **dispel** my friend's fears about her blind date that evening by telling her that my parents met on a blind date.

_B_ *Dispel* means   A. to cause.   B. to eliminate.   C. to communicate.

5 explicit
(ĕks-plĭs′ĭt)
-adjective

● Even though the instructions were **explicit**, we were still unable to put the bookcase together.

● My parents were very **explicit** about what I could and could not do during their three-day absence. They presented me with a detailed list!

_C_ *Explicit* means   A. brief.   B. mysterious.   C. specific.

6 longevity
(lŏn-jĕv′ĭ-tē)
-noun

● Toyotas and Hondas are known for their **longevity**, often outlasting more expensive cars.

● The animal with the greatest **longevity** is the giant land tortoise, which can live several hundred years.

_B_ *Longevity* means   A. form.   B. long life.   C. size.

7 magnitude
(măg′nĭ-tōōd′)
-noun

● Numbers in the billions and trillions are of too great a **magnitude** for most people to grasp.

● When the bank teller realized the **magnitude** of his error, he panicked at the thought of being held responsible for the loss of so large a sum of money.

A *Magnitude* means   A. a great amount.   B. a time.   C. a length.

8 mundane
(mŭn-dān′)
-adjective

● Because Usha teaches belly dancing every day, it is simply one more **mundane** activity to her.

● The most **mundane** activities can turn into extraordinary events. For instance, I met my best friend while washing my clothes at the laundromat.

C *Mundane* means   A. exciting.   B. painful.   C. commonplace.

9 obscure
(ŏb-skyōōr′)
-adjective

● The chemist didn't express his theory clearly, so it remained **obscure** to all but a few scientists.

● The police easily discovered who committed the murder, but even to the best psychiatrists, the killer's motives remained **obscure**.

B *Obscure* means   A. unimportant.   B. unclear.   C. known.

10 render
(rĕn′dər)
-verb

● Don't let the baby near your term paper with that crayon, or she will **render** it unreadable.

● Phyllis added so much red pepper to the chili that she **rendered** it too hot for anyone to eat.

B *Render* means   A. to remember.   B. to make.   C. to wish.

Matching Words with Definitions

Following are definitions of the ten words. Clearly write or print each word next to its definition. The sentences above and on the previous page will help you decide on the meaning of each word.

1. _____dispel_____   To drive away as if by scattering; cause to vanish

2. _____magnitude_____   Size; greatness of size or amount

3. _____mundane_____   Ordinary; everyday

4. _____explicit_____   Stated or shown clearly and exactly

5. _____ambivalent_____   Having conflicting feelings about someone or something

6. _____render_____   To cause (something) to become; make

7. _____obscure_____   Not easily understood; not clearly expressed

8. _____aloof_____   Cool and reserved; distant in personal relations

9. _____augment_____   To increase; make greater, as in strength or quantity

10. _____longevity_____   Length of life; life span

CAUTION: Do not go any further until you are sure the above answers are correct. Then you can use the definitions to help you in the following practices. Your goal is eventually to know the words well enough so that you don't need to check the definitions at all.

Sentence Check 1

Using the answer line provided, complete each item below with the correct word from the box. Use each word once.

A. aloof	B. ambivalent	C. augment	D. dispel	E. explicit
F. longevity	G. magnitude	H. mundane	I. obscure	J. render

_____mundane_____ 1. The best writers can describe something ___ so that it doesn't seem ordinary at all.

_____augment_____ 2. The architect decided to add another pillar to the building to ___ its support.

_____ambivalent_____ 3. "Russell seems ___ toward me," Janice said, "as if he both likes and dislikes me."

_____longevity_____ 4. Recent research suggests that our parents' ___ doesn't necessarily affect how long we will live.

_____aloof_____ 5. When I'm frightened, I try to appear ___ because looking cool and distant helps me feel in control.

_____obscure_____ 6. The essence of my science teacher's genius is that he is able to make complicated, ___ ideas clear to students.

_____render_____ 7. "If you keep walking on the backs of your shoes like that, you will ___ them as flat as the floor," Anya's mother said.

_____dispel_____ 8. If Claude proposes marriage to Jean, he will ___ any doubts she may still have as to whether or not he really loves her.

_____explicit_____ 9. "I try to make my test questions as ___ as possible," said Mr. Baines, "so that my students will know exactly what answers I'm looking for."

_____magnitude_____ 10. I began to realize the ___ of the insect population when I read that there are more kinds of insects living today than all other kinds of animals in the world.

NOTE: Now check your answers to these items by turning to page 179. Going over the answers carefully will help you prepare for the next two practices, for which answers are not given.

Sentence Check 2

Using the answer lines provided, complete each item below with **two** words from the box. Use each word once.

_____longevity_____
_____explicit_____ 1–2. When asked about his ___, ninety-year-old Mr. Greene gives a(n) ___ recipe for a long life: eat well, exercise, and stay away from hospitals. "It's ironic°," he explains, "that I got the worst infection of my life at a hospital."

_____augment_____
_____magnitude_____ 3–4. Harriet was able to ___ the family income by working overtime. Although her fiscal° worries dwindled,° her problems with her husband and children increased in ___ as a result.

_____ambivalent_____
_____render_____ 5–6. I'm ___ about playing with our rock band. The music is a source of elation° for me, but I'm afraid it will ___ me deaf one of these days.

_____aloof_____   7–8. Gail sometimes appears cold and conceited, but she is ___ only toward
_____dispel_____   people whom she strongly dislikes. With all others, her usual genial° and
                              modest manner soon ___s any impression that she is haughty°.

_____obscure_____   9–10. "Does the idea that we don't always see things as they really are seem ___
_____mundane_____   to you?" the teacher asked. "If so, it will become clearer if you relate it to
                              the ___ experience of looking down a road. Doesn't it look narrower in the
                              distance than it really is?"

Final Check: _My Sister's Date_

Here is a final opportunity for you to strengthen your knowledge of the ten words. First read the following selection carefully. Then fill in each blank with a word from the box at the top of the previous page. (Context clues will help you figure out which word goes in which blank.) Use each word once.

I remember watching my older sister, Ruth, as she removed the last spiked curler from her hair. We gaped° at the result. She somehow had (1)_____render_____(e)d her hair limp as spaghetti. When Ruth started to cry, I tried to pacify° her with my usual gentleness: "Why are you such a crybaby about some stupid guy?"

The guy was Steven Meyer. He and Ruth were going to a high-school dance. She'd had a crush on him for years, for reasons that were (2)_____obscure_____ to me. (I had never been able to discern° what she saw in him.)

When Ruth began to (3)_____augment_____ her makeup by applying some more powder, she gave a terrifying scream that probably reduced my (4)_____longevity_____ by at least a year. She informed me between sobs that a pimple had just appeared on her nose, making her "look like a vile° witch." I studied her face, expecting a pimple of truly amazing (5)_____magnitude_____. Instead, I spotted a tiny speck. I tried to (6)_____dispel_____ Ruth's worries: "So, it makes you look like a witch. Don't you want to look bewitching?" But she just began to cry again. I took this opportunity to go downstairs and wait for Steven Meyer.

He arrived a half hour before Ruth was ready. In the interim°, while waiting for Ruth, we talked, and I tried to figure out exactly what Ruth saw in him. Finally, she appeared. Trying to look (7)_____aloof_____, she came downstairs very slowly, wearing a cool, distant expression.

When Ruth returned home later that night, her comment about the evening was both curt° and (8)_____explicit_____: "Totally rotten." She contended° that Steven, far from being extraordinary, had turned out to be deficient° in personality—"the most (9)_____mundane_____ sort of person in the world." It seemed Ruth had bypassed feeling (10)_____ambivalent_____ about Steven and gone straight from love to hate.

It's just as well, since I've been married to Steven for ten years now.

Scores	Sentence Check 2 _____%	Final Check _____%

Enter your scores above and in the **Vocabulary Performance Chart** on the inside back cover of the book.

The box at the right lists twenty-five words from Unit Five. Using the clues at the bottom of the page, fill in these words to complete the puzzle that follows.

Word box:
- aloof
- ambivalent
- avid
- constrict
- depict
- dispel
- fallible
- feign
- furtive
- genial
- implicit
- ironic
- mediate
- mundane
- muted
- nurture
- obscure
- pathetic
- pragmatic
- punitive
- saturate
- sibling
- smug
- sneer
- vivacious

ACROSS

4. To make smaller or narrower, as by squeezing or shrinking
6. Pitifully inadequate or unsuccessful
7. To soak or fill as much as possible
9. Overly pleased with one's own cleverness, goodness, etc.; self-satisfied
13. Having conflicting feelings about someone or something
17. Enthusiastic and devoted
19. Cool and reserved
21. Suggested but not directly expressed
22. Not easily understood or clearly expressed
23. To settle (a conflict) by acting as a go-between
24. A sister or brother

DOWN

1. Lively; full of enthusiasm
2. Giving or involving punishment; punishing
3. Done or behaving so as not to be noticed; secret; sneaky
5. To promote the development of by providing nourishment, support, and protection
7. To show or express contempt or ridicule
8. Practical
10. Softened; toned down; made less intense
11. Friendly, pleasant, and kindly
12. To pretend; give a false show of
14. Ordinary; everyday
15. Opposite to what might be expected
16. Capable of making an error
18. To represent in pictures or words; describe
20. To drive away as if scattering; cause to vanish

PART A

Choose the word that best completes each item and write it in the space provided.

_____pretentious_____ 1. Dean is so ___ that he refers to his position of hamburger cook at a fast-food restaurant as "chef."

      A. punitive   B. transient   C. pretentious   D. muted

_____explicit_____ 2. Peter hasn't been ___ about quitting his job, but he's hinted at it.

      A. explicit   B. avid   C. fallible   D. punitive

_____depicted_____ 3. In talking with the social worker, the abused child ___ a life of horror.

      A. depicted   B. implored   C. intimidated   D. nurtured

_____implicit_____ 4. When my brother complained about a shortage of cash, his ___ message was "Can you lend me some money?"

      A. smug   B. avid   C. implicit   D. vivacious

_____esteem_____ 5. The poker gang laughed when Mom asked to join their game, but their ___ for her rose as she won the first four hands.

      A. esteem   B. longevity   C. legacy   D. magnitude

_____formulated_____ 6. While driving home three hours after her curfew, Lucille ___ an excuse she hoped her parents would believe.

      A. formulated   B. dispelled   C. ruptured   D. intimidated

_____exhaustive_____ 7. After a(n) ___ search during which I crawled around my entire apartment, my "missing" contact lens fell out of my eye.

      A. exhaustive   B. fiscal   C. pretentious   D. vindictive

_____smug_____ 8. Jerome deserves his excellent grades, but he doesn't have to be ___ and say, "Naturally, I got straight A's again."

      A. obscure   B. deficient   C. smug   D. muted

_____ironic_____ 9. It's ___ that my rich uncle is so stingy and my parents, who aren't rich, are always lending money to family members.

      A. exhaustive   B. ironic   C. furtive   D. pragmatic

_____feigned_____ 10. Although he had heard about his grandmother's aches and pains a million times, Dennis ___ interest whenever she complained to him.

      A. implored   B. feigned   C. mediated   D. intimidated

(Continues on next page)

PART B

On the answer line, write the letter of the choice that best completes each item.

_C_ 11. "I'm not **fallible**," my older sister insists. She means that she never makes
    A. money.   C. mistakes.
    B. meals.   D. good grades.

_D_ 12. The **habitat** of a cactus is
    A. very prickly.   C. grayish-green.
    B. capable of storing water.   D. the desert.

_A_ 13. A **mundane** experience, in most people's opinion, would be
    A. grocery shopping.   C. sky-diving.
    B. meeting one's future spouse.   D. having major surgery.

_C_ 14. "This new comedy show is **devoid** of humor," wrote the television critic, meaning that the show
    A. is always funny.   C. completely lacks humor.
    B. is funny some of the time.   D. is going to win an award.

_D_ 15. When Isaac **implored** his sister to lend him ten dollars, he
    A. blackmailed her into lending him the money.   C. refused her offer to lend him the money.
    B. demanded that she lend him the money.   D. begged her to lend him the money.

_C_ 16. A person who begins honking and yelling, "Go, go!" at other drivers the second a traffic light turns green is **deficient** in
    A. vision.   C. patience.
    B. rudeness.   D. speed.

_A_ 17. A reliable way to **infuriate** a teacher is to
    A. skip class, refuse to do assignments, and talk back rudely in class.
    B. hold the door open for him or her and offer to help clean up the classroom.
    C. take education courses in college and eventually get a student-teaching assignment.
    D. ask for clarification when you do not understand an assignment.

_D_ 18. Roger realized Anitra's interest in him had **dwindled** when she began to
    A. ask his friends if he was dating anyone special.
    B. object to his seeing other women.
    C. come up with excuses to call him at home.
    D. avoid his phone calls and visits.

_B_ 19. When my father **mediates** a quarrel, he
    A. intentionally angers the people involved because he wants them to fight.
    B. helps settle the quarrel by acting as a go-between.
    C. takes one person's side in order to make the other one even angrier.
    D. refuses to become involved in the quarrel in any way.

_C_ 20. Although Vanessa developed a crush on her classmate Josh, the feeling was **transient** because
    A. she asked him out on a date.
    B. Josh was in all her classes.
    C. she soon met the boy she called her "true love."
    D. Josh returned Vanessa's feelings.

Score (Number correct) _____ x 5 = _____%

PART A

Complete each item with a word from the box. Use each word once.

A. **ambivalent**	B. **condone**	C. **contemplate**	D. **evoke**	E. **feasible**
F. **fiscal**	G. **inhibition**	H. **jeopardize**	I. **legacy**	J. **magnitude**
K. **muted**	L. **reconcile**	M. **sibling**		

_____muted_____ 1. To make the bright green a more ___ shade, the painter added a few drops of black.

_____evoke_____ 2. Music in a minor key often ___s sad feelings in the listener.

_____magnitude_____ 3. No one realized the ___ of Nora's depression until she tried to kill herself.

_____ambivalent_____ 4. Isabel has ___ feelings about her job. She loves the work but hates her boss.

_____contemplate_____ 5. Why ___ dropping out of school when you've got only two semesters to go?

_____feasible_____ 6. It isn't ___ to grow roses in our back yard. There's too much shade back there for roses.

_____condone_____ 7. Rosa has ___(e)d her son's temper tantrums for so long that he thinks they're acceptable behavior.

_____legacy_____ 8. My love of the outdoors is a(n) ___ from my grandfather, who often hiked in the mountains.

_____fiscal_____ 9. The company is in such bad ___ shape that over half the employees will soon lose their jobs.

_____jeopardize_____ 10. Dick ___(e)d his chances of getting the job when he addressed the interviewer by the wrong name.

_____sibling_____ 11. My ___s will be coming from California and Arkansas to celebrate our parents' twenty-fifth anniversary.

_____inhibition_____ 12. At first, Tiffany was reluctant to sit in Santa Claus's lap, but she overcame her ___s when she saw that he was handing out candy canes.

_____reconcile_____ 13. As the wedding drew near, Brenda had to ___ herself to the fact that her son would marry a woman she disliked.

(Continues on next page)

PART B

Write **C** if the italicized word is used **correctly**. Write **I** if the word is used **incorrectly**.

___I___ 14. *Saturate* the washcloth by wringing it out.

___I___ 15. I asked Sal to *augment* the stereo because it was giving me a headache.

___C___ 16. An *avid* reader, Judy spends much of her time enjoying newspapers, magazines and books.

___I___ 17. Sonia *sneered* at the rock star who was her idol and asked him to autograph her CD.

___I___ 18. Being a *pragmatic* person, my brother values music and poetry more than practical things.

___C___ 19. Barry didn't let his children stay up late last night because he didn't want to set a *precedent* for future nights.

PART C

On the answer line, write the letter of the word that is the **synonym** of the boldfaced word.

Example: ___A___ **dwindle** A. lessen B. increase C. turn

___C___ 20. **aloof** A. angry B. friendly C. reserved

___C___ 21. **nurture** A. starve B. establish C. nourish

___A___ 22. **render** A. make B. prevent C. return

PART D

On the answer line, write the letter of the word that is the **antonym** of the boldfaced word.

Example: ___B___ **dwindle** A. lessen B. increase C. turn

___A___ 23. **genial** A. unpleasant B. kindly C. inborn

___A___ 24. **pathetic** A. admirable B. required C. sorry

___C___ 25. **intimidate** A. delay B. frighten C. encourage

Score (Number correct) _____ x 4 = _____ %

Enter your score above and in the **Vocabulary Performance Chart** on the inside back cover of the book.

Each item below starts with a pair of words in CAPITAL LETTERS. For each item, figure out the relationship between these two words. Then decide which of the choices (A, B, C, or D) expresses a similar relationship. Write the letter of your choice on the answer line.

_A_ 1. INTROVERT : SHY ::
    A. firefighter : brave   C. showoff : modest
    B. timid : shyness   D. recipe : ingredients

_C_ 2. SIBLING : BROTHER ::
    A. niece : aunt   C. parent : father
    B. baby : infant   D. twins : triplets

_D_ 3. VIVACIOUS : SLUGGISH ::
    A. lively : active   C. spirited : cheerleader
    B. curious : interested   D. passionate : uncaring

_C_ 4. FURTIVE : SPY ::
    A. tall : mouse   C. dishonest : criminal
    B. sly : sneaky   D. tiptoe : walk

_B_ 5. GAPE : AMAZING ::
    A. smile : sad   C. yawn : exciting
    B. laugh : humorous   D. interrupt : conversation

_C_ 6. PUNITIVE : PENALTY ::
    A. liberating : shackles   C. instructive : lesson
    B. punishing : reward   D. verdict : evidence

_B_ 7. CRYPTIC : CODE ::
    A. spicy : carrot   C. wealthy : beggar
    B. encouraging : cheerleader   D. mystical : magical

_A_ 8. DETRIMENTAL : SMOKING ::
    A. beneficial : exercise   C. snakebite : antidote
    B. physician : health   D. harmful : medicine

_D_ 9. RUPTURE : PIPE ::
    A. sweep : dustcloth   C. inhale : exhale
    B. dirt : shovel   D. malfunction : computer

_A_ 10. VINDICTIVE : FORGIVING ::
    A. neglectful : attentive   C. expensive : costly
    B. local : nearby   D. take : revenge

(Continues on next page)

_A_ 11. CONSTRICT : SHRINK ::
   A. commonplace : usual   C. fracture : bone
   B. vanish : appear   D. fire : ash

_B_ 12. GENIAL : GRUMPY ::
   A. gentle : mild   C. selective : picky
   B. elegant : awkward   D. legible : readable

_C_ 13. VILE : SPOILED FOOD ::
   A. rude : good manners   C. shiny : new coin
   B. striped : long lines   D. medicine : bitter taste

_D_ 14. ESTEEM : ROLE MODEL ::
   A. admiration : enemy   C. respect : fondness
   B. familiarity : stranger   D. contempt : bully

_C_ 15. MUTED : BLARING ::
   A. coarse : rough   C. functional : useless
   B. quiet : silence   D. external : outside

_B_ 16. PACIFY : ENRAGED ::
   A. calm : asleep   C. preach : sermon
   B. heal : wounded   D. delay : tardy

_B_ 17. DISPEL : FALSE RUMOR ::
   A. expose : conceal   C. sneeze : cold
   B. seal : crack   D. enclose : container

_A_ 18. EXPLICIT : OBSCURE ::
   A. frequent : rare   C. expire : lapse
   B. usual : everyday   D. sow : seeds

_C_ 19. MUNDANE : ORDINARY ::
   A. stone : diamond   C. sparkling : shiny
   B. bright : night   D. childish : adult

_D_ 20. MAGNITUDE : MOUNTAIN ::
   A. agility : tortoise   C. magnify : microscope
   B. dampness : desert   D. sweetness : candy

Score   (Number correct) _____ x 5 = _____ %

Appendixes

A. Limited Answer Key

IMPORTANT NOTE: Be sure to use this answer key as a learning tool only. You should not turn to this key until you have considered carefully the sentence in which a given word appears.

Used properly, the key will help you to learn words and to prepare for the activities and tests for which answers are not given. For ease of reference, the title of the "Final Check" passage in each chapter appears in parentheses.

Chapter 1 (Joseph Palmer)

Sentence Check 1

1. adamant
2. encounter
3. malign
4. amiable
5. amoral
6. epitome
7. absolve
8. antagonist
9. animosity
10. eccentric

Chapter 2 (Telephone Salespeople)

Sentence Check 1

1. dilemma
2. wary
3. inclination
4. curt
5. sabotage
6. demoralize
7. subsequent
8. irate
9. zeal
10. retort

Chapter 3 (A Cruel Sport)

Sentence Check 1

1. tangible
2. obsolete
3. acclaim
4. adjacent
5. escalate
6. engross
7. exploit
8. methodical
9. terminate
10. elicit

Chapter 4 (Bald Is Beautiful)

Sentence Check 1

1. infirmity
2. implication
3. infringe
4. succinct
5. sparse
6. innovation
7. revitalize
8. subjective
9. inequity
10. deterrent

Chapter 5 (No Luck with Women)

Sentence Check 1

1. mercenary
2. allusion
3. altruistic
4. assail
5. euphemism
6. taint
7. appease
8. syndrome
9. arbitrary
10. banal

Chapter 6 (A Taste of Parenthood)

Sentence Check 1

1. audience
2. sympathetic
3. childhood
4. pendant
5. quartet
6. nonessential
7. happily
8. unicycle
9. annually
10. hypertension

Chapter 7 (Accident and Recovery)

Sentence Check 1

1. calamity
2. ponder
3. flagrant
4. comprehensive
5. conventional
6. persevere
7. rehabilitate
8. turmoil
9. fluctuate
10. venture

Chapter 8 (Animal Senses)

Sentence Check 1

1. enhance
2. attest
3. dispatch
4. exemplify
5. enigma
6. nocturnal
7. discern
8. orient
9. mobile
10. attribute

Chapter 9 (Money Problems)

Sentence Check 1

1. predominant
2. concurrent
3. constitute
4. prerequisite
5. nominal
6. decipher
7. recession
8. default
9. confiscate
10. hypothetical

Chapter 10 (The New French Employee)

Sentence Check 1

1. suffice
2. sinister
3. vulnerable
4. intricate
5. implausible
6. sanctuary
7. incoherent
8. scrutiny
9. degenerate
10. intercede

Chapter 11 (A Cruel Teacher)

Sentence Check 1

1. immaculate
2. blight
3. gloat
4. blatant
5. contrive
6. garble
7. retaliate
8. gaunt
9. qualm
10. plagiarism

Chapter 12 (It's Never Too Late)

Sentence Check 1

1. exclaimed
2. biorhythm
3. patricide
4. homeward
5. inflexible
6. forceful
7. semiprivate
8. finalists
9. humanitarian
10. humiliated

Chapter 13 (Learning to Study)

Sentence Check 1

1. Intermittent
2. devastate
3. incorporate
4. indispensable
5. incentive
6. rigor
7. squander
8. curtail
9. digress
10. succumb

Chapter 14 (The Mad Monk)

Sentence Check 1

1. intrinsic
2. alleviate
3. virile
4. cynic
5. infamous
6. covert
7. revulsion
8. speculate
9. benefactor
10. demise

Chapter 15 (Conflict Over Holidays)

Sentence Check 1

1. aspire
2. benevolent
3. diversion
4. mandatory
5. abstain
6. deficit
7. dissent
8. affiliate
9. agnostic
10. lucrative

Chapter 16 (Dr. Martin Luther King, Jr.)

Sentence Check 1

1. Conversely
2. extrovert
3. poignant
4. prevalent
5. contend
6. proponent
7. charisma
8. contemporary
9. traumatic
10. quest

Chapter 17 (Relating to Parents)

Sentence Check 1

1. prone
2. congenial
3. flippant
4. prompt
5. rapport
6. impasse
7. relentless
8. perception
9. reprisal
10. rationale

Chapter 18 (Held Back by Fears)

Sentence Check 1

1. boyish
2. Wisdom
3. discouraged
4. immobile
5. produced
6. magnified
7. duplicate
8. psychoanalyst
9. intensify
10. claustrophobia

Chapter 19 (Interview with a Rude Star)

Sentence Check 1

1. comprise
2. redundant
3. haughty
4. libel
5. glib
6. benign
7. blasé
8. facade
9. condescend
10. pseudonym

Chapter 20 (The Nightmare of Gym)

Sentence Check 1

1. detract
2. ominous
3. averse
4. elation
5. nullified
6. endow
7. expulsion
8. disdain
9. divulge
10. mortified

Chapter 21 (Skipping Church)

Sentence Check 1

1. latent
2. designate
3. deviate
4. credible
5. interim
6. cursory
7. secular
8. improvise
9. shun
10. simulate

Chapter 22 (A Model Teacher)

Sentence Check 1

1. waive
2. commemorate
3. deplete
4. transcend
5. complacent
6. niche
7. menial
8. diligent
9. consensus
10. empathy

Chapter 23 (My Talented Roommate)

Sentence Check 1

1. bizarre
2. repertoire
3. falter
4. conducive
5. gist
6. hamper
7. viable
8. paradox
9. frenzy
10. flaunt

Chapter 24 (Fascinating Courses)

Sentence Check 1

1. actor
2. geochemistry
3. omnipresent
4. asterisk
5. director
6. theologian
7. misplace
8. contradict
9. Monogamy
10. populated

Chapter 25 (Cal and His Sisters)

Sentence Check 1

1. vivacious
2. implore
3. devoid
4. introvert
5. jeopardize
6. sibling
7. infuriate
8. sneer
9. intimidate
10. smug

Chapter 26 (Shoplifter)

Sentence Check 1

1. gape
2. contemplate
3. precedent
4. feasible
5. condone
6. fiscal
7. furtive
8. pathetic
9. feign
10. punitive

Chapter 27 (A Nutty Newspaper Office)

Sentence Check 1

1. deficient
2. rupture
3. ironic
4. detrimental
5. inhibition
6. depict
7. vindictive
8. cryptic
9. saturate
10. implicit

Chapter 28 (Roughing It)

Sentence Check 1

1. vile
2. genial
3. reconcile
4. constrict
5. formulate
6. exhaustive
7. Pretentious
8. habitat
9. pragmatic
10. fallible

Chapter 29 (Getting Scared)

Sentence Check 1

1. pacify
2. evoke
3. dwindle
4. muted
5. nurture
6. transient
7. esteem
8. avid
9. legacy
10. mediate

Chapter 30 (My Sister's Date)

Sentence Check 1

1. mundane
2. augment
3. ambivalent
4. longevity
5. aloof
6. obscure
7. render
8. dispel
9. explicit
10. magnitude

B. Dictionary Use

It isn't always possible to figure out the meaning of a word from its context, and that's where a dictionary comes in. Following is some basic information to help you use a dictionary.

How to Find a Word

A dictionary contains so many words that it can take a while to find the one you're looking for. But if you know how to use guidewords, you can find a word rather quickly. *Guidewords* are the two words at the top of each dictionary page. The first guideword tells what the first word is on the page. The second guideword tells what the last word is on that page. The other words on a page fall alphabetically between the two guidewords. So when you look up a word, find the two guidewords that alphabetically surround the word you're looking for.

● Which of the following pair of guidewords would be on the page with the word *skirmish*?

    (**skimp / skyscraper**)   **skyward / slave**   **sixty / skimming**

The answer to this question and the questions that follow are given on the next page.

How to Use a Dictionary Listing

A dictionary listing includes many pieces of information. For example, here is a typical listing. Note that it includes much more than just a definition.

> **driz•zle** (drĭz′əl) *v.* **-zled, -zling.** To rain gently and steadily in fine drops.
> — *n.* A very light rain. —**driz′zly,** *adj.*

Key parts of a dictionary entry are listed and explained below.

Syllables. Dots separate dictionary entry words into syllables. Note that *drizzle* has one dot, which breaks the word into two syllables.

● To practice seeing the syllable breakdown in a dictionary entry, write the number of syllables in each word below.

    glam•our __2__   **mi•cro•wave** __3__   **in•de•scrib•a•ble** __5__

Pronunciation guide. The information within parentheses after the entry word shows how to pronounce the entry word. This pronunciation guide includes two types of symbols: pronunciation symbols and accent marks.

Pronunciation symbols represent the consonant and vowel sounds in a word. The consonant sounds are probably very familiar to you, but you may find it helpful to review some of the sounds of the vowels—*a, e, i, o,* and *u.* Every dictionary has a key explaining the sounds of its pronunciation symbols, including the long and short sounds of vowels.

    Long vowels have the sound of their own names. For example, the *a* in *pay* and the *o* in *no* both have long vowel sounds. Long vowel sounds are shown by a straight line above the vowel.

    In many dictionaries, the *short vowels* are shown by a curved line above the vowel. Thus the *i* in the first syllable of *drizzle* is a short *i.* The pronunciation chart on the inside front cover of this book indicates that the short *i* has the sound of *i* in *ill.* It also indicates that the short *a* has the sound of *a* in *apple,* that the short *e* has the sound of *e* in *end,* and so on.

● Which of the words below have a short vowel sound? Which has a long vowel sound?

    drug __short__   **night** __long__   **sand** __short__

Another pronunciation symbol is the *schwa* (ə), which looks like an upside-down *e*. It stands for certain rapidly spoken, unaccented vowel sounds, such as the *a* in *above*, the *e* in *item*, the *i* in *easily*, the *o* in *gallop*, and the *u* in *circus*. More generally, it has an "uh" sound, like the "uh" a speaker makes when hesitating. Here are three words that include the schwa sound:

in•fant (ĭn′fənt)   **bum•ble** (bŭm′bəl)   **de•liv•er** (dĭ-lĭv′ər)

● Which syllable in *drizzle* contains the schwa sound, the first or the second? _____second_____

Accent marks are small black marks that tell you which syllable to emphasize, or stress, as you say a word. An accent mark follows *driz* in the pronunciation guide for *drizzle,* which tells you to stress the first syllable of *drizzle*. Syllables with no accent mark are not stressed. Some syllables are in between, and they are marked with a lighter accent mark.

● Which syllable has the stronger accent in *sentimental*? _____third_____

sen•ti•men•tal (sĕn′tə-mĕn′tl)

Parts of speech. After the pronunciation key and before each set of definitions, the entry word's parts of speech are given. The parts of speech are abbreviated as follows:

noun—*n.*   pronoun—*pron.*   adjective—*adj.*   adverb—*adv.*   verb—*v.*

● The listing for *drizzle* shows that it can be two parts of speech. Write them below:

_____noun_____   _____verb_____

Definitions. Words often have more than one meaning. When they do, each meaning is usually numbered in the dictionary. You can tell which definition of a word fits a given sentence by the meaning of the sentence. For example, the word *charge* has several definitions, including these two: **1.** To ask as a price. **2.** To accuse or blame.

● Show with a check (✓) which definition (1 or 2) applies in each sentence below:

The store charged me less for the blouse because it was missing a button.   1 ✓   2 ___

My neighbor has been charged with shoplifting.   1 ___   2 ✓

Other information. After the definitions in a listing in a hardbound dictionary, you may get information about the *origin* of a word. Such information about origins, also known as *etymology,* is usually given in brackets. And you may sometimes be given one or more synonyms or antonyms for the entry word. *Synonyms* are words that are similar in meaning to the entry word; *antonyms* are words that are opposite in meaning.

Which Dictionaries to Own

You will find it useful to own two recent dictionaries: a small paperback dictionary to carry to class and a hardbound dictionary, which contains more information than a small paperback version. Among the good dictionaries strongly recommended are both the paperback and the hardcover editions of the following:

The American Heritage Dictionary
The Random House College Dictionary
Webster's New World Dictionary

Answers to the Dictionary Questions

Guidewords: *skimp/skyscraper*	Accent: stronger accent on third syllable *(men)*
Number of syllables: 2, 3, 5	Parts of speech: noun and verb
Vowels: *drug, sand* (short); *night* (long)	Definitions: 1; 2
Schwa: second syllable of *drizzle*	

C. Topics for Discussion and Writing

NOTE: The first three items for each chapter are intended for discussion; the last three, for writing. Feel free, however, to either talk or write about any of the items.

Chapter 1 (Joseph Palmer)

1. Do you ever watch TV programs in which real-life antagonists appear and malign each other as the audience cheers and shouts? What do you think of these shows?

2. Think of some amiable people you know and also people who seem to feel a lot of animosity toward others. How do their relationships with others differ? Why might they deal with others as they do?

3. Do you think amoral people are born that way? Or is there another explanation for why some people have no conscience?

4. Write a paper on a point of view about which you are adamant. For example, you might feel strongly that children should be given a voice in certain family decisions. Or you might stubbornly insist that the government should offer free health care for all citizens regardless of age or income. In your paper, explain your reasoning.

5. Select a person in entertainment, sports, or politics who you think is the epitome of something—for example, the epitome of courage or talent or kindness. Write a paper in which you describe this person and give evidence for your opinion. You might begin with a sentence such as this: *Former President Jimmy Carter is the epitome of service to humankind.*

6. Who is the most eccentric person you have ever had an encounter with? Write a paper about two or three unusual things this person has done.

Chapter 2 (Telephone Salespeople)

1. Do you enjoy salespeople who make their sales pitches with great zeal? Or does such enthusiasm make you wary? Give an example of a strong sales pitch you've heard recently, either in person, on TV, or on the radio.

2. Have you had to deal with classmates or coworkers who were frequently curt? Do you retort sarcastically to make them realize how rude they are? Is there a better way to handle such a situation?

3. When you are faced with a difficult dilemma, what is your inclination: to make a decision quickly, or to put off deciding as long as possible? For instance, how have you decided to take one course instead of another, or choose one job or project instead of another?

4. When has a careless comment from someone demoralized you? How did you react? Judging from your subsequent conversations with that person, did he or she mean to make you feel bad? Write a paper explaining the comment and the context in which it was given, how the comment affected you, and how you eventually came to view it.

5. What in your day-to-day life really makes you irate? Write about a situation (or person) that regularly angers you.

6. Do you know, or know about, a person who acts in self-destructive ways, creating problems for himself or herself? Write about a person who sabotages his or her own life. Here's a sample main idea for your paper: *My brother has sabotaged his own future by thinking only of the present.*

Chapter 3 (A Cruel Sport)

1. Do people who wear fur exploit animals, or are they making appropriate use of resources? Do you feel the same way about people who wear leather and eat meat?

2. Have you ever been in a conversation that was at first calm but then escalated into an angry argument? How did you (or the other person involved) eventually terminate the fight?

3. Name a book or movie that truly engrossed you and that you think is deserving of acclaim. What specifically about the book or movie elicits such admiration from you?

4. Pretend you're an advice columnist. One of your readers writes, "Dear _____, Occasionally, on the bus I take to work (or school), an attractive person sits in the seat adjacent to mine. How can I make contact?" Write a humorous, methodical plan for this reader to follow in order to meet the attractive stranger.

5. Will calculators and computer spell-check programs make basic math and spelling obsolete? Write a paper in which you defend one of these two points: (1) Public schools should stop spending so much time on math and spelling, or (2) Despite the common use of calculators and computer spell-check programs, public schools should continue to emphasize math and spelling.

6. Select one of the following types of people: an athlete, a musician, an artist, a slob, a neat freak, a pack rat, or an animal lover. Write a paper in which you describe this imaginary person's apartment. What tangible evidence in the apartment would give hints of the owner's identity?

Chapter 4 (Bald Is Beautiful)

1. Have you ever noticed barriers to wheelchairs in your town? If you had to use a wheelchair, would you feel not being able to enter shops, restaurants, and theaters was just one of those things you had to get used to? Or would you feel it was an inequity that should be corrected?

2. In recent years, we have seen more and more people willing to put their divorces, lawsuits, family problems, dating lives, and even marriages on television for the entertainment of strangers. What are the implications of this trend in TV entertainment—for both the participants and the audience?

3. With the move of many businesses to malls, many old business areas have boarded-up buildings and only sparse attractions for local residents. What are a few things that could be done to revitalize such an area in your town?

4. What innovations might make your school a better place? Write a few suggestions in the form of a memo to school administrators. Be as succinct as possible—the officials are busy people.

5. Do any of the campaigns against teenage smoking, drinking, and drug use actually succeed as deterrents? Write a paper explaining your view.

6. Abortion is a topic about which people have strong, highly subjective views. How far do you feel anti-abortion protesters should be allowed to go? Should they be able to picket abortion centers, for instance, as long as they do not interfere with traffic? How about protesters who infringe on the ability of others to obtain abortions by blocking the entrance to such a center? Write a paper about your thoughts.

Chapter 5 (No Luck with Women)

1. Which is the most **banal** TV show you've ever seen? Explain your choice by naming one or two ways in which the show lacks originality.

2. Are there rules and regulations at your school or workplace that seem **arbitrary**? Why do you think such seemingly unreasonable rules exist? Whom might they be intended to **appease**?

3. As you were growing up, what topics did people in your family consider unpleasant or offensive? Did family members tend to use **euphemisms** and make only vague **allusions** to these subjects? Or did they speak about them directly? Give an example to illustrate your point.

4. Who is the most **mercenary** of your friends or acquaintances? At the other end of the scale, which of your friends or acquaintances is the most **altruistic**? Write a paper that describes both people and indicates which one you prefer and why.

5. Do you sometimes feel **assailed** by homework, tests, and other school demands? Write a humorous paper about "Tired Student **Syndrome**," describing the symptoms of this imaginary "disease."

6. Has anyone ever spread a rumor about you that has **tainted** your reputation? If not, have you seen someone else's reputation damaged by rumors? Write about the rumor and its effects.

Chapter 7 (Accident and Recovery)

1. Pretend the superintendent of a prison for youthful criminals wants to **rehabilitate** the inmates and has consulted you. With your classmates, brainstorm ideas for such a program. The program can be as **comprehensive** as you like, involving any kind of treatment or education you think might help these young people turn their lives around.

2. Whom can you think of whose clothing and appearance are quite **conventional**? On the other hand, whom can you think of whose clothing and appearance show a **flagrant** disregard for what is considered normal? Describe in detail the two people's appearances, and suggest why they might have decided to look or dress as they do.

3. Think of someone you admire because of a risk he or she has taken. Perhaps the person gave up a steady but boring job to do something he or she really believed in, or maybe the person **ventured** failure by going back to school after being out of it for some time. What happened? In your opinion, is the person happy he or she took that risk?

4. Do you know anyone whose life seems to involve one **calamity** after another? Write a paper about this person, giving examples of events that have caused his or her life to be in **turmoil**. Do you think that the person has more than his or her share of bad luck? Or does he or she somehow contribute to the problems?

5. Think of a situation in your life in which you were tempted to give up, but kept trying. Perhaps you've struggled with a class, a sport, a personal relationship, or a job. In a paper, describe the situation and explain what made you **persevere** instead of giving up. Alternatively, write about such a situation in the life of someone you know.

6. Write about a difficult decision you've had to make. Describe how your thoughts **fluctuated** as you **pondered** what course of action to take. What did you finally decide to do, and why?

Chapter 8 (Animal Senses)

1. Which appeals to you more: living your life in one community where you'd "put down roots," or living a more mobile life, moving from place to place? Explain which way of life you'd prefer and why.

2. Think of a time when a friend has done something to enhance his or her appearance. Did you discern the change right away, or did it take some time? How did you react to the change?

3. Everyone seems to know at least one "Odd Couple," two people who seem so different that their attraction to one another is an enigma. Whom do you know, or know about, who exemplify such a mismatched couple? Why might they be together?

4. If you could design your own town, what attributes would it include? Write a paper listing and explaining some characteristics you feel would contribute to good lives for residents and make it easy for newcomers to orient themselves.

5. Choose a place you are familiar with both during the day and at night. Write a paper contrasting the place's daytime and nocturnal appearances. What sights, sounds, and other sensations might one experience at each time of day? You might describe, for instance, how a place that is unattractive in daylight becomes more attractive at night, when its ugliness is hidden. Or you might describe a place that is pleasant during the day but scary after dark.

6. Choose a character trait of one of your relatives. Then write a paper in which you attest to this trait's influence on your family life. For example, you might write about how your sister's bad temper has ruined some family activities or how your uncle's sense of humor has helped others get through some bad times. Add interest to your paper by using colorful descriptions and quotations.

Chapter 9 (Money Problems)

1. What, in your mind, constitutes lying? Does it occur only when a person says something he or she knows is not true? What about this hypothetical situation? Bill has a paper due the next day. The library is closed, and he doesn't have a computer at home. He says to his friend Ned, "I sure wish I knew someone who could let me use his computer." Ned says, "Good luck," and goes home. Then someone mentions to Bill that Ned has a computer at home. Later, Bill accuses Ned of lying, and Ned responds, "I never said I didn't have a computer. You never asked." Did Ned lie?

2. In your career as a student, what book have you been required to read that you found hardest to decipher? What was so difficult about it, and what (if anything) did you finally get out of it?

3. During a recession, soup kitchens, homeless shelters, and places that distribute donated clothing and food are very active. If you were in charge of such a place, would you provide services to the unemployed free of charge, or do you think it would be better to charge nominal fees? Explain your answer.

4. Imagine that you face two concurrent job offers: one paying $100,000 a year, and the other giving you the opportunity to travel for a year at someone else's expense. You can't accept both offers. There is no guarantee that either job will be available to you if you don't take it now. Write about the choice you would make and why you would make it.

5. What do you think are the predominant reasons so many people default on their car and house payments? Write a paper listing two or three of those reasons and explaining some ways to avoid failing to make such payments.

6. We often hear about situations in which authorities have confiscated children, taking them out of abusive or neglectful situations and placing them in foster homes. These situations might be avoided if people were better prepared for the enormous responsibility of parenthood. Write a paper in which you explain two or three helpful prerequisites for people thinking about having children.

Chapter 10 (The New French Employee)

1. Which is easier to get away with—a simple lie or an intricate one? Give examples.

2. When you see the relationship between two friends or family members degenerate, what do you think is your best response? Should you intercede on behalf of the person you think is in the right, or should you keep your distance? Use situations from your experience to illustrate your points.

3. What are some implausible excuses you've heard (or perhaps given!) for not completing homework? Did any suffice to satisfy the teacher?

4. In school, people who are different in any way are often vulnerable to teasing, criticism, and even attack. Write a paper about a person you've known who was targeted for abuse because he or she was in some way different. Did anyone come to this person's defense?

5. Foster homes should be sanctuaries for children who, for whatever reasons, cannot stay in their own homes. Tragically, foster parents may have sinister motives for taking in children. Pretend that you are in charge of checking out would-be foster parents. Write a paper about the kind of scrutiny you would give them before approving them. You might begin with a main idea such as this: *If I were in charge of checking out would-be foster parents, I'd look for three things.*

6. Some people find it easy to speak up in public, while others tend to be incoherent when trying to speak in a group. Which are you? Write a paper about at least one experience that shows how easy or difficult speaking up in public is for you. If you like, use exaggeration to achieve a humorous tone.

Chapter 11 (A Cruel Teacher)

1. Why do you think plagiarism is considered such a bad thing in school and elsewhere? What is the most blatant case of plagiarism you've heard about?

2. After you have (or someone else has) retaliated against someone who has hurt or offended you, how do you usually feel? Do you gloat, bragging that you've gotten back at him or her? Or do you have some qualms about having sunk to that person's level? Give an example.

3. Telephone messages are easy to garble. Describe a time that a message you've left—or one you've received—was so jumbled that its meaning became confused.

4. How strongly are young people influenced by images on TV and in magazines? For instance, do very slender models and actresses encourage young girls to become unhealthily gaunt? Write a paper about a few ways young people imitate what they see in the media. Use detailed examples to support your points.

5. Where do you fall on the neatness scale? Are you a total slob? Does it drive you crazy if your room or house is anything less than immaculate? Write a humorous paper describing your housekeeping methods. Your main point might be stated something like this: *My housekeeping methods are weird but effective.*

6. What, in your opinion, is the single biggest blight on society today? Drugs? Guns? Child abuse? Pollution? Something else? Write a paper in which you explain your opinion as well as one or two solutions you've contrived for dealing with the problem.

Chapter 13 (Learning to Study)

1. Describe a time when you tried to curtail a bad habit, such as eating too much, smoking, or biting your nails. Did it help to provide yourself with incentives, such as rewarding yourself with new jeans if you'd lose five pounds?

2. When you imagine losing all your belongings in a fire, you realize what is indispensable to you. If such a tragedy occurred and you could rescue only one object, what would it be? What are two other objects it would devastate you to lose?

3. Describe your perfect vacation. Where would it take place, and what activities would you incorporate into it?

4. "Youth is wasted on the young," one writer said, meaning young people (in the eyes of their elders, anyway) often squander their opportunities. What opportunity do you wish you had made better use of? What happened to keep you from taking full advantage of the situation—did you succumb to laziness, the bad example of friends, or something else? Write a paper about an opportunity you missed.

5. Write a paper that describes a mentally or physically exhausting experience you have had. Use sharp details to make the reader feel the rigor of the experience. Don't digress into other topics, such as why you were there or who else was with you. Simply write about the difficulty.

6. Who is the most effective teacher you have ever had? Write a paper that explains what made him or her so good. Also mention whether you always appreciated him or her, or whether your good opinion was intermittent—interrupted by periods when you thought the teacher was, for example, too tough or unfair.

Chapter 14 (The Mad Monk)

1. In your opinion, what really makes a male virile? Is it how he looks? How he treats other people? How he handles his responsibilities? What qualities are intrinsic to a manly male?

2. While most people regard accused killers with revulsion, it is a strange fact that some women are fascinated by them. Infamous characters such as O. J. Simpson and Charles Manson receive love letters, even offers of marriage, from such women. Speculate on the reasons such men attract women's attention.

3. Have you had a favorite pet that died? What led to its demise? Explain what made the pet so special to you.

4. Cynics say that no one does anything simply to be kind. Write a paper that either agrees with or contradicts that view. If you hold the opposing view, offer the example of someone who has served as a benefactor to you, or to someone else, without expecting a reward.

5. What's the best way you know to alleviate the blues? Write a paper on a way (or ways) you cheer yourself up. Include a colorful example of each method you mention.

6. Children often carry on covert activities. For example, they may hide the fact that they use a flashlight to read under the blanket when they should be sleeping. Or they may try to keep adults from learning that they've skipped school. As a young child, what secret activities did you take part in? Write a paper describing one or more such activities. Tell what the experiences were like for you and what methods you used to keep from being caught. If you ever *were* caught, explain how you were caught and what the consequences were.

Chapter 15 (Conflict Over Holidays)

1. When you were younger, were there rules about mandatory behavior in your household that created dissent between you and your parents? What were they?

2. What career do you aspire to? Does that career attract you primarily because it is lucrative, or are there other reasons you are drawn to it?

3. Tell about your daily diet. Does it have a deficit of certain kinds of food? Too much of others? What do you consider a healthy diet for someone your age?

4. Who is the most benevolent person you know? Write a paper about that person and his or her acts of generosity, describing one or more such acts in detail.

5. What role does television play in your life? Is it an occasional diversion, a constant companion, or something in between? How much of a problem would it be for you to abstain from watching it for a week? A month? Write a paper describing television's role in your life and how you think you'd manage if you had to give it up.

6. Are you affiliated with any groups, such as social clubs, study groups, or volunteer organizations? Write a paper explaining the group's role in your life. What type of group is it? Why did you join? What activities are you involved in? Has your view of the group changed since you've joined it?

Chapter 16 (Dr. Martin Luther King, Jr.)

1. Which famous athletes and entertainers would you say have charisma? In your opinion, are the people who have that quality necessarily extroverts, or can a quiet person be magnetic and charming as well?

2. What do you think of NASA's quest for a way to put astronauts on Mars and maybe even to establish a human colony there? Are you a proponent of further space exploration, or do you think the government's money could be better spent in other ways?

3. Describe the most poignant book, movie, or television show that you've read or seen lately. Include details that show just what was so touching about it.

4. What traumatic event do you remember from your childhood? Conversely, what is one of your happiest childhood memories? Write a paper about either event, telling what happened and explaining what made the event so painful or happy for you.

5. Who is a contemporary figure that you greatly admire? Write a paper in which you explain which qualities in that person you particularly respect. Begin with a main idea similar to this: *I admire and respect _____ largely because of two of his/her special qualities.*

6. What do you contend are the two best reasons for going to college? Write a paper explaining and defending your point of view.

Chapter 17 (Relating to Parents)

1. Brothers and sisters, even those who are usually on congenial terms, sometimes tease and play tricks on one another. If you had a brother or sister (or a cousin or close friend) when you were younger, did you sometimes do things to annoy him or her? What was the reprisal, if any?

2. People's perceptions of behavior often differ. For instance, have you ever been accused of being flippant when you were in fact being serious? Do people sometimes think you're grouchy when you're not feeling that way at all? Explain. How do you convince people of your true intent or feelings?

3. With whom in your family do you have the best rapport? How is communicating with that person different from talking with other members of your family?

4. Write a paper about a time when you and another individual—perhaps a friend, a coworker, or a family member—had a disagreement and reached an impasse. What happened next? What was your rationale for how you acted?

5. Imagine that you have a friend who has a self-destructive habit. Perhaps he or she is relentless about smoking, drinking, overeating, or taking drugs. Write a paper about two or three techniques you might try in order to prompt your friend to give up the unhealthy habit.

6. When you are faced with a decision, are you prone to make it quickly—or to put it off as long as possible? Think about, for instance, how long it takes you to select which classes to sign up for, what gifts to buy, when to get a haircut, and whether to ask someone out on a date. Write a paper in which you give examples of your usual decision-making style.

Chapter 19 (Interview with a Rude Star)

1. Should celebrities have the same protection from libel as people who aren't famous? Since celebrities invite fame and the media attention that comes with it, is it unrealistic for them to complain when the media publish things they don't like?

2. Today's families comprise a bigger variety of relationships than ever. Take a poll in your class, asking your classmates, "What types of relationships does your family include?" How many families include a mother, a father, and their biological children? How many others include stepparents, step-siblings, half-siblings, adopted children, foster children, and single parents? What conclusions can be drawn?

3. People who appear to be "stuck up" are sometimes shy and unsure of themselves, and actually quite friendly once you get to know them. Can you think of a person who seemed haughty to you at first, but who turned out to have quite a benign personality? How did you discover the truth about this person?

4. Think of an activity that you once believed was great fun, but about which you've become blasé. At what point did it cease being fun and original? Why do you think your opinion of it changed? Write quickly, without thinking much about your choice of words. Then look carefully at your paper to find redundant parts, if any, and cross them out or reword them.

5. Write a paper describing a building you find impressive—perhaps an old mansion, theater, or museum, or a modern house or storefront with some special appeal. Describe the building's facade so your reader can picture it clearly.

6. Every school has its social cliques—groups of students who hang out together because of some shared characteristics. Write a paper that describes several cliques in your school. Was (or is) there a lot of interaction between those cliques, or did (or do) members of one group refuse to condescend to mix with members of the others?

Chapter 20 (The Nightmare of Gym)

1. Of all the movies you've ever seen, which would you say had the most ominous atmosphere? What made it so ominous?

2. If a troublesome student views school with disdain, does it do any good to threaten him with expulsion? What might be more effective ways of dealing with students' bad behavior?

3. Is it ever right to nullify the results of an election? Under what conditions?

4. We all have memories of special childhood occasions when we were filled with elation. Write a paper describing such an occasion in your childhood. Include any details and explanations needed for your reader to understand why the experience filled you with such joy or pride.

5. Although the details may be embarrassing to divulge, write a paper about an experience that really mortified you. Be sure to include specific information so that the reasons for your feelings will make sense.

6. Of the people you know, who is endowed with the best combination of physical, mental, and/or emotional qualities? Write a paper describing that person. Since no one is perfect, include one or two characteristics that detract from the person's otherwise outstanding personality and/or appearance. Your main idea for this paper might be similar to this: *Although Veronica does have her faults, she has a wonderful combination of personal qualities.*

Chapter 21 (Skipping Church)

1. Think of a time you (or someone you know) had to improvise a false story to get out of an uncomfortable situation. Was the story credible enough to be believed? What happened as a result?

2. Should public schools be completely secular, or do you think it's all right to have, for instance, prayer in schools or a teacher talking about his or her religious beliefs? Explain.

3. There are actually people who earn their livings as "life coaches": they advise their clients on issues ranging from school and career choices to their love lives. If you had to designate a person you know—or know about—to be your life coach, who would that person be, and why?

4. What would you like to be doing in ten years? What will you do in the interim in order to make that goal happen? In addition, what might you wish to shun so that you can achieve your goal? Write a paper that describes your goals and what you plan to do to reach them.

5. Most people have an interest or two they'd like to explore if they had more time and/or money. What's a latent interest of yours that you've never really developed? Write a paper explaining that interest and why it appeals to you. Also tell how you might follow this interest one day when you have time for it.

6. Write about a time in your life when you deviated from what you knew was right. What happened? How did you feel afterward?

Chapter 22 (A Model Teacher)

1. What are the two menial household tasks that you dislike the most? Is there a consensus on this question among your classmates?

2. When you imagine the lives of celebrities, surrounded by adoring fans and making incredible amounts of money, it's not hard to understand why these people develop attitude problems. Do you think you could deal with sudden wealth and fame without becoming complacent? How might you transcend the pressures of being a celebrity and remain a "regular person"?

3. Think about your future. What niche do you see yourself filling in ten years? What type of work do you think you'd like to be doing? What could you do now to learn about that activity to see if it's really what you imagine it to be?

4. Write a paper about two people in your life. One is a person for whom you have a lot of empathy because you think this person is trying hard to do a good job of managing his or her life. The other is a person who has depleted your store of sympathy, perhaps because he or she seems to be a complainer who does little to improve his or her situation. In your paper, contrast how the two people manage their lives and problems.

5. What do you wish you had been more diligent about when you were younger? Studying a particular subject? Practicing a musical instrument? Learning an athletic skill? Write a paper describing what you wish you'd worked harder at, and why.

6. Write a paper, humorous or serious in tone, in which you answer the following question: After your death many years from now, your friends and/or family want to commemorate your life in some fashion. What would be a suitable celebration held or memorial established in your honor? Your paper might take the form of instructions to your friends and family.

Chapter 23 (My Talented Roommate)

1. Homeless people are sometimes the victims of mental illness or other conditions that make them look, act, and speak strangely. What examples of bizarre behavior have you noticed among homeless people? How do passersby tend to react?

2. You may have heard the saying, "If you've got it, flaunt it." What does that statement mean? Are there times when that guideline is not appropriate? If the characteristic one wishes to flaunt is modesty, does the saying become a paradox?

3. Without going into too much detail, describe the gist of your all-time favorite book, movie, or television program. See if you and your classmates can come up with "Ten Best" lists for each of these types of entertainment.

4. Your room/house/apartment is a mess. The phone rings. Someone who means a great deal to you is coming to see you in twenty minutes. You go into a frenzy of tidying up. What tricks do you have in your housecleaning repertoire to help you make the most of your time? Do you, for example, hide dirty dishes in a closet? Stuff clothes under the bed? Write a description of how you would make your place presentable for the unexpected guest.

5. Think of one problem with your school—an aspect of it that you dislike or that doesn't work well. Write a paper in which you explain the problem and then propose a viable solution.

6. You've been asked to help new students at your school succeed. What atmosphere do you find most conducive to doing schoolwork? What conditions hamper study? Write a paper that contrasts those two situations and makes suggestions for successful studying.

Chapter 25 (Cal and His Sisters)

1. Describe a recent experience that infuriated you. What happened? Why did it make you so angry?

2. Which member of your family (or which of your friends) is particularly vivacious? Which could be called an introvert? How do these very different people get along?

3. Describe someone you know—perhaps a teacher, an employer, a fellow student or teammate—who intimidated you. What did he or she do to make you feel that way? Sneer at your mistakes? Make impossible demands? With your classmates, brainstorm suggestions for dealing with such people.

4. Write a paper about a time you saw a friend or family member involved in something you believed jeopardized his or her well-being, and you tried to help. The danger could have been to your friend's emotional or physical health, reputation, or general happiness. When you implored your friend to think about the behavior, what was his or her response?

5. When we say, "He (or she) is like a brother (or sister) to me," we mean that a person is very close to us and that we understand one another in a special way. Write a paper about someone who is "like a sibling" to you. In your paper, describe the ways in which the relationship is special to you.

6. Of all the classes you have taken or organizations you have joined, which would you say was most devoid of interest or value to you? Write a paper describing what the class or organization was like and why it failed to interest you.

Chapter 26 (Shoplifter)

1. Everyone knows the tendency of drivers to slow down and gape at the scene of an accident. What do you think is the reason for this tendency? What drives people to stare at a horrible sight?

2. Do you condone using physical punishment, such as spanking, for children? Or do you think there are punitive techniques that work more effectively? What would these be? Explain.

3. When you were little, did you ever feign an illness in order to get out of doing something? Were you skillful enough to get away with it, or were your attempts to act sick pretty pathetic?

4. Write a paper comparing two routes your future might take. One route should be quite feasible—a practical, realistic plan. The other should be less realistic, even wildly unlikely, but lots of fun. Use humor to make your paper enjoyable to write and to read.

5. What's your fiscal style? Do you save for a future need? Spend money as soon as you have it? And how did you develop your style—are you following the precedent your family set for you? Write a paper about how you behave with money and why. You might state your main idea like this: *My money-management habits can be improved in a couple of ways.*

6. As you contemplate everything you've done in the current school year, which of your accomplishments are you proudest of? Why? Write a paper about your reasons for choosing this particular accomplishment.

Chapter 27 (A Nutty Newspaper Office)

1. You would think that when people grew up with situations that were detrimental to their well-being—for instance, with an abusive parent or with family members who are alcoholics—that they would be determined never to repeat that situation. It's an ironic fact, though, that people often do re-create those painful situations when they become adults. Why do you think people tend to repeat behaviors that they themselves have been hurt by? What might be done to help them change?

2. Do you know someone who seems to have an unusual number of inhibitions? Maybe the person refuses to do anything in public, such as dance or try a new activity, that might make him or her look silly. Are these people deficient in self-confidence, or could there be other reasons for their inhibitions?

3. How are chores divided up in your family? Has the family formally decided who should do what, or is there more of an implicit understanding about general areas of responsibility?

4. Write a paper in which you depict, hour by hour, a typical school day for you. Which parts of it do you enjoy the most? The least?

5. Have you, or has someone you know, ever been the victim of a vindictive act? Write a paper describing what the other person did and why—and what happened as a result.

6. Write about a time when a friend's cryptic behavior left you puzzled or disturbed. Perhaps someone with whom you'd been on good terms suddenly began acting unfriendly, or someone seemed busy with an activity he or she wouldn't talk about. Be sure to explain just what was puzzling about the behavior. If you eventually figured out what was going on, include that in your paper as well.

Chapter 28 (Roughing It)

1. When you hear about battles between housing developers and environmentalists concerned about protecting animals' habitats, whose side are you usually on? Which do you think is more important: to take care of people's housing needs, or to protect animals' homes? Explain your view.

2. A pretentious, know-it-all character appears in many TV comedies and movies. Think of such a character and describe how he or she makes a show of his or her importance.

3. Is there a situation in your life that you're not very pleased with, but you've had to reconcile yourself to? For example, maybe someone you care about is friendly with someone you don't care for. Or maybe a relative or employer is grouchy, but there doesn't seem to be much you can do about it. Explain what you've had to do to accept the situation.

4. We are probably all fallible in our first judgments of others. Write about a time when your initial judgment of another person was wrong. Perhaps you thought someone was unfriendly at first, but the person turned out to be quite genial when you got to know him or her better. Give specific examples of the person's behavior so that your reader can understand your reactions.

5. Think of a minor problem that's annoying you right now—such as a faucet that is leaking, a cat that is scratching the furniture, or your losing an assignment or a library book. In a paper, explain that problem. Then formulate a pragmatic solution to the problem, and explain that as well.

6. What do you know how to do very well? Paint a room perfectly? Make a divine salad? Buy holiday gifts on a strict budget? Write exhaustive directions for doing something you're skilled in so a reader wishing to follow your instruction will benefit from your experience and have no trouble achieving good results.

Chapter 29 (Getting Scared)

1. Think of one legacy—a talent, an interest, a part of your physical appearance or way of behaving—that you've inherited from a relative. Tell about the relative and the legacy you've inherited. Are you glad or sorry that you have this trait in common?

2. What in your opinion are some of the most important things parents can do to nurture their children? Why might these things be so important to a growing child?

3. Have you ever been asked to mediate a disagreement between friends or family members? How did you respond? Were you successful in helping to pacify both people, or did one end up thinking he or she had been treated unfairly? Explain.

4. Write a paper about someone you once liked and respected, but who has lost your esteem. What happened to make your good opinion of this person dwindle?

5. Have you had the opportunity to revisit a place you knew well as a child—perhaps your or a relative's old home, your elementary school, or a place where you used to play? Write a paper about the experience of revisiting that place and the feelings and memories it evoked in you. Were those memories clear and strong, or dim and muted?

6. Write about an interest that you were avid about at one point in your life—a hobby or subject in which you were deeply involved. How did you become interested in it? Have you retained that interest, or was it transient?

Chapter 30 (My Sister's Date)

1. When have you faced a decision about which you were ambivalent? What made the decision so difficult? Did something finally happen to render the decision a little easier for you?

2. Do you enjoy reading material that is new and challenging, or do you prefer something more mundane? Give examples. Also, what are your techniques for dealing with reading assignments that are somewhat obscure?

3. Is there someone you've been friends with for many years? What do you think has contributed to the longevity of your friendship?

4. Write a description of someone who you think is aloof. Include explicit details about exactly what the person does that makes him or her seem so cool and distant.

5. Imagine that a friend who had dropped out of school was considering going back. But he or she is scared and says, "I don't know if I can succeed." Write a letter to your friend in which you do your best to dispel his or her fears. Include in your letter the point that education augments a person's chances for a successful career.

6. Write a paper about an important decision you've had to make recently. What about the decision made it a matter of great magnitude to you? How did you know it was the right decision?

D. List of Words and Word Parts

NOTE: Word parts are in *italics*.